PAUL D. SANSONE, O.F.M.

DOCUMENTS OF JEWISH SECTARIES

THE LIBRARY
OF
BIBLICAL STUDIES

Edited by

Harry M. Orlinsky

TWO VOLUMES IN ONE

DOCUMENTS OF JEWISH SECTARIES

VOLUME I

FRAGMENTS OF A ZADOKITE WORK

EDITED

FROM HEBREW MANUSCRIPTS IN THE CAIRO GENIZAH COLLECTION
NOW IN THE POSSESSION OF THE UNIVERSITY
LIBRARY, CAMBRIDGE

AND PROVIDED WITH

AN ENGLISH TRANSLATION, INTRODUCTION AND NOTES

BY

S. SCHECHTER, M.A., LITT.D. (CANTAB.)
President of the Jewish Theological Seminary of America in New York

PROLEGOMENON BY

JOSEPH A. FITZMYER, S.J.

KTAV PUBLISHING HOUSE, INC.
1970

First Printed 1910
Reprinted By Permission of Cambridge University Press

© New Matter Copyright 1970
Ktav Publishing House, Inc.
SBN 87068-016-1

Library of Congress Catalog Card Number: 69-10671
Manufactured in the United States of America

CONTENTS

PLATES

Facsimile of page 1, Text A, *to face* p. 1

„   „   „   20,   „   B, *between* pp. lxiv *and* 20

TABLE OF CONTENTS FOR VOLUME TWO.

For the convenience of the reader consecutive pagination has been introduced.

TO

THE HONOURABLE JACOB H. SCHIFF

ἔοικε μὲν οὖν ἡ μεγαλοψυχία οἷον κόσμος τις εἶναι
τῶν ἀρετῶν.

ARISTOTLE, *Ethics*.

PROLEGOMENON

The work now being reprinted, *Documents of Jewish Sectaries,* was first made available to the scholarly world sixty years ago. Since that time it has been the object of much discussion and consultation, even though it has recently been difficult to secure a copy of it. It represents one of the major publications of documents that came from the "Cairo Genizah." This collection of thousands of ancient Jewish documents from many periods is now famous, even though some of them apparently still await publication. But no little reason for the fame of this collection is the text which was first published as volume I in his work. *The Wisdom of Ben Sira: Portions of the Book of Ecclesiasticus from Hebrew Manuscripts* (Cambridge: University Press, 1899) and the *Fragments of a Zadokite Work* represent the two most famous publications of texts in that collection. At the time of their original publication no one realized the role that the Zadokite Fragments would play in the next half-century of scholarly research and discussion. The latter is not yet at an end, and hence the advisability of the reprinting of this work. The second volume of the work contains the text of a sectarian writing of lesser importance and of later date, *Fragments of the Book of the Commandments by 'Anan;* but it too has been a major contribution to the history of medieval Judaism.

The editor of this two-volume work, as well as of the *Wisdom of Ben Sira* from the Cairo Genizah, was Dr. Solomon Schechter, a renowned Talmudic scholar, esteemed teacher, and a leader of English-speaking Jewry. Born in the small village of Fokshan (Focșani) in Rumania in 1847, he eventually fulfilled his boyhood dreams of travelling widely and learning much about his venerable Jewish heritage. His biographers[1] tell of his running away from home to get an education. He began his early studies at Piatra (in Rumania) and Lemberg; they were later continued in Vienna (1875), and at the Hochschule für die Wissenschaft des Judentums and the university in Berlin. These studies

9

so developed him that he became in time a pioneer in the modern critical study of Talmudic literature. Though he received the rabbinical diploma in 1879, he never functioned as a rabbi.

Influenced by Claude G. Montefiore, he came to England in 1882 and soon took the post of a lecturer on the Talmud at Jews' College, London. In 1887 he published the text of *Aboth de Rabbi Nathan* and married Mathilda Roth. She was originally of Breslau and eventually bore him a son and two daughters.

His association with Cambridge University began in 1890, when he was appointed reader in Talmud and Rabbinical Literature. In this capacity he published *Some Aspects of Rabbinic Theology*—originally essays which appeared in the *Jewish Quarterly Review*, and later in expanded form as a book (1909). These essays established his reputation as a Jewish theologian and talmudist. His theological interests were clearly manifested in this "presentation of Rabbinic opinion on a number of theological topics as offered by Rabbinic literature, and forming an integral part of the religious consciousness of the bulk of the nation or 'Catholic Israel'." A scholarship to study Hebrew manuscripts in Italy took him to Rome in 1893 and a lecture tour brought him to Philadelphia in 1895.

About this time rumors had been circulating in Europe for several years about a cache of ancient Jewish documents in Cairo which would be of considerable interest to Jewish history. Indeed, some had already found their way to England and Russia. In May of 1896 Mrs. Agnes Lewis and Mrs. Gibson, two Scottish women interested in ancient Near Eastern texts, brought a collection of manuscripts and fragments from Egypt and Palestine to Cambridge. They showed them to Schechter and he identified one of the pieces as a part of the Hebrew text of the Wisdom of Ben Sira (or Ecclesiasticus). He announced his discovery in an article in the *Expositor* 5/4 (1896) 1-15, and this article enabled A. Neubauer and A. E. Cowley to identify further fragments of the text that had been acquired by the Bodleian Library in Oxford.

This discovery and the suspicion that there might be still more available in Egypt created the need for a trip to Cairo to see whether more of the cache could not be brought to Cambridge. Through the influence of C. Taylor, the master of St. John's College, and with a commission from Cambridge University, Schechter was able to travel to Cairo in 1896. He succeeded in getting permission from the Grand Rabbi of Cairo and from the Jewish community to transport the hoard of ancient documents stored there to England. For centuries the Jews in Cairo had been storing away in the genizah of the Ezra Synagogue of Old Cairo (Fustat) documents of a very diverse nature. They lay in a room without windows and difficult of access and were covered with the dust of time. The operation in which Schechter was engaged in transporting the documents to Cambridge was arduous and his health suffered from it. After various difficulties Schechter succeeded in bringing a great part of that cache of ancient documents to England. The number of texts he acquired has been variously reported, but it must have been in the neighborhood of

90,000 fragments.[2] Over these fragments he poured during his remaining days in England; when he eventually came to America, he also brought some of the texts with him.

Besides further fragments of the Wisdom of Ben Sira, which he found among the texts he brought from the genizah, he discovered the two manuscripts known today as the *Zadokite Fragments* (or, quite often, the *Damascus Document*) and the Fragments of the *Book of the Commandments by 'Anan*, the two texts being reprinted in this work.

In 1897 Schechter was named the Goldsmid Professor of Hebrew at the University of London, and in the following year Cambridge University conferred on him an honorary doctor's degree.

The contacts that he had already made with American Jewish leaders resulted in an invitation to him to become the president of the Jewish Theological Seminary of America in New York. This post he accepted in 1892 and thereby entered in a very significant way into American Jewish life. During his presidency the Seminary developed its scholarly tradition and became a real center of Conservative Judaism in America. It was as president that Schechter published the present work, *Documents of Jewish Sectaries* (1910). In the following year Harvard University conferred on him the degree of Doctor of Letters, and he became the first Jew to receive this distinction. In 1913 Schechter founded the United Synagogue of America, a movement of Conservative Judaism which sought to offset the Reform movement. During his career as president, Schechter also became one of the editors of the *Jewish Quarterly Review,* of the *Jewish Encyclopedia,* and of the translation of the Bible published by the Jewish Publication Society. This translation, however, did not appear until after his death, which occurred on November 15, 1915.

Schechter's name lives on for many reasons today, but not the least because of his connection with the documents of the Cairo Genizah. Indeed, the collection of them that he brought to Cambridge University is now known as the Taylor-Schechter collection. Over a decade after his death he was honored with a memorial volume: *Genizah Studies in Memory of Doctor Solomon Schechter* (Texts and Studies of the Jewish Theological Seminary of America, 7–9; New York: Jewish Theological Seminary, 1928–29).

The Hebrew text of the *Damascus Document* and the strange Hebrew-Aramaic text of the *Book of the Commandments by 'Anan* were unknown prior to their discovery in the Cairo Genizah. Today both of them are recognized as sectarian writings, as documents from distinctive groups or sects of Jews. The identity of the group from which the *Damascus Document* comes is not universally agreed on today, but there is little doubt that the *Commandments of 'Anan* is a writing from the medieval Karaite sect that emerged toward the end of the eighth century and flourished chiefly from the ninth to the twelfth centuries.

This writing has been called the manifesto of 'Anan ben David, a Persian Jew who was the legislator, if not the founder, of the Karaites, and who composed it *ca.* A.D. 770. He set himself up as an exilarch and advocated the discarding of the rabbinic interpretation of biblical Law; he thus challenged the authority of the rabbis and the teachers of the Talmud. This opposition resulted in his being regarded as an antinomian, but in reality he actually advocated a rigorous interpretation of the Torah, which he considered to be self-explanatory and in no need of man-made traditions to interpret it. The Karaites developed eventually an interpretation of the Bible that would rival that of the Rabbis. For his opposition to the rabbinic tradition, 'Anan ben David found himself eventually imprisoned by the Khalif Mansur, but he is said to have later won his freedom with the help of Abu Hanifa, the founder of the Hanifi school. 'Anan was a relatively obscure figure in Jewish history, prior to the discovery of the Genizah texts. When Schechter published Volume II of this work, it duplicated in part fragments of the *Book of Commandments* that had been published a few years earlier by A. E. Harkavy (*Likkute Kadmoniot II: Zur Geschichte des Karaismus und der karäischen Literatur* [Studien und Mittheilungen aus der kaiserlichen oeffentlichen Bibliothek, 8; St. Petersburg, 1903], pp. 1–172). These too were Genizah fragments, but Schechter's edition added considerably to the bulk of the composition and helped to lift the veil of obscurity from 'Anan ben David.

This fragmentary Karaite text has not been studied or discussed very much. Schechter himself did not attempt to translate it, leaving the task to such scholars as S. Poznański, "who, I hope, will soon furnish us with the necessary explanation to the contents of these fragments as well as with an essay bearing on their relation to the works of other early Karaite writers" (p. vi.).[3] Schechter confined his publication to the presentation of the texts of four manuscripts of the *Book of Commandments:* ms. A (pp. 3–29), ms. B (pp. 30–32), ms. C (pp. 33–34), ms. D (pp. 35–36). He also added a list of Scripture references and a few critical remarks on readings. Poznański subsequently revealed that ms. D. "does not properly belong to the Book of Commandments, but to another work of 'Anan, viz. the one called *Fadhâlika* (*pdlkh*), which is a sort of compendium to the *Book of Commandments*, and which was similarly composed in Aramaic" (*The Jewish Review* 2 [1911–12] 279). Poznański also noted that with the publication of this material one saw for the first time that " 'Anan closely followed the style of the Geonim, whose disciple he was, and the method of the Talmud, of which he was the opponent; only that he often followed this method *ad absurdum*" (*ibid.*).

Poznański sought to sort out the various parts of the *Book of the Commandments,* noting that there is no certainty today about the order of the laws in the preserved fragments. But he called attention to the need to transpose pp. 31 and 32 in ms. B (since 'Anan is there following the order of Lev 18, explaining 18:18 on p. 32 and 18:22 on p. 31). Again, in ms. A four parts may be distinguished: pp. 3–22 (with a lacuna between pp. 4–5), pp. 23–24, pp. 25–26, pp. 27–29 (with a lacuna between pp. 28–29). He sought to correlate the material in Schechter's volume with that in Harkavy's publication, and distinguished legislation on the following points:

Schechter saw a remote connection between the *Book of the Commandments by 'Anan* and the *Damascus Document*. It was not merely that they were writings stemming from Jewish sectaries, but he sought to explain the anti-rabbinical attitude of the Karaites as rooted in the attitude of a pre-Christian Jewish sect, which he called the Zadokites (and more specifically Dositheans) and believed were somehow related to the Sadducees. The Pharisaic tradition had persisted by and large in the teaching of the rabbis; but the tradition of the Sadducees disappeared in Jewish history in a surprising way. The *Damascus Document* (CD) seemed to refer to its members as *benê Ṣādôq*, "sons of Zadok"; indeed, according to 4:3, they are the *beḥîrê Yiśrā'ēl*, "the elect of Israel." Whatever this would have meant in the concrete, it is certain that the group, referring to itself in this way, regarded itself as privileged. Medieval opponents of 'Anan, such as Saadia and his rabbinical contemporaries, claimed that the Karaites were simply repeating the errors of a pre-Christian Jewish sect, the Zadokites. Little credence was given to this medieval accusation by historians; and yet the striking thing is that the teachings of the medieval Karaites exhibit no little similarity to the halachic regulations of the group of Jews depicted in the *Damascus Document*.[5] Thus Schechter's suspicion was not unfounded. It was not based merely on such extrinsic criteria as the discovery of the two texts in the same Genizah, or the fact that the two manuscripts of the *Damascus Documents* were medieval copies (ms. A. from the tenth century and ms. B from the twelfth), or even the likelihood that the medieval Karaites had made use of the *Damascus Document* in their opposition to the rabbinical and talmudic tradition. It was rather the obvious intrinsic similarity of tenets and practices that were represented in the two groups. It seemed assured that the medieval Karaites were somehow tributary to the group of Jews who produced the *Damascus Document* and that these Jews lived several centuries earlier, perhaps even in pre-Christian times.

But who were the *b*ᵉ*nê Ṣādôq,* "the sons of Zadok," the people of the *Damascus Document?* The answer to this question caused much debate during the decades that followed the original publication of the writing in 1910. Many identifications were proposed. E. Meyer considered them to be a Jewish community of the Seleucid period, and toyed with the idea that they might be Essenes.[6] Schechter called them Zadokites, and more specifically Dositheans, relating them indirectly to the Sadducees, because he believed that the document contained an attack on the Pharisees. On the other hand, attempts were made to identify the sect as Pharisaic. G. Margoliouth wrote a series of articles, maintaining that the people involved were Sadducean Christians in Damascus.[7] Scholars such as A. Büchler, A. Mamorstein, S. Zeitlin, and P. R. Weis have argued with varying nuances that the *Damascus Document* represents a medieval composition, some even saying that it is "indeed a karaitic work."[8] So the debate went until the late 40's, when the discovery of the Qumran scrolls was announced to the world. Indeed, even afterwards the identification of the sect as Zadokite persisted.[8a]

Prior to the discovery of the Qumran scrolls, however, one other small fragment from the Cairo Genizah, which undoubtedly was related to the *Damascus Document,* was published by I. Lévi; it apparently belonged to some medieval copy of the same text.[9] It is a small piece of parchment, containing the central portion of about nine lines; it bears the siglum *pergCfr* (i.e., parchment Cairo fragment). This fragment also mentions "the sons of Zadok."

1. . . .] *khn*	. . .] priest.
2. . . .] *'t ywrwny mbny*[	. . .] time they will instruct me by the sons of [
3. . . .] *'dt bny ṣdwq* [	. . .] the congregation of the sons of Zadok [
4. . . .] *'l ḥwq ṭm' wt*[*hwr*	. . .] about the statute of impurity and pu[rity
5. . . .] *mšpṭyw yšpwṭ*[	. . .] he will issue his judgments [
6. . . [*y*]*qdyšw wḥwl*[	. . .] they will sanctify, and the profane [they will . . .
7. . . [*š*]*m yswbw dwkny*[	. . t]here they will sanctify my table [
8. . . [*b*]*šyr yhllw 'w*[*tw*	. . wi]th a hymn they will praise h[im . . .
9. . . .]*yy 'z l'mw ytn*[	. . .]yy he will give strength to his people [

Once the *Manual of Discipline* of Qumran Cave I was published,[10] it did not take scholars long to realize that there was a connection between it and Schechter's *Damascus Document.*[11] There is little doubt today that the *Manual of Discipline* represents a rule book of a pre-Christian Jewish sect of

Palestine; the convergence of archaeological, historical, literary, and palaeographical data to give information about this sect, yield what is almost historical certitude regarding its date. The palaeographic work done on the Qumran scrolls in recent years[12] has resulted in a date for the *Manual of Discipline* from Cave I (IQS) as *ca.* 100 B.C. Whether it is the oldest copy of that text or not does not concern us now; it shows at least the pre-Christian origin of this Jewish sect.

In 1952 the same Bedouins of the Ta'amireh tribe who had discovered Cave I came upon another hoard of texts in what has since been named Cave IV. Though this cave yielded no complete manuscript, fragments in the neighborhood of 30,000 were recovered from it. When the giant jig-saw puzzle was completed—to the extent that it can ever be completed, since there are hundreds of "hopeless cases," tiny fragments whose pertinence cannot be established because of missing pieces—seven, or possibly eight, further fragmentary copies of the *Damascus Document* itself were recovered. They are known today as 4QD[a–g(h)] but have not yet been published. J. T. Milik, the editor to whom they have been entrusted for publication, has already revealed a certain amount of information about them.[13] Though there are different recensions of this work, which had been known ever since Schechter's publication of mss. A. and B from the Cairo Genizah, the Cave IV material reveals further recensional differences, which will be discussed below. However, there is no doubt that the Qumran Cave IV fragments belong to the same text as Schechter's *Damascus Document*. Having worked on these 4Q texts in the Palestine Archaeological Museum in Jerusalem myself, as part of a team preparing a concordance for the non-biblical texts from Cave IV, I can testify to their relationship, even though the 4Q copies are still unpublished.

Further fragments of the *Damascus Document* turned up in Qumran Caves V and VI,[14] and even though they are small, they make their contribution to the over-all evidence for the pre-Christian dating of the sect.

But who were the Jews who formed the Qumran community? Among the first to identify the Qumran community as Essene was A. Dupont-Sommer; this identification has been acknowledged also by the team of scholars who have been most intimately connected with the study of them—by the chief archaeologist of Qumran, Roland de Vaux; by the international team which has been entrusted with the 4Q fragments; by Y. Yadin, who has published or commented on important Qumran texts in Israel. This view is widely accepted today, despite some obvious difficulties that it has always had to face. These stem mainly from the fact that the classical descriptions of the Essenes in Pliny the Elder, Josephus, Philo, and Hippolytus have not always been easy to square with passages in the texts that have come from the Qumran caves. I do not intend to discuss here the pro's and con's of this issue; in the present state of our knowledge I personally think that this identification is the best and the difficulties that a small group of scholars bring up against it are not serious enough to contest it.[15]

Part of the problem itself, and one that does concern the rest of this prolegomenon, is the relation of the *Damascus Document* to the *Manual of Discipline.* This is probably the most difficult question to handle in the discussion of Qumran literature today; it complicates the identification of the Jewish group from which the documents have come. Though the *Damascus Document* is clearly related to the *Manual of Discipline,* as has been pointed out above and as can be shown by a comparison of a number of points, there are obvious differences (e.g., whereas the Damascus community regards itself as the "new covenant," borrowing a phrase from Jer 31:31, this title does not appear in 1QS; there is also a different community structure; etc.). The *Damascus Document* often speaks of "camps" (e.g., CD 7:6; 12:23; 13:4,5,7,13,16,20), in which some of the community dwells, and this item has been used to explain different sorts of Essene communities. The phrase, "the land of Damascus," which occurs in CD 6:5,19; 8:21; 19:34, has also affected this problem. It has been the subject of much debate: Does it refer to a sojourn of the community in Damascus during a period of exile? Does it suggest that certain groups of Essenes were dwelling in camps in the Damascene area? Is it merely a figurative or "prophetic" (so F. M. Cross, Jr.) name for the desert of Qumran itself? [16] Whatever the solution to this last problem might be, I am still attracted by Milik's suggestion that one should really distinguish four different kinds of Essenes: (1) Those who lived at Qumran during the various phases of community existence there; it should be regarded as the "mother-house" of the community, and life there would have been regulated by the *Manual of Discipline.* (2) Those who lived in camps in the land of Damascus (or Hauran), in which the community structure was not the same as that at Qumran and life was regulated by the *Damascus Document.* (3) Those who lived in towns and villages of Palestine, of whom Josephus speaks (*JW* 2.8,4 #124) and about whom we have little information. It is not at all certain that they lived the same communal form of life and possibly "the order of the assembly of the cities of Israel" (CD 12:19) refers to them. (4) The Therapeutae in Egypt, a group of Jewish solitaries who lived near Lake Mareotis in the vicinity of Alexandria, about whom Philo writes (*De vita contemplativa,* 3–11 #21–90). They seem to be related to the Syro-Palestinian groups of Essenes. [17]

Such a distinction prevents one from facilely depicting the Essenes as a monolithic organization, allows one to explain the diversity of the details in different texts, and reckons with Josephus' own testimony that there was more than one order of Essenes (*JW* 2.8,13 #160). This remark he made in the context of explaining that there were some Essenes who married. However one may explain this remark, which occurs at the very end of Josephus' discussion of the Essenes in the *Jewish Wars,* it may refer to two contemporary forms of Essene life. The evidence in the *Manual of Discipline* by and large supports the view that the Qumran community was celibate,[18] whereas the appendix to it (1QSa 1:8–11) and the *Damascus Document* envision a community in which at least some members married (CD 7:8–10).[19]

If one accepts this fourfold division of the ancient Essenes and ascribes the two differing rule books to at least two of them—since it is possible that those who lived in the towns and villages of Palestine might also have conducted themselves according to one or other of these books—one has a plausible explanation of the relation of the *Damascus Document* to the *Manual of Discipline*. The finding of a multiple number of copies of the *Damascus Document* at Qumran itself, and indeed in several caves (IV, V, VI), may even suggest that it had been in use there too. This possibility has to be envisaged; but then too the multiple copies could be due to the work of copyists in the Qumran mother-community who made them for the related, scattered communities.

A definitive answer to this question of the relation of the *Damascus Document* must await the publication of the fragments from Qumran Cave IV, for these reveal that the text itself was copied in different recensions and undoubtedly reflect differing stages of the community's existence. The same is also true of the *Manual of Discipline*.[20] The fact that both rule books grew by accretion and reflect different stages of community development complicates the judgment about their relationship.

Schechter's main text, ms. A (T.-S. 10 K 6), contains sixteen columns and his secondary text, ms. B (T.-S. 16 311), two lengthy columns, which he numbered 19 and 20, skipping 17–18. The first is dated to the tenth century; the second to the twelfth. The latter is an expanded version of cols. 7–8 of ms. A. Milik has revealed that the texts from Qumran Cave IV agree substantially with that of ms. A from the Cairo Genizah, but that there are some noteworthy additions to the text.

Specifically, he indicates the following changes that one has to reckon with in the study of this text:

> On the evidence of two manuscripts [from Qumran Cave IV], we have now to change the order of pages proposed by Schechter and followed by all subsequent editors of the Cairo manuscript. Pages XV and XVI precede page IX *directly;* these two pages and the beginning of page IX both give laws relating to oaths and vows. After page VIII and the conclusion to the historical section (missing in A, preserved in B, page XX, . . .), but before page XV, we can detect the loss of several pages in the Cairo manuscript A. Numerous fragments from the Cave IV manuscripts belong to this missing section. These contain prescriptions concerning the cultic purity of priests and sacrifices; a more detailed treatment of the law of diseases (Lev. 13.29ff.) and an expanded version of Lev. 15 (fluxes of men and women), laws of marriage, prescription relating to agricultural life, the payment of tithes, relations with pagans, relations between the sexes, a prohibition of magic, etc.
>
> To sum up, the original order of the work was as follows: Opening columns (4Q, missing in Cairo manuscript), CD. I-VIII (and a text parallel to *fin.* XIX-XX), missing part (partly preserved in 4Q), XV-XVI, IX-XIV, final columns (4Q: penal code, and liturgy for the feast of the Renewal of the Covenant, cf. pp. 116f.).[21]

This is based on Milik's preliminary report, and we shall have to await the publication of the documents to check it.

The following outline may suggest the shape of the *Damascus Document*, as one can reconstruct it from the various data available:

The Damascus Document

(This tentative outline utilizes the Cairo Geniza copy and the fragments from Qumran Caves IV, V, VI, arranged according to the indications of J. T. Milik, given above. These indications are drawn from the manuscripts that he has provisionally labeled 4QD[b, c].)

(I)   [4Q columns]; 1:1–8:21; 19:1–20:34 *An Exhortation: God's Saving Plan in Man's History*

    (A)   Introductory Columns in 4Q texts

    (B)   Meditation on the Lessons of History (CD 1:1–2:1)

    (C)   Predestination of the Upright and the Wicked (2:2–13)

    (D)   A Second Meditation on the Lessons of History (2:14–4:12a)

    (E)   The Three Nets of Belial (4:12b–6:1)

    (F)   The Community of the New Covenant (6:2–7:9a; [19:1–5a = 7:5b–9a])

    (G)   Diverse Fates of Those Who are Faithful to the Covenant and of Apostates (7:9b–8:21 [= 19:5b–34]; 19:35–20:34)

[Further sections, missing in CD, but partly preserved in 4Q fragments]

(II)   15:1–16:20; 9:1–14:22 *The Constitution: Life in the New Covenant*

    (A)   Rules for Entrance into the Covenant and for Oaths (15:1–16:16)

        (a) The Oath by Which to Swear (15:1–5a)

        (b) Admission into the Community (15:5b–19)

        (c) Oath on Entering the Covenant (16:1–6a)

        (d) The Validity of Oaths (16:6b–12)

        (e) Voluntary Gifts (16:13–16)

    (B)   Regulations within the Community (9:1–10:10a)

        (a) Fraternal Correction (9:1–8a)

        (b) Judicial Oaths (9:8b–16a)

        (c) Witnesses (9:16b–10:3)

        (d) Judges (10:4–10a)

    (C)   Rites to be Observed in the Community (10:10b–12:18)

        (a) Purification with Water (10:10b–13)

        (b) Sabbath Regulations (10:14–11:18a)

        (c) Sundry Regulations (11:18b–12:11a)

            (1) Sacrificial Offerings through an Unclean Intermediary (11:18b–21a)

            (2) Entrance into the Temple in a State of Uncleanness (11:21b–23)

            (3) Defilement of the Sanctuary (12:1–3)

            (4) Profanation of the Sabbath (12:3b–6a)

            (5) Killing or Robbing Pagans (12:6b–8a)

            (6) Commerce with Outsiders (12:8b–11a)

        (d) Ritual Purity (12:11b–18)

(D) The Organization of the Community (12:19–14:19)
     (a) Preamble (12:19–13:2a)
     (b) Local Communities (13:2b–7a)
     (c) The Overseer of the Camp (13:7b–14:2)
     (d) Functionaries of the Community (14:2–12a)
     (e) The Works of the Community (14:12b–19)
(E) The Penal Code (14:20–22)

As the writing can be reconstructed today on the basis of the various information available, it falls into two main parts. The first (1:1–8:21 and 19:1–20:34) presents an exhortation addressed to the community of the "sons of Zadok." Written somewhat in imitation of the Deuteronomist historian, it summons the members of the community to reflect on God's mighty acts in the course of Israel's history. The author appeals to what God has done for Israel, points an accusing finger at Israel's infidelity, and exhorts the community—now regarded as the remnant of Israel and the new covenant —to turn to the Lord. The exhortation is not well written; it is repetitious and rhetorical. It draws many examples from the biblical narratives of past sinners and their fate. The author thus presents his case for the sectarian life of the community, which has separated itself from the surrounding Jewish world. The author is not the Righteous Teacher, since he is referred to (in CD 1:9–11; 20:14) as having belonged to an earlier phase of the community's life.

The second part of the *Damascus Document* (4Q fragments; 15:1–16:20; 9:1–14:22) deals with detailed regulations for life within the community, especially in the camps "in the land of Damascus." The foregoing outline indicates the details. It seems rather obvious that part I was intended as a theoretic introduction to the specific regulations to be set forth in part II.

Schechter included in his original publication of the *Damascus Document* an introduction, the Hebrew text, an English translation of the Hebrew text, some notes, several lists of corrections to the Hebrew text and notes, and an index. Save for a photo of page 1 of ms. A and a photo of page 20 of ms. B, he failed to provide the scholarly world with an adequate reproduction of this important text, for no one was able to check the readings of the text that he had published. No less a scholar than R. H. Charles, who had been refused access to the manuscript in the Cambridge University Library because an arrangement had been made that no scholar would be allowed to inspect it for five years after Schechter's edition, criticized the latter severely and judged that it was "carelessly done." "Even if Dr. Schechter's edition were thoroughly satisfactory this extraordinary action on his part could hardly fail to call forth the reprobation of scholars generally. . . . If Dr. Schechter chooses to edit his text so carelessly that is of course his own concern, but in that case he ought at all events to have published a facsimile of the entire MSS.—only a matter of eighteen pages."[22] Such a judgment did not make Schechter happy, and he replied caustically.[23] He explained that he was contemplating a second edition of the text, in which he planned to use the criticisms of others; but alas! he never lived to see it through.

It was not until 1952 that photographs of the manuscripts were made available; these were published in relatively legible reproductions by S. Zeitlin in his monograph, *The Zadokite Fragments: Facsimile of the Manuscripts in the Cairo Genizah Collection in the Possession of the University Library, Cambridge, England.*[24]

The text of the *Damascus Document* that Schechter published will be consulted for its historical value as the *editio princeps*. It was a pioneer publication and the reading of the text has been improved by the studies of other scholars since 1910. Schechter himself included two lists of corrections in the publication (pp. lvii-lix, lix-lx); further corrections can be found at times in the notes on his translation of the Hebrew text. To facilitate the use of the text in this reprinting of Schechter's work, I am including a list of the principal corrections and restorations that have been considered. These include those important corrections that Schechter himself made, the restorations of other scholars, and a few suggestions of my own (based on a study of clear photographs of the text supplied by the Library of Cambridge University). Many of the corrections supplied below agree with the readings in the handy edition of the *Damascus Document* published by C. Rabin, *The Zadokite Documents*. In the following list, the page and line numbers refer to Schechter's edition:

Page	Line	Instead of[25]	Read
1	4	š'ryt	š'yryt
2	3	wtwšwyh	wtwšyyh
	6	bw	(possibly) *by* (i.e., *by<d>*)
	9	qṣytm	qṣyhm
	10	wnhyyt*	wnhywt (see CD 13:8)
	12	whw'	wḥwzy
	13	'mt wbprwš*	'mtw bprwš
	13	šmw	{šmw}
	16	w'ny	w'<y>ny
	18	'ydy	'yry
	20	kl bśr hyh	kl bśr 'šr hyh
3	1	t'y*	t'w
	1	wmšpḥh.hm	wmšpḥwtyhm
	2	wy'. . . hb	wy'[l 'w]hb
	4	lpny*	lp{n}y
	8	mṣwt	<wlw' h'zynw> mṣwt
	10	ḥbw	hbw
	18	brwy	brzy
	21	(?)	(nothing)
4	1	mqdšw	mqdšy
	2	m'lyhm	m'ly hm
	3	whnlwym*	w<hlwym hm> hnlwym
	6	hqwdš šwnym*	<'nšy> hqwdš <hr'>šwnym

Page	Line	Instead of[25]	Read
	16	*byśr'l**	*b<yt> yśr'l*
	16	*pnyhm**	*<l>pnyhm*
	17		*ḥḥwn* (though the ms. clearly reads *ḥḥyn*)
5	3	*nptḥ*	*npḥt* (crossed out) *nptḥ*
	4	*wywš'* (with an accent)	{*wywš'*} (with superscript *w* between *š* and ')
	5	*nglh*	*<wl'>nglh*
	6	*hm*	*<l>hm*
	8	*'ḥyhm* (pointed)	*'ḥyhm* (with *m* crossed out and *w* written above)
	12	*l'md*	*l'mr*
	13	*zyqy*	*zyqwt*
	16	*b'lylwtm*	*b'lylwtyhm*
6	1	*bmšyḥw*	*bmšyḥy*
	2	*wyqḥ*	*wyqm*
	3	*wyšm'm*	*wyšmy'm*
	12	*mzbḥw*	*mzbḥw ḥnm*
	13	*ysgyr*	*ysgwr*
	13	*dltw**	*dlty*
	16	*'lmnwt*	*'lm[nw]t*
	19	*bmṣ'. .*	*kmṣ't*
7	5	*yswrw**	*yswry*
	10	*kbw'*	*bbw'*
	12	*b'w*	*<l'> b'w*
	13	*hsgrw* (accented)	*hsgrw* (with superscript *w* or *y* after *h*)
	17	*wkynwy*	(possibly) *wkynyy*
	17	*wkywn ḥṣlmym*	{*wkywn ḥṣlmym*}
8	7	*wytnkrw*	*wytgbrw*
	11	*bhm*	(nothing)
	12		*bhm* (at the beginning of the line)
	13	*mbwhl*	*šwql*
	17	*hw'yrw*	*hy'ydw*
9	2		*mby'y* (though ms. clearly has *mby'w*)
	13		*whtwdh* (though ms. clearly has *whtwrh*)
	13	*hmwšb*	*hmyšb*
	14		(The blank space actually precedes *hkl*)
	17	*wywdy'hw*	*wydy'hw*
	22	*. . klw*	*yqblw*
	23	*w'l 'ḥd*	*w'l <py 'yd> 'ḥd*
	23	*hṭhrh*	*<mn> hṭhrh*
	23	*yqwm*	*yqwbl*
10	6	*ḥḥgw*	*ḥḥgy* (i.e., *heh°gî*)
	6	*wbyswdy**	*wbyswry*
	14	*ḥš . . t*	*ḥš[b]t*

Page	Line	*Instead of*[25]	*Read*
	15		*ml* (erased at beginning of the line)
	18	*yšpwṭ*	(possibly) *yšpwkw*
	20	*ḥpṣy*	*ḥpṣw*
	21	*’d*	*’* (crossed out ?)
	23	. . . *h*	[*bṡ*]*dh*
11	2	*kl kly*	*kl kl<y>*
	3	*bgw*	*bgz*
	8	*bmwbh*	*bswkh*
	9	*pṭh*	*<y>pṭh*
	13		*tpwl* (though ms. clearly has *tpyl* [an Aramaism?])
12	2	*’šr* (second one)	(nothing)
	14	*nšpk*	*nš*[*p*]*k*
	18	*ytm’*	*wṭm’w*
	21	*klhw*	*kl ḥy*
	21	. .	*‘t*
	23	. . . . . *thl*	[*h*]*m*[*ḥnwt*] *hmthlkym b’lh*
	23	*mšwḥ*	*mšyḥ*
13	2	*wbqwm*	*wbmqwm*
	2	*hhgw*	*hhgy*
	5	*mšpš*	*mšpṭ*
	8	*pl’y*	*pl’w*
	8	*bprtyh**	*bptryh*[*m*]
	9	*wyš* . . .	*wyš*[*yb*]
	9	*mdḥwbm*	*mdḥwbm*
	10	*l . my . . dym*	*lblty hywt*
	11	*lm . ṡyw*	*lm‘ṡyw*
	12	*yhwtw*	*hywtw*
	12	*h* . . .	*h’*[*wr*] (cf. 1QM 13:9)
	14	*’l yš’l ’l*	*’l ’l yš’l w’l*
	14	. . *bny hšḥr*	*lbny hšḥt k*[*y*]
	15	*’yš*, etc.	*’yš ḥbr lmqḥ wlmmkr ky ’m hwdy‘*
	16	*w‘ṡh*, etc.	*w‘ṡh ’mnh wl’ yš*[ ]*h ’š*[
	18	*ḥṭ* . . *’l yṭh* . . *hb*	*ḥsd ’l yṭwr lhm*
14	2	*wn‘n*	*wn‘nš*[*w*]
	7	*’š*	* ’š*
	7	*w‘d*	*‘d*
	8	. . .	[*hhgy*]
	8	*lhbrm*	*ldbrm*
	9	*w‘d*	*‘d*
	10	*rm . pry.*	*lmšpḥwtm*
	13	*trwmtn hm*	[*š*]*ny ymym*
	13	. *hm* . . . *t*	*lm*[*m*]*‘t*
	14	. . *‘m w . mny*	[*ytw*]*mym wmmnw*
	14	*bh*	*byd*
	15	*yg‘ wl’*	*ynw*[*g‘*] *wl’šr*
	16	. . . . *r*	[*’yn*] *lh g*[*w’*]*l wln*[*‘r ’*]*šr*
	16	. . *wl’*	*hḥbr wl’*

Page	Line	Instead of[25]	Read
	19	. . . . . ’hrn	[‘d ‘mwd mšy]ḥ ’hrn
	19	‘wnnw	‘wnm
	20	. . . . . r . qr	’[š]r [yš]qr bmmwn
	22	. . .’ bmš	l’ bmšpṭ [wn‘nš] šnh
15	1	. .‘	[yš]b‘
	1	šbw‘h hb . .	šbw‘t h[skm]
	5	. mwt	[y]mwt
	5	’š	’šr ygy‘w
	6	yqwmw	yqymw
	9	lš[ ] l̀[ ]sh	lš[wb ’]l twrt mšh
	10	bm . . . ṣ . . .	bk[l q]ṣ [hrš‘]
	10	yydy‘hw	ywdy‘hw
	11	.’.	šmh
	13	. . . ym . .	. . .’ym hm
	13	’m r . . . l . .	’m ym [‘]l
	13	lryb	lrwb
	14	. . . š . . bw	[ ]h whw’ šwh bw
	14	wy . . .	wylmd
16	6	nymwl	nymwl b (crossed out)
	8	l‘śwt	l[‘ś]wt
	9	. . .’yš	[yqy]m ’yš
	9	l . . . .‘d	lswr m[n htw]rh ‘d
	10		[‘]l (at the beginning of the line)
	10	’m . . .šh	’m[r l]’yšh
	11	.d‘ . . dm	[y]d‘nh ’m
	13	h . .wt	hndbwt
	13	’yš	’[yš]
	14	. .hnym	[hkw]hnym
	14	. . . . yqdš	[’l] yqdš
	15	. . .l .y	p[yhw l’]l ky
	15	’t ‘.dw	’t r‘yhw
	15	. .w ḥrm	yṣ[w]dw ḥrm
19	1	kb	kk
	2	mṣwty	mṣwtyy
	2	kḥwqy	ksrk
	11	yhzq’l	yḥzq’l (crossed out)
	16	b’w	b’w bsw (the latter is crossed out)
	17	wyt‘llw	wytgllw
	20	b‘ynyw	b‘yny[w]
	35	l.	l’
	35	wbktbw	wbktbm
20	4	kmw	kmy
	4	yzkyrwwhw	ywkyḥwhy
	5	m‘wt	d‘wt
	12	bbryt	bbryt ’l (the latter is possibly deleted)
	13	htwrh	htwr[h]
	14	ywryh	ywrh

14	*hlkw*	*šbw*
17	*pšʿ y. . .*	*pšʿ yʿqb*
17	*. . nd . . .*	*yd[br]*
18	*rʿ. . l. . . n. . .*	*rʿhw lhṣdyq ʾyš*
20	*y ʿlh*	*yglh*
23	*wṭmʾw*	*wyṭmʾw*
24	*nsyk*	*w[yś]k*
25	*qdš*	*hqdš*
29	*blktm*	*blktnw*
33	*ʾl*	*ʾt*

Future work on the *Damascus Document* will certainly be related to the studies of the Qumran fragments of this writing. Little can be done on this text that is of lasting value before the full publication of the Cave IV material. Once that is available, then a full critical text will be needed with an adequate apparatus criticus. Then it will be possible to write an extensive commentary on this ancient Jewish rule book. Even Rabin's edition of the *Zadokite Documents,* for all its usefulness, gives only the barest commentary and the skimpiest of notes on many of the most crucial problems that the text raises.

A major problem that will then be able to be discussed in detail is the relation of this writing to the *Manual of Discipline,* the problem that we have already mentioned above. In the study of both of these texts the most urgent thing is source analysis, because both of them exist in different recensional forms and both have grown in various stages.

Then too it will be possible to study a number of minor problems that the *Damascus Document* raises, for instance, the use of the Old Testament in this writing, the attitude toward the Sabbath and marriage that it reflects, etc.

Much has already been written on the *Damascus Document,* and it is scarcely all digested at the moment. Some of it appeared in the decade after Schechter's first publication, much of it since the discovery of the Qumran Scrolls. As an aid to the further study of the text, I am including here a bibliography of the most important discussions and studies of the text.

BIBLIOGRAPHY

(A) *Text* (reproduced in whole or in part)

Cantera Burgos, F. and F. Pérez Castro, *Antología hebraica postbíblica* (Madrid: Instituto Arias Montano, 1953), pp. 6-7.

Habermann, A. M., *'Edah we-'Eduth: Three Scrolls from the Judaean Desert: The Legacy of a Community* (Jerusalem: Maḥbaroth le-Sifruth, 1952), pp. 89-123.
    Megilloth midbar Yehudah: The Scrolls from the Judean Desert (Jerusalem: Maḥbaroth le-Sifruth, 1959), pp. 71-88.

Lohse, E., "Die Damaskusschrift," *Die Texte aus Qumran hebräisch und deutsch: Mit masoretischer Punktation, Übersetzung, Einführung und Anmerkungen* (Munich: Kösel, 1964), pp. 63-107.

Rabin, C., *The Zadokite Documents: I. The Admonition; II. The Laws* (Oxford: Clarendon, 1954; 2nd ed., 1958).

Rost, L., *Die Damaskusschrift neu bearbeitet* (Kleine Texte, 167; Berlin: de Gruyter, 1933).

Segal, M. H., *"Sepher bᵉrît Dammeśeq,"* *Haš-šilôaḥ* 26 (Odessa, 1912) 390-406, 483-506.

(B) *Translations of CD* (partial or entire)

Baron, S. W. and J. L. Blau, *Judaism: Postbiblical and Talmudic Period* (New York: Liberal Arts Press, 1954), pp. 91-94.

Barrett, C. K., *The New Testament Background: Selected Documents* (London: S.P.C.K., 1956), pp. 257-62.

Böhl, F. M. T., "Neugefundene Urkunden einer messianischen Sekte im syrisch-palaestinensischen Judentum," *Theologisch tijdschrift* 46 (1912) 1-35, 93.

Bonsirven, J., *La Bible apocryphe: En marge de l'Ancien Testament* (Paris: Fayard, 1953), pp. 171-89.

Brongers, H. A., *De gedragsregels der Qumrangemeente* (Amsterdam: Proost en Brandt, 1958).

Burrows, M., *The Dead Sea Scrolls* (New York: Viking, 1955), pp. 349-64.

Charles, R. H., "Fragments of a Zadokite Work," *Apocrypha and Pseudepigrapha of the Old Testament* (Oxford: Clarendon, 1913), 2. 785-834.

Cothenet, E., "Le Document de Damas," *Les textes de Qumran* (2 vols.; ed. J. Carmignac and P. Guilbert; Paris: Letouzey et Ané, 1961, 1963), 2. 129-204.

Dupont-Sommer, A., *The Dead Sea Scrolls: A Preliminary Survey* (tr. E. M. Rowley; Oxford: Blackwell, 1952), pp. 53-68.

   The Essene Writings from Qumran (tr. G. Vermes; Meridian Book 44; Cleveland: World, 1962), pp. 114-63; *Les écrits esséniens découverts près de la Mer Morte* (Paris: Payot, 1959), pp. 129-78.

Edelkoort, A. H., *De handschriften van de Dode Zee* (Baarn: Bosch en Keuning, n.d.), pp. 74-119.

Gaster, T. H., *The Dead Sea Scriptures in English Translation* (Anchor A378; rev. ed.; Garden City, N. Y.: Doubleday, 1964), pp. 70-97.

   The Scriptures of the Dead Sea Sect (London: Secker and Warburg, 1957), pp. 71-94.

Hvidberg, F. F., *Menigheden af den Nye Pagt i Damascus* (Copenhagen: G. E. C. Gad, 1928).

Lagrange, M.-J., "La secte juive de la Nouvelle Alliance au pays de Damas," *RB* ns 9 (1912) 213-40, 321-60.

Lamadrid, A. G., *Los descubrimientos de Qumran* (Madrid: Instituto español de estudios eclesiasticos, 1956), pp. 308-45.

Lévi, I., "Un écrit sadducéen antérieur à la destruction du Temple," *REJ* 61 (1911) 161-205; 63 (1912) 1-19.

Lohse, E., "Die Damaskusschrift," see above.

Maier, J., *Die Texte vom Toten Meer. I: Übersetzung; II: Anmerkungen* (Munich: E. Reinhardt, 1960), 1. 46-70.

Medico, H. E. del, *L'énigme des manuscrits de la Mer Morte: Etude sur la provenance et le contenu des manuscrits découverts dans la grotte I de Qumrân* (Paris: Plon, 1957), pp. 116-34, 533-89.

Michel, A., "Le Document de Damas," *Les manuscrits hébreux du désert de Juda* (ed. A. Vincent; Paris: Fayard, 1955), pp. 163-99.

Nielsen, E., *Handskrift fundene i Juda ørken: Dødehavsteksterne* (Copenhagen: G. E. C. Gad, 1956), pp. 102-19.

Rabin, C., *The Zadokite Documents,* see above.

Riessler, P., "Sadokitisches Werk," *Altjüdisches Schrifttum ausserhalb der Bibel* (Augsburg, 1928; reprinted: Heidelberg: F. H. Kerle, 1966), pp. 920-41, 1323-25.

Schreiden, J., *Les énigmes des manuscrits de la Mer Morte* (Wetteren: Editions Cultura, 1961; 2nd ed., 1964), pp. 374-98.

Schousboe, J., *La secte juive de l'alliance nouvelle au pays de Damas et le christianisme naissant* (Copenhagen, 1942).

Staerk, W., *Die jüdische Gemeinde des neuen Bundes in Damaskus* (Beiträge zur Förderung christlicher Theologie, 27/3; Gütersloh: C. Bertelsmann, 1922).

Sutcliffe, E. F., *The Monks of Qumran as Depicted in the Dead Sea Scrolls* (London: Burns and Oates, 1960), pp. 131-48.

Vellas, V. M., *Peri ta cheirographa tēs Nekras Thalassēs: Ta hebraika cheirographa tēs koinotētos tēs Damaskou* (Athens: Phrontistēriakē, 1961), pp. 1-58.

Vermes, G., *Discovery in the Judean Desert* (New York: Desclée, 1956), pp. 157-85; *Les manuscrits du Désert de Juda* (Tournai: Desclée, 1954), pp. 159-84.

   The Dead Sea Scrolls in English (Pelican A551; Baltimore: Penguin, 1965), pp. 95-115.

(C) *Studies Devoted to Particular Passages in CD*

1:1   Denis, A.-M., *Les thèmes de connaissance dans le Document de Damas*
           (Studia hellenistica, 15; Louvain: Publications universitaires,
           1967).

1:1ff.   Soloff, R. A., "Toward Uncovering Original Texts in the Zadokite
           Documents," *NTS* 5 (1958-59) 62-67.

1:1ff.   Wernberg-Møller, P., "*Ṣedeq, ṣaddîq, ṣādôq* in the Zadokite Fragments
           (CDC), the Manual of Discipline (DSD) and the Habakkuk-
           Commentary (DSH)," *VT* 3 (1953) 310-15.

1:4   Collins, R. F., "The Berîth-Notion of the Cairo Damascus Covenant
           and Its Comparison with the New Testament *diatheke*," *ETL* 39
           (1963) 555-94.

1:4   LeDéaut, R., "Une citation de Lévitique 26, 45 dans le *Document de
           Damas*, I, 4; VI, 2," *RQ* 6 (1967-68) 289-91.

1:5   Rabinowitz, I., "A Reconsideration of 'Damascus' and '390 Years' in
           the 'Damascus' ('Zadokite') Fragments," *JBL* 73 (1954) 11-35.

1:5   Rowley, H. H., "The 390 Years of the Zadokite Work," *Mélanges
           bibliques rédigés en l'honneur de André Robert* (Paris: Bloud et
           Gay, 1957), pp. 341-47.

1:5-6   Sacchi, P., "Il problema degli anni 390 nel Documento di Damasco
           I, 5-6," *RQ* 5 (1964-65) 89-96.

1:5-6   Walker, N., "Concerning the 390 Years and the 20 years of the
           Damascus Document," *JBL* 76 (1957) 57-58.

1:6   Walker, N., "An Awkward Reading in the Damascus Document,"
           JBL 79 (1960) 169-70.

1:11   Weingreen, J., "The Title Môreh Sedek," *JSS* 6 (1961) 162-74.

1:14   Richardson, H. N., "Two Addenda to 'Some Notes on *Lîṣ* and Its
           Derivatives,' " *VT* 5 (1955) 434-36.

2:12   Deichgräber, R., "Zur Messiaserwartung der Damaskusschrift," *ZAW*
           78 (1966) 333-43.

2:12   Rabin, C. and J. L. Teicher, "On a Puzzling Passage in the Damascus
           Fragments," *JJS* 6 (1955) 53-55, 111.

2:12   Teicher, J. L., "Puzzling Passages in the Damascus Fragments," *JJS*
           (1954) 139-47.

2:12   Yadin, Y., "Three Notes on the Dead Sea Scrolls," *IEJ* 6 (1956)
           158-62.

2:14-15   Bergmeier, R., "Glaube als Werk? Die 'Werke Gottes' im Damaskus-
           schrift, II, 14-15 und Johannes 6, 28-29," *RQ* 6 (1967-69)
           253-60.

3:4   Kimbrough, S. T., Jr., "The Concept of Sabbath at Qumran," *RQ* 5
           (1964-65) 483-502.

3:21   Teicher, J. L., "Priests and Sacrifices in the Dead Sea Scrolls," *JJS*
           5 (1954) 93-99.

4:1   North, R., "The Qumrân 'Sadducees,' " *CBQ* 17 (1955) 44-68 [164-
           88].

4:4   Daniélou, J., "Eschatologie sadocite et eschatologie chrétienne," *Les
           manuscrits de la Mer Morte: Colloque de Strasbourg, 25-27 mai
           1955* (Paris: Presses universitaires, 1957), pp. 111-25.

4:4   Huppenbauer, H. W., "Zur Eschatologie der Damaskusschrift," *RQ* 4 (1963-64) 567-73.

4:12   Kosmala, H., "The Three Nets of Belial (A Study in the Terminology of Qumran and the New Testament)," *ASTI* 4 (1965) 91-113.

4:19   Winter, P., "Two Non-Allegorical Expressions in the Dead Sea Scrolls," *PEQ* 91 (1959) 38-46.

4:20-21   Winter, P., "Sadoqite Fragments IV 20, 21 and the Exegesis of Genesis 1, 27 in Late Judaism," *ZAW* 68 (1956) 71-84, 264.

5:5-6   Sutcliffe, E., "The Translation of CDC 5:5-6," *VT* 11 (1961) 91-94.

5:8   Krauss, S., "Die Ehe zwischen Onkel und Nichte," *Studies in Jewish Literature Issued in Honor of Prof. Kaufmann Kohler* (Berlin: G. Reimer, 1913), pp. 165-75.

6:1   Winter, P., "The Holy Messiah," *ZNW* 50 (1959) 275.

6:5   Jaubert, A., " 'Le pays de Damas,' " *RB* 65 (1958) 214-48.

6:5   North, R., "The Damascus of Qumran Geography," *PEQ* 87 (1955) 34-48.

6:7   Winter, P., "Notes on Wieder's Observations on the *Dwrš htwrh* in the Book of the New Covenanters of Damascus," *JQR* 45 (1954-55) 39-47.

6:10   Carmignac, J., "Le retour du Docteur de Justice à la fin des jours?" *RQ* 1 (1958-59) 235-48.

7:6   Fensham, F. C., " 'Camp' in the New Testament and Milḥamah," *RQ* 4 (1963-64) 557-62.

7:9-21   Kosmala, H., "Damascus Document 7, 9-21," *Essays on the Dead Sea Scrolls in Memory of E. L. Sukenik* (Jerusalem: Hekhal Ha-Sefer, 1961), pp. 183-90.

7:12-21   Daniélou, J., "L'étoile de Jacob et la mission chrétienne à Damas," *VC* 11 (1957) 121-38.

8:11   Dupont-Sommer, A., " 'Le chef des rois de Yâwân' dans l'Ecrit de Damas," *Semitica* 5 (1955) 41-57.

9:1   Falk, Z. W., *"Beḥuqey hagoyim* in Damascus Document IX, 1," *RQ* 6 (1967-69) 569.

9:1   Winter, P., "Sadoqite Fragments IX, 1," *RQ* 6 (1967-68) 131-36.

9:1   Delcor, M., "Les tribunaux de l'église de Corinthe et les tribunaux de Qumran," *Studiorum paulinorum congressus internationalis catholicus 1961* (Analecta biblica, 17-18; Rome: Pontifical Biblical Institute, 1963), pp. 535-48.

         "The Courts of the Church of Corinth and the Courts of Qumran," *Paul and Qumran* (ed. J. Murphy-O'Connor; Chicago: Priory, 1968), pp. 69-84.

9:18   Goetz, K. G., "Ist der *mbqr* der Genizafragmente wirklich das Vorbild des christlichen Episkopats?" *ZNW* 30 (1931) 89-93.

9:18   Osten-Sacken, P. von der, "Bemerkungen zur Stellung des Mebaqqer in der Sektenschrift," *ZNW* 55 (1964) 18-26.

10:6   Goshen-Gottstein, M. H., " 'Sefer Hagu'—The End of a Puzzle," *VT* 8 (1958) 286-88.

11:21-23   Talmon, S., "A Further Link Between the Judean Covenanters and the Essenes," *HTR* 56 (1963) 313-19.

12:15-17 Baumgarten, J. M., "The Essene Avoidance of Oil and the Laws of Purity," *RQ* 6 (1967-69) 183-92.

13:7-8 Marcus, R., *"Bprtyh* in the Damascus Covenant XIII. 7-8," *JNES* 15 (1956) 184-87.

13:8 Milik, J. T., "Un termino enigmatico del Documento di Damasco *bprtyh, CD* 13, 8," *Biblos-Press* 6/4 (1965) 110-12.

13:20 Rosenthal, J., "The Sabbath Laws of the Qumranites or the Damascus Covenanters," *Biblical Research* 6 (1961) 10-17.

14:12-16 Teicher, J. L., "Restoration of the 'Damascus Fragments' xiv, 12-16," *JJS* 3 (1952) 53-55, 87-88.

14:19 Priest, J. F., "Mebaqqer, Paqid, and the Messiah," *JBL* 81 (1962) 55-61.

18:21 Carmignac, J., "L'utilité ou l'inutilité des sacrifices sanglants dans la 'Règle de la communauté' de Qumran," *RB* 63 (1956) 524-32.

20:1 Maier, J., "Zum Begriff *yḥd* in den Texten von Qumran," *ZAW* 72 (1960) 148-66.

20:1 Dombrowski, B. W., *"Hyḥd* in 1QS and *to koinon:* An Instance of Early Greek and Jewish Synthesis," *HTR* 59 (1966) 293-307.

20:1 Philonenko, M., "Un titre messianique de Bar Kokeba," *TZ* 17 (1961) 434-35.

(D) *More General Studies*

(1) *Up to 1947*

[Anonymous], "A New Discovery in Early Christian History," *The Independent* 69 (1910) 1337-39.

[Anonymous], "Mr. Margoliouth's Dream," *The Independent* 71 (1911) 555-56.

Adler, E. N., "The Sadducean Christians of Damascus," *Athenaeum* (London) 4345 (4 Feb., 1911) 128.

Bacher, W., "Zu Schechters neuestem Geniza-Funde," *Zeitschrift für hebräische Bibliographie* 15 (1911) 13-26.

Barnes, W. E., "Fresh Light on Maccabean Times," *JTS* 13 (1911) 301-3.

Beer, G., Review of W. Staerk, *Die jüdische Gemeinde, TLZ* 49 (1924) 33-34.

Bertholet, A., "Damaskusschrift," *RGG*² 1 (1927) 1775-76.

   "Zur Datierung der Damaskus-Schrift," *Karl Budde zum siebzigsten Geburtstag* (BZAW 34; ed. K. Marti; Giessen: Töpelmann, 1920), pp. 31-37.

Bousset, W., "Literatur und Religion des Spätjudentums und des rabbinischen Judentums," *ThRu* 18 (1915) 41-58, esp. pp. 51-58.

Bousset, W. and H. Gressmann, *Die Religion des Judentums im späthellenistischen Zeitalter* (HNT 21; 4th ed.; Tübingen: Mohr, 1966 [reprint]), pp. 15-16.

Büchler, A., "Schechter's 'Jewish Sectaries,' " *JQR* ns 3 (1912-13) 429-85.

Eerdmanns, B. D., "De Zadokieten," *Theologisch tijdschrift* 45 (1911) 282-85.

Eisler, R., "The Sadoqite Book of the New Covenant: Its Date and Origin," *Occident and Orient: Being Studies . . . in Honour of . . . M. Gaster's 80th Birthday* (eds. B. Schindler and A. Marmorstein; London: Taylor's Foreign Press, 1936), pp 110-43.

Foakes-Jackson, F. J. and K. Lake, "The Covenanters of Damascus," *The Beginnings of Christianity* (London: Macmillan) I/1 (1920) 97-101.

Frey, J. B., "Apocryphes de l'Ancien Testament: 5. Le Document Sadocite," *DBS* 1 (1928) 395-403.

Ginzberg, L., "Eine unbekannte jüdische Sekte," *MGWJ* 55 (1911) 666-98; 56 (1912) 33-48, 285-307, 417-48, 546-66, 664-89; 57 (1913) 153-67, 284-308, 394-418, 666-96; 58 (1914) 16-48, 143-77, 395-429. Reprinted as a book: *Eine unbekannte jüdische Sekte* (New York, 1922).

Gressmann, H., "Anzeigen," *ZDMG* 66 (1912) 491-503.

"Eine neuentdeckte jüdische Schrift aus der Zeit Christi," *Internationale Wochenschrift für Wissenschaft, Kunst und Technik* 5 (1911) 257-66.

"Mitteilung," *TLZ* 37 (1912) 541.

Gutmann, J., "Damaskusschrift," *Encyclopaedia judaica* 5 (1930) 750-53.

Hitchcock, G. S., "The Jewish Sect of the New Covenant at Damascus," *The Catholic University Bulletin* 19 (1913) 533-46.

Hölscher, G., "Zur Frage nach Alter und Herkunft der sogen. Damaskusschrift," *ZNW* 28 (1929) 21-46.

[Jacobs, J.], "Dr. Schechter's New 'Find,'" *American Hebrew* 88 (1910-11) 226-27.

Kohler, K., "Dositheus, the Samaritan Heresiarch, and His Relations to Jewish and Christian Doctrines and Sects (A Study of Professor Schechter's Recent Publication)," *AJT* 15 (1911) 404-35.

Landauer, S., Review of S. Schechter, *Documents*, I, *TLZ* 37 (1912) 261-64.

Lauterbach, S., "Midrash und Mishnah: A Study in the Early History of Halakah," *JQR* ns 5 (1914-15) 503-27; 6 (1915-16) 23-95, 303-23.

"The Sadducees and Pharisees," *Studies in Jewish Literature Issued in Honor of Prof. Kaufmann Kohler* (Berlin: G. Reimer, 1913), pp. 176-98.

Leszynsky, R., "Der neue Bund in Damaskus," *Jahrbuch für jüdische Geschichte und Literatur* 17 (1914) 97-125.

Die Sadduzäer (Berlin: Mayer und Müller, 1912), pp. 142-67.

"Observations sur les *Fragments of a Zadokite Work* édité par Schechter," *REJ* 62 (1911) 190-96.

Lévi, I., "Notes sur les observations de M. Leszynsky," *REJ* 62 (1911) 197-200.

"Le tétragramme et l'écrit sadokite de Damas," *REJ* 68 (1914) 119-21.

Lightley, J. W., "The Recently-Discovered Zadokite Fragments," *London Quarterly Review* 123 (1915) 15-31.

Margoliouth, D. C., "The Zadokites," *Expositor* 8/6 (1913) 157-64.

Margoliouth, G., "Fragments of a Zadokite Work," *International Journal of Apocrypha* 37 (1914) 36-37.

"The Calendar, the Sabbath and the Marriage Law in the Geniza-Zadokite Document," *ExpTim* 23 (1911-12) 362-65; 24 (1912-13) 553-58; 25 (1913-14) 560-64.

"The Sadducean Christians of Damascus," *Bibliotheca sacra* 69 (1912) 421-37.

"The Sadducean Christians of Damascus," *Athenaeum* 4335 (26 Nov., 1910) 657-59; 4349 (4 Mar., 1911) 249.

"The Sadducean Christians of Damascus," *Expositor* 8/2 (1911) 499-517; 8/3 (1912) 213-35.

"The Two Zadokite Messiahs," *JTS* 12 (1910-11) 446-50.

"The Zadokites Once More," *Jewish Review* 2 (1911-12) 361-69.

Marmorstein, A., "Eine unbekannte jüdische Sekte," *Theologisch tijdschrift* 52 (1918) 92-122.

Meyer, E., "Die Gemeinde des neuen Bundes im Lande Damaskus: Eine jüdische Schrift aus der Seleukidenzeit," *Abh. der preussischen Akademie der Wissenschaften* (Berlin), Philos.-hist. Kl. 1919, Nr. 9, pp. 1-65.

Montgomery, J. A., "A Lost Jewish Sect," *Biblical World* 38 (1911) 373-83.

Moore, G. F., *Judaism in the First Centuries of the Christian Era* (3 vols.; Cambridge: Harvard, 1927-30), 1. 200-204; 2. 27, 32-33, 121-22; 3. 58-59.

"The Covenanters of Damascus: A Hitherto Unknown Jewish Sect," *HTR* 4 (1911) 330-77.

Poznański, S., "More about Schechter's 'Fragments of a Zadokite Work,'" *Jewish Review* 2 (1911-12) 443-46.

Review of S. Schechter, *Documents,* I-II, *Jewish Review* 2 (1911-12) 273-81.

"Allegorische Gesetzesauslegung bei den älteren Karäern," *Studies in Jewish Literature Issued in Honor of Prof. Kaufmann Kohler* (Berlin: G. Reimer, 1913), pp. 237-59.

Preisker, H., "Zum Streit um die Geniza-Texte der jüdischen Gemeinde des neuen Bundes in Damaskus," *Theologische Studien und Kritiken* 98-99 (1926) 295-318.

Reicke, B., "The Jewish 'Damascus Documents' and the New Testament," *Symbolae biblicae upsalienses* 6 (1946) 1-24.

Revel, B., "Inquiry into the Sources of Karaite Halakah," *JQR* ns 2 (1911-12) 517-44; ns. 3 (1912-13) 337-96.

Schechter, S., "Announcement," *JQR* ns 3 (1912-13) 485.

"Reply to Dr. Büchler's Review of Schechter's 'Jewish Sectaries'," *JQR* ns 4 (1913-14) 449-74.

Schlatter, A., *Geschichte Israels von Alexander dem Grossen bis Hadrian* (3rd ed.; Stuttgart: Calwer Vereinsbuchhandlung, 1925), pp. 250, 432-33.

Segal, M. H., "Additional Notes on 'Fragments of a Zadokite Work,'" *JQR* ns 3 (1912-13) 301-11.

"Notes on 'Fragments of a Zadokite Work,'" *JQR* ns. 2 (1911-12) 133-41.

Ward, W. H., "The 'Zadokite' Document," *Bibliotheca sacra* 68 (1911) 429-56.

Weir, T. H., "Survey of Recent Archaeology in Relation to Palestine," *Review of Theology and Philosophy* 8 (1912-13) 7-8.

Westphal, G., "Die Inschrift aus der Kairoer Geniza," *Theologischer Jahresbericht* (Leipzig) 31/1 (1911) 238-39.

(2) *Since 1947*

Amusin, I. D., *Rukopisi Mertvogo morya* (Moscow: Akademiy Nauk SSSR, 1960), pp. 103-7.

Baillet, M., "Damasco, Documento de," *Enciclopedia de la Bíblia* 2 (Barcelona, 1963) 756-62.

Baltzer, K., *Das Bundesformular* (Wissenschaftliche Monographien zum Alten und Neuen Testament, 4; 2nd ed.; Neukirchen: Neukirchener Verlag, 1964), pp. 117-27.

Bardtke, H., *Die Handschriftenfunde am Toten Meer: Die Sekte von Qumran* (2nd ed.; Berlin: Evangelische Hauptbibelgesellschaft, 1958), pp. 257-76.

Betz, O., "Zadokite Fragments," *IDB* 4 (1962) 929-33.

Bietenhard, H., "Sabbatvorschriften von Qumran im Lichte des rabbinischen Rechts und der Evangelien," *Qumran-Probleme* (ed. H. Bardtke; Deutsche Akademie der Wissenschaften zu Berlin: Sektion für Altertumswissenschaft, 42; Berlin, 1963), pp. 53-74.

Brand, J., "The Scroll of the Covenant of Damascus and Date of Composition," *Tarbiz* 28 (1958-59) 18-39.

Braun, H., *Spätjüdisch-häretischer und frühchristlicher Radikalismus* (Tübingen: Mohr, 1957), 1. 90-139.

Brownlee, W. H., "A Comparison of the Covenanters of the Dead Sea Scrolls with Pre-Christian Jewish Sects," *BA* 13 (1950) 50-72.

Bruce, F. F., *Biblical Exegesis in the Qumran Texts* (Grand Rapids: Eerdmans, 1959) pp. 28-36 (ch. 3).

Carmignac, J., "Comparaison entre les manuscrits 'A' et 'B' du Document de Damas," *RQ* 2 (1959-60) 53-67.

Cavaignac, E., "Damas de 125 à 29 av. J. C.," *Mélanges bibliques rédigés en l'honneur de André Robert* (Paris: Bloud et Gay, 1957), pp. 348-53.

Delcor, M., "Contribution à l'étude de la législation des sectaires de Damas et de Qumrân," *RB* 61 (1954) 533-53; 62 (1955) 60-75.

Dupont-Sommer, A., "L'écrit de Damas," *Evidences* #59 (1956) 13-27; #60 (1956) 25-36.

     Nouveaux aperçus sur les manuscrits de la Mer Morte (L'orient ancien illustré 5; Paris: Maisonneuve, 1953), pp. 109-40.

Eissfeldt, O., *The Old Testament: An Introduction* (tr. P. R. Ackroyd; New York: Harper and Row, 1965), pp. 649-52.

Fitzmyer, J. A., "The Use of Explicit Old Testament Quotations in Qumran Literature and in the New Testament," *NTS* 7 (1960-61) 297-333.

Ford, J. M., "Can We Exclude Samaritan Influence from Qumran?" *RQ* 6 (1967-69) 109-29, esp. 117-19.

Haapa, E., *Qumran Kuolleen meren löydöt 1950-luvun tutkimuksessa* (Porvoo-Helsinki: W. Söderström, 1960).

Hahn, S., "Zur Chronologie der Qumran-Schriften," *Acta orientalia* 11 (1960) 181-89.

Iwry, S., "Was There a Migration to Damascus? The Problem of *šby yśr'l*," *W. F. Albright Volume* (Eretz-Israel, 9; Jerusalem: Israel Exploration Society, 1969), pp. 80-88.

Kahle, P., "The Community of the New Covenant and the Hebrew Scrolls," *Opera minora* (Leiden: Brill, 1956), pp. 96-112.

     "Die Gemeinde des neuen Bundes und die hebräischen Handschriften aus der Höhle," *TLZ* 77 (1952) 401-12.

     The Cairo Geniza (2nd ed.; Oxford: Blackwell, 1959), pp. 17-28.

Kirkasios, T. G., "To Damaskēnon ē Sadōkikon eggraphon kai hē hairesis tēs neas diathēkēs," *Theologia* (Athens) 31 (1960) 151-66.

Kuhn, K. G., *Konkordanz zu den Qumrantexten* (Göttingen: Vandenhoeck und Ruprecht, 1960).

Margoliouth, M., "Mib-b^{e}rît Dammeśeq 'ad serek hay-yaḥad," *Sinai* 30 (1951-52) 9-21.

Molin, G., *Die Söhne des Lichtes: Zeit und Stellung der Handschriften vom Toten Meer* (Wien: Herold, 1954), pp. 108-18.

Quanbeck, P. A., *The Use of the Old Testament in the Damascus Document Compared with Normative Judaism and the Synoptic Gospels* (Princeton: Dissertation, Theological Seminary, 1958).

Rabin, C., "Notes on the Habbakuk Scroll and the Zadokite Document," *VT* 5 (1955) 148-62, esp. 160-62.

Rabinowitz, I., "Sequence and Dates of the Extra-biblical Dead Sea Scroll Texts and 'Damascus' Fragments," *VT* 3 (1953) 175-85.

Reicke, B., "Die Ta'āmire-Schriften und die Damaskus-Fragmente," *Studia theologica* 2 (1949-50) 45-70.

Roberts, B. J., "Some Observations on the Damascus Document and the Dead Sea Scrolls," *BJRL* 34 (1951-52) 366-87.

Romeo, A., "Sadoquita, Documento," *Enciclopedia de la Bíblia* 6 (Barcelona, 1965) 335-44.

Rost, L., "Damaskusschrift," *RGG*³ 2 (1958) 24-25.

    "Das Verhältnis von 'Damaskusschrift' und 'Sektenrolle,'" *TLZ* 77 (1952) 723-26.

    "Zur Struktur der Gemeinde des neuen Bundes im Lande Damaskus," *VT* 9 (1959) 393-98.

Rowley, H. H., "Some Traces of the History of the Qumran Sect," *TZ* 13 (1957) 530-40.

    "The Covenanters of Damascus and the Dead Sea Scrolls," *BJRL* 35 (1952) 111-54.

    "The Qumran Sect and Christian Origins," *BJRL* 44 (1961-62) 119-56.

    The Zadokite Fragments and the Dead Sea Scrolls (Oxford: Blackwell, 1952).

Rubinstein, A., "Notes on Some Syntactical Irregularities in Text B of the Zadokite Documents," *VT* 7 (1957) 356-61.

    "Urban Halakhah and Camp Rules in the 'Cairo Fragments of a Damascus Covenant,'" *Sefarad* 12 (1952) 283-96.

Schubert, K., "Bemerkungen zum Verständnis einiger Termini in den Handschriften von 'En Feśḥa und im Damaskusdocument," *TLZ* 77 (1952) 329-36.

    "Damaskusschrift," *Lexikon für Theologie und Kirche*² 3 (1957) 135-36.

Schwarz, O. J. R., *Der erste Teil der Damaskusschrift und das Alte Testament* (Diest: Lichtland, 1965).

Segal, M. H., "The Habakkuk 'Commentary' and the Damascus Fragments," *JBL* 70 (1951) 131-47.

Teglbjaerg, J. O., "Det litteraere slaegtskab mellem Damaskusskriftet og Manual of Discipline," *Dansk teologisk tidsskrift* 18 (1955) 241-47.

Teicher, J. L., "The Damascus Fragments and the Origin of the Jewish Christian Sect," *JJS* 2 (1951) 115-43.

Trinquet, J., "Les liens 'sadocites' de l'écrit de Damas, des manuscrits de la Mer Morte et de l'Ecclésiastique," *VT* 1 (1951) 287-92.

Vogt, E., "Communitas Qumrân," *Biblica* 34 (1953) 269-70.

Wernberg-Møller, P., "Some Passages in the 'Zadokite' Fragments and Their Parallels in the *Manual of Discipline*," *JSS* 1 (1956) 110-28.

"The Nature of the *Yaḥad* according to the *Manual of Discipline* and Related Documents," *The Annual of Leeds University Oriental Society* 6 (1966-68: Dead Sea Scroll Studies, 1969) 56-85.

Wiesenberg, E., "Chronological Data in the Zadokite Fragments," *VT* 5 (1955) 284-308.

Review of C. Rabin, *The Zadokite Documents, PEQ* 86 (1954) 101-106.

The foregoing bibliography, though lengthy, can scarcely claim to be exhaustive. In any case, it attests to the importance of the first volume of the present work that is now being reprinted. Hopefully, it will serve as a starting point for further research in this area.

JOSEPH A. FITZMYER, S.J.
The University of Chicago

Nov. 1969

List of Abbreviations

AJT	*American Journal of Theology*
ASTI	*Annual of the Swedish Theological Institute*
BA	*Biblical Archaeologist*
BJRL	*Bulletin of the John Rylands Library*
CBQ	*Catholic Biblical Quarterly*
DBS	*Dictionnaire de la Bible, Supplément*
ETL	*Ephemerides theologicae lovanienses*
ExpTim	*Expository Times*
HTR	*Harvard Theological Review*
IDB	*Interpreter's Dictionary of the Bible*
IEJ	*Israel Exploration Journal*
JBL	*Journal of Biblical Literature*
JJS	*Journal of Jewish Studies*
JNES	*Journal of Near Eastern Studies*
JSS	*Journal of Semitic Studies*
JTS	*Journal of Theological Studies*
JQR	*Jewish Quarterly Review*
MGWJ	*Monatschrift für Geschichte und Wissenschaft des Judentums*
NTS	*New Testament Studies*
PEQ	*Palestine Exploration Quarterly*
RB	*Revue biblique*
REJ	*Revue des études juives*
RGG	*Religion in Geschichte und Gegenwart*
RQ	*Revue de Qumran*
ThRu	*Theologische Rundschau*
TLZ	*Theologische Literaturzeitung*
TZ	*Theologische Zeitschrift*
VC	*Vigiliae christianae*
VT	*Vetus Testamentum*
ZAW	*Zeitschrift für die alttestamentliche Wissenschaft*
ZDMG	*Zeitschrift des deutschen morgenländischen Gesellschaft*
ZNW	*Zeitschrift für die neutestamentliche Wissenschaft*

NOTES

[1] See Norman Bentwich, *Solomon Schechter: A Biography* (Philadelphia: Jewish Publication Society of America, 1938); *Selected Writings, Solomon Schechter* (Oxford: East and West Library, 1946), pp. 9-31; A. Eisenberg, *Fill a Blank Page: A Biography of Solomon Schechter* (New York: United Synagogue Commission of Jewish Education, 1965).—Cf. A. S. Oko, *Solomon Schechter, M.A., Litt.D.: A Bibliography* (Cambridge: University Press, 1938).

[2] The full number of documents that came from the Cairo Genizah is much greater; a recent estimate speaks of "a quarter of a million" leaves, which are mainly fragments of Hebrew books. Collections of Cairo Genizah material are widely scattered over the world. For an idea of the extent of this material, which concerns mainly the history of medieval Judaism (from the tenth to the thirteenth centuries), see S. Shaked, *A Tentative Bibliography of Geniza Documents* (The Hague: Mouton, 1964); cf. P. Kahle, *The Cairo Geniza* (2nd ed.; Oxford: Blackwell, 1959).

[3] Selections from the *Book of Commandments* can be found in a modern translation in L. Nemoy, *Karaite Anthology: Excerpts from the Early Literature* (Yale Judaica series, 7; New Haven: Yale University Press, 1952), pp. 11-20. For some studies of 'Anan's writing, see S. Poznański, "Anan et ses écrits," *REJ* 44 (1902) 161-87; 45 (1902) 50-69, 176-203; J. Mann, "'Anan's Liturgy and His Half-Yearly Cycle of the Reading of the Law," *Journal of Jewish Lore and Philosophy* 1 (1919) 329-53; L. Nemoy, "'Anan ben David: A Re-appraisal of the Historical Data," *Semitic Studies in Memory of Immanuel Löw* (ed. A. Scheiber; Budapest: Publications of the Alexander Kohut Memorial Foundation, 1947), pp. 239-48; "Early Karaism," *JQR* 40 (1949-50) 307-15.

[4] Lines 8-22 are unrelated; cf. Harkavy, pp. 69-72.

[5] See N. Golb, "The Dietary Laws of the Damascus Covenant in Relation to Those of the Karaites," *JJS* 8 (1957) 51-69; "Literary and Doctrinal Aspects of the Damascus Covenant in the Light of Karaite Literature," *JQR* 47 (1957) 354-74.

[6] "Die Gemeinde des neuen Bundes im Lande Damaskus: Eine jüdische Schrift aus der Seleukidenzeit," *Abh. der preussischen Akademie der Wissenschaften* (Berlin), Phil.-hist. Kl. 1919, Nr. 9, pp. 1-65.

[7] "The Sadducean Christians of Damascus," *Expositor* 8/2 (1911) 499-517; 8/3 (1912) 213-35. See further the bibliography below.

[8] A. Büchler, "Schechter's 'Jewish Sectaries,'" *JQR* ns 3 (1912-13) 429-85; A. Marmorstein, "Eine unbekannte jüdische Sekte," *Theologische tidjschrift* 52 (1918) 92-122; S. Zeitlin, Review of R. T. Herford, *The Pharisees, JQR* ns 16 (1925-26) 385-86; P. R. Weis, "The Date of the Habakkuk Scroll," *JQR* 41 (1950-51) 125-54, esp. pp. 137-42.

[8a] E.g., in the title of C. Rabin's edition of the text, *The Zadokite Documents* (Oxford: Clarendon, 1954).

[9] "Document relatif à la 'Communauté des fils de Sadoc,'" *REJ* 65 (1913) 24-31. Cf. A. M. Habermann, *'Edah we-'Eduth*, p. 124; *Megilloth Midbar Yᵉhudah*, p. 166; S. Talmon, "The 'Manual of Benedictions' of the Sect of the Judaean Desert," *RQ* 2 (1959-60) 475-500.

[10] M. Burrows, *The Dead Sea Scrolls of St. Mark's Monastery: II. Plates and Transcription of the Manual of Discipline* (New Haven: American Schools of Oriental Research, 1951).

[11] For example, H. H. Rowley, "The Covenanters of Damascus and the Dead Sea Scrolls," *BJRL* 35 (1952) 111-54; A. Dupont-Sommer, *Aperçus préliminaires sur les manuscrits de la Mer Morte* (L'orient ancien illustré, 4; Paris: Maisonneuve, 1950); *The Dead Sea Scrolls: A Preliminary Survey* (tr. E. M. Rowley; Oxford: Blackwell, 1952), pp. 53-68.

[12] See F. M. Cross, Jr., "The Development of the Jewish Scripts," *The Bible and the Ancient Near East* (Essays in Honor of William Foxwell Albright; ed. G. E. Wright; Anchor A 431; Garden City, N.Y.: Doubleday, 1965), pp. 133-202; N. Avigad, "The Palaeography of the Dea Sea Scrolls and Related Documents," *Aspects of the Dead Sea Scrolls* (Scripta hierosolymitana, 4; Jerusalem: Magnes Press, 1958), pp. 56-87. The conclusion of these scholars has been contested by S. Zeitlin, who maintains that "there is no proof whatsoever that these Fragments belong to a very early period" (*The Zadokite Fragments* [see n. 24 below], p. 7).

13 See [P. Benoit, *et al.*,] "Le travail d'édition des fragments manuscrits de Qumrân," *RB* 63 (1956) 49-67, esp. p. 61; "Editing the Manuscript Fragments from Qumran," *BA* 19 (1956) 75-96. J. T. Milik, *Ten Years of Discovery in the Wilderness of Judaea* (SBT 26; Naperville, Ill.: Allenson, 1958), pp. 38-39, 151-52.—Milik has published a fragment of one of the 4Q texts of the Damascus Document, 4QDᵃ 1 xvii 1-16; see "Fragment d'une source du psautier (4QPs 89) et fragments des Jubilés, du Document de Damas, d'un phylactère dans la grotte 4 de Qumran," *RB* 73 (1966) 94-106. It corresponds, however, to nothing in the Cairo Genizah text, but belongs to the additional material that precedes 15:1 (see the outline below).

14 J. T. Milik, "**12.** Document de Damas," in M. Baillet, J. T. Milik, and R. de Vaux, *Les 'Petites Grottes' de Qumrân* (Discoveries in the Judaean Desert of Jordan, III; Oxford: Clarendon, 1962), p. 181. This text (5QD or 5Q*12*) contains five fragmentary lines that correspond to CD 9:7-10, except for the first line which corresponds to an addition that is found in 4QDᵉ 10 iii 20 (as yet unpublished).—See also M. Baillet, "**15.** Document de Damas," *ibid.*, pp. 128-31. This text, of which the siglum is 6QD or 6Q*15*, consists of five fragments, which correspond to CD 4:19-21; 5:13-14; 5:18-6:2; 6:20-7:1; the fifth fragment (with five fragmentary lines) corresponds to nothing in CD, and apparently to nothing in the 4Q texts either. Cf. M. Baillet, "Fragments du Document de Damas: Qumrân, Grotte 6," *RB* 63 (1956) 513-23 (+ pl. II); see also his preliminary notice on p. 55.

15 For the defense of a minority view (i.e., Zealot identification), see G. R. Driver, *The Judaean Scrolls: The Problem and a Solution* (Oxford: Blackwell, 1964); C. Roth, *The Historical Background of the Dead Sea Scrolls* (Oxford: Blackwell, 1958). But cf. R. de Vaux, "Esséniens ou Zélotes? A propos d'un livre récent," *RB* 72 (1965) 212-35 (English translation, *NTS* 13 [1966-67] 89-104; H. H. Rowley, "The Qumran Sectaries and the Zealots: An Examination of a Recent Theory," *VT* 9 (1959) 379-92. For still another view, see S. Zeitlin, "History, Historians, and the Dead Sea Scrolls," *JQR* 55 (1964-65) 97-116; also his previous studies, "The Essenes and Messianic Expectations" and "The Pharisees," respectively in *JQR* 45 (1954-55) 83-119 and 52 (1961-62) 97-129.

16 See F. M. Cross, Jr., *The Ancient Library of Qumran* (Anchor A272; rev. ed.; Garden City, N.Y.: Doubleday, 1961), pp. 81-82; R. North, "The Damascus of Qumran Geography," *PEQ* 87 (1955) 34-48; A. Jaubert, " 'Le pays de Damas,' " *RB* 65 (1958) 214-48; M. H. Segal, "The Habakkuk 'Commentary' and the Damascus Fragments," *JBL* 70 (1951) 131-47; C. T. Fritsch, "Herod the Great and the Qumran Community," *JBL* 74 (1955) 173-81; J. T. Milik, *Ten Years*, p. 90.

17 J. T. Milik, *Ten Years*, pp. 87-93.

18 See the references in F. M. Cross, Jr., *The Ancient Library of Qumran*, p. 79, n. 42.

19 There is the further question of the skeletons of women and children that have been found at Khirbet Qumran. Though more than a thousand graves have been counted there, marked by a low rectangular mound of stones (which in most cases have been kicked about over the centuries), only about 50 of the graves were originally opened by the excavators. Most of the skeletons were male, especially those found in the center of the cemetery; but female skeletons and those of children were found on the periphery and in an annexed area (see R. de Vaux, *L'archéologie et les manuscrits de la Mer Morte* [Schweich Lectures, 1959; London: Oxford University Press, 1961], pp. 38, 47). Cf. S. H. Steckoll, "Preliminary Excavation Report on the Qumran Cemetery," *RQ* 6 (1967-69) 323-36.

20 There are at least ten different fragmentary copies of the *Manual of Discipline* among the Cave IV fragments (see C. Burchard, *Bibliographie zu den Handschriften vom Toten Meer* [BZAW 89; Berlin: Töpelmann, 1965], pp. 337-38). There is possibly one fragmentary copy from Cave V (see J. T. Milik, DJD 3. 180-81, 5Q*11*).

21 *Ten Years*, pp. 151-52.

22 *The Apocrypha and Pseudepigrapha of the Old Testament* (Oxford: Clarendon, 1913), 2. 796-97.

23 *JQR* NS 4 (1913-14) 474. For an attempt to gloss over this matter, see N. Bentwich, *Solomon Schechter, A Biography*, p. 266.

24 JQR Monograph series, 1 (Philadelphia: Dropsie College, 1952). Pp. 1-32; pls. I-XVI, XIX-XX. The facsimiles of the mss. published by Zeitlin are preceded by an Introduction (32 pp.) which summarizes his views on this writing.

25 An asterisk appended to words in the first column indicates that they are clearly read as Schechter presents them, but they must be regarded as scribal errors. Square brackets [ ] indicate editorial restorations of lacunae; angular brackets < > editorial corrections of omitted letters or words; braces { } editorial deletions of extra letters added by a scribe.— One should also consult the comments of S. Zeitlin (*The Zadokite Fragments*, pp. 6-7) for some idea of the difficulties in reading these medieval copies of the text.

PREFACE

THE two groups of fragments appearing herewith under the title of DOCUMENTS OF JEWISH SECTARIES, were all discovered in the Cairo Genizah, the greatest part of which is now in the possession of the Cambridge University Library, England, and marked as the Taylor-Schechter Collection. They are published here for the first time, each group in a separate volume. The first volume contains the group bearing the title FRAGMENTS OF A ZADOKITE WORK, which title was supplied by me on a hypothesis. The second volume reproduces FRAGMENTS OF THE BOOK OF THE COMMANDMENTS BY ANAN, which title was also supplied by me, but which may be accepted as a certainty. The importance of the first volume, which I have little doubt will prove a valuable contribution to the history of early Jewish Sects, suggested to me the advisability of furnishing the student with an English translation accompanying the text. The risk of giving a translation of such a defective text as the FRAGMENTS OF A ZADOKITE WORK unfortunately represent, was great indeed, and I was fully aware of it. This risk I felt not less when writing the Introduction and the Notes to the text, but I preferred to be blamed for my mistakes and be corrected, than be praised for my prudence of non-committal, which policy I do not always think worthy of a student. All I could do was both in the Introduction and in the Notes to call the attention of the reader to the unfortunate condition of our text. In the Notes in particular, I have especially marked many passages as obscure, the meaning of which was unclear to me. The literalness of the translation, to which I kept throughout, will, I believe, make the inherent shortcomings of the original fairly transparent. Words or phrases based on an emendation of the original which was evident to me are marked by asterisks. No student who has had experience in editing texts can fail to see at once that very little can be taken for certain, and the largest part of the commentary and the conclusions based on it in the Introduction can only be regarded as tentative.

The divisions into paragraphs were supplied by me, so as to enable the student to form some notion of the variety of matter touched upon in our fragments. I must further point out that by some oversight, which is excusable enough in view of the distance of my residence from the

v

(39)

place of publication, I had no opportunity to read the last proof of Text A of the first volume. I therefore collated this text again with the manuscript, and this collation resulted in a few new readings, which are incorporated in the Corrections and Additions at the end of the volume, to which especial attention is called. I have added also a facsimile of a page of text A and text B, thus offering an opportunity to scholars to make a fresh search in Genizah material. Nobody will rejoice more than I, if this should lead to the discoveries, though they be made "almost simultaneously," of fresh fragments, which will further elucidate the history of the sect, even should they prove to upset my theories.

Much less was the labour spent upon the second volume, קונטרסים מספר המצות לענן Fragments of the Book of the Commandments by Anan. My contribution to its elucidation consists only in giving at the end of the text the necessary references to the Bible. Occasionally references will also be found to Dr A. Harkavy's *Studien und Mittheilungen*, part 8 (לקוטי קדמוניות, 2nd part, St Petersburg, 1903). I have no further comment to make on it, as the subject does not fall within the province of my studies, except that I hope it will prove a valuable contribution to the early Karaitic literature, and form a subject of discussion by specialists.

In conclusion, it gives me much pleasure to record here my thanks to Professor Israel Friedlaender, of the Jewish Theological Seminary of America, in New York, and Professor Henry Malter, of the Dropsie College, in Philadelphia, who were helpful in furnishing me with translations from Kirkisani and other Arabic texts, quoted in my first volume. I have further to record here my thanks to Professor Alexander Marx, of the Seminary, who enriched this volume with many a suggestion. His experience in the reading of manuscripts proved also many a time of great aid to me. To my friend Norman Bentwich of London I am also under obligations for aid given to me in various directions. The Index was prepared by Mr Joseph B. Abrahams, Secretary of the Seminary, who was always at my call during the correction of the proofs, and to whom I express here my best thanks.

S. SCHECHTER.

New York,
June 1910.

INTRODUCTION

THE two texts included in this volume reproduce the contents of two fragments in MS. coming originally from the Cairo Genizah and now in the possession of the University Library of Cambridge, England. They form a part of the Taylor-Schechter Collection, and bear the class-marks: T.-S. 10 K 6 and T.-S. 16 311. They will be designated here as Text A and Text B.

TEXT A extending from page 1 to 16 (inclusive) consists of eight leaves, or sixteen pages, measuring $8\frac{1}{2} \times 7\frac{1}{8}$ in. The first four leaves, or eight pages, count 21 lines on each page, whilst the last four leaves (or eight pages) differ in the number of lines, pp. 9—12 having 23 lines. Pages 13—16 are mutilated at the bottom of each page, so that it is impossible to determine with any accuracy how many lines they may have had, but it was assumed in the notes that they contained 23 lines as the preceding four pages. The writing is ancient Oriental, in square characters, but rather stiff, and there is very little consistency in such letters as ', ו, the latter being occasionally so long as almost to be taken for a final ן, whilst the ' is sometimes so large as to be confused with a ו. The ה also greatly resembles the ח, the left stroke reaching the roof of the letter, but this is a feature common to all ancient Oriental MSS. The MS. probably dates from the 10th century. Here and there we have letters provided with Babylonian or Palestinian vowel-points (p. 1, ll. 9, 10, 11, 18, 20, 21; p. 2, ll. 11, 16, 19; p. 3, ll. 8, 9; p. 5, ll. 8, 12, 16, 21; p. 6, ll. 6, 13), but the latter seem to have been added by a hand of a more recent date. Some words are crossed through by the scribe (p. 11, ll. 13, 16; p. 12, l. 17), as indicated in the text. The MS. is possibly defective at the beginning and is certainly so at the end. Pages 13—16 are badly mutilated, both on the edges and at the bottom of the page. The MS. is also torn and obliterated in some other places, by which a few words or letters are affected[1]. Besides the missing pages at the end and at the beginning, there is a lacuna between p. 8 and p. 9, the MS. breaking up at the end of a line, and perhaps in the middle of a sentence. It is impossible to determine how many pages may be missing here. I have also indicated such a lacuna at the end of p. 12, but have subsequently

---

[1] See texts and notes of p. 3, l. 2; p. 6, l. 19; but especially the text and notes of the last four pages.

come to the conclusion to consider it as continuous. As will be seen from the Notes, we have here to deal with a very careless scribe, who not only may have had a very poor copy before him, but also disfigured his text in several places by his inability to read his MS. correctly (p. 1, l. 12; p. 3, l. 7; p. 5, l. 15; p. 8, l. 3; p. 10, l. 21; p. 11, l. 9; p. 13, l. 6; p. 16, l. 2, text and notes).

TEXT B, covering pages 19 and 20, consists of one leaf, or two pages, measuring $13\frac{1}{2} \times 8$ in., written in square characters, but already with a tendency to cursive. Some words are also provided with Babylonian and Palestinian vowel-points (p. 19, ll. 2, 15, 34, 35; p. 20, ll. 2, 3, 7, 8, 11, 14, 16, 19, 20, 24, 33); other words, again, are cancelled by the scribe himself (p. 20, ll. 5--6). It is undoubtedly of a later date than Text A (perhaps the 11th or 12th century), but the scribe must have been more careful and also had a better copy before him. Perhaps it will be more correct to speak of it as another recension of the same Text, as the differences are of such a nature that they cannot always be accounted for by the mere carelessness of the scribe of Text A or by such mere variants inevitable in two MSS. of the same text. This will be best seen by a comparison of the two texts, which on pp. 7—8 overlap each other, and the English translation of which appears in parallel columns.

Apart from the defective state of the MS. owing to age, or the carelessness of the scribe, its whole contents, at least as they are represented by Text A, are in a very fragmentary state, leaving the impression that we are dealing with extracts from a larger work, put together, however, in a haphazard way, with little regard to completeness or order. This is particularly discernible in the legal part. Thus we have on p. 7, l. 8 (=p. 19, l. 5) a reference to the laws concerning vows, which is practically not taken up again till p. 16, l. 5. Page 10, ll. 4—10, again forming the beginning of what we may call the constitution of the Sect and its organization, is suddenly broken off by laws bearing upon Levitical purity, covering about four lines, from which the scribe abruptly passes to Sabbath laws, covering the last ten lines of p. 10, and the whole of p. 11. Then he gives us another law of Levitical purity, covering about a line and a half, but followed by laws bearing upon the Sabbath, upon the relation of the Sect to heathens, upon dietary laws, taking up the larger part of p. 12 (from line 2 to line 15), and concluding with two Levitical purity laws, condensed in two short paragraphs (p. 11, ll. 15—18). It is here where he returns again to the constitution of the Sect and its organization, extending to about the end of p. 14; whilst pp. 15 and 16 represent laws relating to oaths and vows (p. 11, ll. 1--4); laws bearing upon the treatment of penitents (p. 15, l. 5 to end); and again, laws relating to vows and free offerings to the altar. In other parts of the MS. we have the same feeling of abruptness and incompleteness; as for instance, on p. 3, ll. 12—16, where we may assume that the reference to the seasons and festivals was followed by a lengthy exposition of the calendar of the Sect. Possibly the scribe omitted it as being in his view a mere repetition of the Book of Jubilees. Page 4, l. 4, again, הנה פרוש etc., we could expect a list of the names of the leaders of the Sect, and their history; but of this no trace is left in our text.

The language of the MS. is for the most part pure Biblical Hebrew. The first three pages rise even to the dignity of Scriptural poetry, though a good deal of it is obscured by the unfortunate condition in which the text is at present. But there are in it terms and expressions which occur only in the Mishna or even only in the Rabbinic literature dating from the first centuries of the Middle Ages. Such are:

ופרוש p. 2, l. 9; p. 4, l. 4; etc.; cf. especially p. 6, l. 14. חבו p. 3, l. 10. העריות p. 5, l. 9. הרואה את דם זובה p. 5, l. 7. ויסוד הבריאה p. 4, l. 21. למשכים p. 10, l. 19. גלגל השמש p. 10, l. 14. זכו לשוב p. 10, l. 3. המוכן p. 10, l. 22. במובה p. 11, l. 8. גוי and גוים (in the sense of the Gentiles) p. 11, l. 13 and p. 12, l. 9. להרשותו p. 11, l. 20. חבור ישראל p. 12, l. 8. בממון p. 14, l. 20. מדוקדק p. 16, l. 2. מדרש התורה p. 20, l. 7.

The term בית השתחות (p. 11, l. 22) for a place of worship, even suggests a much later influence. It is, however, not impossible that all such expressions pointing to a later date are mere substitutions by the later scribe for the original terms. The term סרך again (p. 7, l. 6, etc.), occurring frequently in the sense of custom (= מנהג or משפט), is almost entirely unknown otherwise in the Hebrew literature. Strange also is the way in which citations from the Scriptures extending over the greatest part of the Bible are introduced without regard to strict consistency. The usual שנאמר is entirely absent and replaced by כאשר אמר, or ואשר א' (p. 4, l. 20; p. 7, ll. 8, 14, 16; p. 9, l. 2; p. 16, ll. 6, 15; p. 20, l. 16), followed occasionally by the name of the prophet, as אמר משה, or ומשה א' (p. 5, l. 8; p. 8, l. 14; p. 19, l. 26) or אשר אמר ישעיה (p. 6, l. 7) or אשר אמר יחזקאל (p. 19, l. 11). Sometimes, we have even כאשר אמר אל or אשר אמר אל (p. 6, l. 13; p. 8, l. 9; cf. p. 9, l. 7). The same expression is also used with reference to the *Pseudepigrapha* [2] אשר אמר עליהם לוי בן יעקב. In other places we have the more familiar כתוב ביד or ככתוב or כאשר כתוב (p. 5, l. 1; p. 7, l. 19; p. 9, l. 5; p. 11, ll. 17, 20; p. 19, ll. 1, 7). Sometimes, however, we have embedded whole groups of verses from the Scriptures without any introductory formula whatever, which in some places at least may be due to a mere clerical error (p. 5, l. 13; p. 8, l. 2). Altogether, the quotations from the Scriptures

---

[2] See also with reference to other non-Canonical books, p. 8, l. 20; p. 10, ll. 9, 10.

b 2

are seldom correctly given, so that sometimes the source is hardly recognizable (p. 2, l. 11; p. 5, l. 14 seq.; p. 7, l. 11; p. 8, l. 3). As a rule these deviations from the Massoretic text are mere textual corruptions of a careless scribe and not to be explained by the variae lectiones suggested by any known version, or quotation by any ancient authority. A specially noteworthy feature to which attention should be drawn is the absence of the Tetragrammaton or any other Biblical appellation for God besides אל, which is consistently used in both texts.

The contents of the MS. are in their present state about equally divided between Hagada and Halacha. The first part (pp. 1—8), dealing largely with matter of an historical and doctrinal nature, and the second part being chiefly occupied with subjects of a rather legal character. The Hagada as well as the Halacha represent apparently the constitution and the teachings of a Sect long ago extinct, but in which we may perhaps easily detect the parent of later schisms with which history dealt more leniently.

The defective state of the MS. and the corrupt condition of the text in so many places make it impossible to draw a complete picture of the Sect. Yet what remains offers us a few distinct features and salient points enabling us to catch a few glimpses of the history of the Sect, its claims and its relation to the rest of the nation.

First, as to its history: After the completion of 390 years, forming the End of the Wrath (p. 1, l. 5) or as it is termed in another place, "the end of the desolation of the land" (p. 5, l. 20), begun with the delivering of Israel into the hands of Nebuchadnezzar, the King of Babylon, God, we are told, made bud from Israel and Aaron a branch to inherit his land (p. 1, ll. 6, 7). This would bring us to within a generation of Simon the Just, who flourished about 290 B.C. For twenty years, however, closely following the End of the Wrath, Israel was blind, groping its way, because of the evil effects of the erroneous teachings (or waters of lies) of the Man of Scoffing, who led Israel astray. This brings us into the midst of the Hellenistic persecutions preceding the Maccabean revolt (about 176 B.C.). But at last, as it would seem, this scion from Aaron and Israel overcame all difficulties, and was recognized as the Teacher of Righteousness whose mission is to make Israel walk in the ways of God (p. 1, l. 11, and also p. 6, l. 11; p. 20, l. 31), and to undo the evil wrought in a former generation (p. 1, l. 12 and notes).

This Teacher is also called the "Only Teacher," or the "Only One" (p. 20, ll. 1, 32), and is identical with "the Lawgiver who Interprets the Law" (p. 6, l. 7) referred to in connection with the princes and nobles "who went forth out of the land of Judah" (p. 6, ll. 5, 6, 8). The activity of these latter, though representing both Aaron and Israel (p. 6, ll. 2, 3), consisted only in continuing and carrying out the precepts (p. 6, l. 9 במחוקקות)[3] of the Lawgiver, in which they were "to walk in them for all end of the wickedness" (p. 6, l. 10, text and notes). This seems to be the period intervening between the *first* appearance of the Teacher of Righteousness (p. 1, l. 11) (the founder of the Sect) who was gathered in[4] (or died), and the *second* appearance of the Teacher of Righteousness who is to rise in "the end of the days" (p. 6, l. 11, text and notes). Moreover, the Only Teacher, or Teacher of Righteousness is identical with משיח or the Anointed One from Aaron and Israel, whose advent is expected by the Sect through whom He made them know His holy spirit (p. 2, l. 12), and in whose rise the Sect saw[5] the fulfilment of the prophecy, "there shall come a star out of Jacob" (p. 7, l. 18; cf. note 18). Apparently this Anointed One was rejected by the great bulk of the nation who "spoke rebellion" against him (p. 5, l. 21; p. 6, l. 1). What must be especially noted is that the Messiah of the Sect is a priest, a descendant from Aaron and Israel[6]. Of a Messiah descending from Judah, there is no mention in our text[7]. Indeed, "after the completing of the end... one shall not join the house of Judah," whilst the princes of Judah, the removers of the bound, will be visited by the wrath of God (p. 4, l. 11; p. 8, l. 3, text and notes). Among these princes, King David is also included, who is held in slight estimation by the Sect (see below, p. xvii). As a contrast to and substitute for David, and his dynasty, the Sect put up Zadok, and his descendants (the sons of Zadok).

These differences, in addition to those still to be discussed, led to a complete separation of the Sect from the bulk of the Jewish nation. We are further told that they left the land of Judah for the North, and settled in the city of Damascus (p. 6, l. 5; p. 7, l. 19; p. 8, l. 21; p. 19, l. 34; p. 20, l. 12). They emigrated there under the leadership of the Star (p. 7, ll. 18, 19), where they established a New Covenant[8]. Unfortunately, there is a lacuna in our text at the end of p. 8, where the story of the Sect in Damascus was probably continued, but we gather from another passage that the Only Teacher found his death in Damascus, but is expected to rise again (p. 19, l. 35; p. 20, l. 1; cf. also p. 6, l. 11). This disappearance, as it seems,

---

[3] The meaning of the word is not quite certain, but the sense seems to be "the legislative rules laid down by the מחוקק."

[4] The death, or the gathering in of the Teacher is stated in p. 19, l. 35; p. 20, l. 1. See also p. 20, l. 14.

[5] See p. 12, l. 23 (משוח—אהרן), p. 19, l. 10 (משיח אהרן), p. 20, l. 1 (משיח מאהרן), which latter reading is supported by p. 1, l. 7. In p. 14, l. 19 the word משיח or משוח was probably torn off.

[6] Rather obscure is the meaning of וישראל in all

these places, unless it indicates that the mother of the Messiah will descend from a lay family. As it appears from p. 6, ll. 2, 3, the Sect insisted that the lay element should be represented in all important functions.

[7] Cf. Test. Reuben **6** 8, and Introduction of Dr Charles, p. xcvii.

[8] See p. 6, l. 19 and references given there, and p. 8, l. 21.

led to backsliding and apostacy from the Sect, but the backsliders were expelled from the Congregation, and admonished to come back to the Station of men of perfect holiness (p. 20, ll. 3, 4 and 5). In case they persisted in their apostacy, they and their families had no longer a "share in the House of the Torah" (p. 20, ll. 10, 13). They are regarded as the men of scoffing (p. 20, ll. 10, 11), and are cursed by the saints of the Most High (p. 20, l. 8), and no one is to associate with them in wealth and in work (p. 20, l. 7).

Neither these apostacies, however, nor the death of the Only Teacher, affected the fortunes of the Sect to such a degree as to be followed by its immediate extinction. Apparently the Sect continued its existence for a considerable time after these events had taken place. The Sect was constituted of four estates: Priests, Levites, Israelites and Proselytes (p. 14, ll. 3, 6). Its government, however, was placed in the hands of the first three estates (p. 10, ll. 4, 5)[9] consisting of a body of ten men selected of the Congregation, in which the tribe of Levi and Aaron were represented by four and the Israelites by six men (p. 10, ll. 5, 6). Only men between the age of twenty-five and sixty were eligible, who had to be learned in the Book of the Hagu and in the foundations of the Covenant (p. 10, ll. 6—8). At the head of the governing body stood two men, the one a regular priest whilst the other bore the title of Censor (מבקר) an office otherwise unknown in Judaism (p. 13, ll. 2, 5, 6; p. 14, ll. 6, 8). The priest, who had to be a man between thirty and sixty, was expected to be learned in the Book of the Hagu, in all the laws of the Torah (p. 13, l. 2; p. 14, ll. 8, 9), and a part of his office was to record in writing all the members of the settlement by their names in the following order: Priests, Levites, Israelites and Proselytes, as well as to give decisions in certain cases (p. 14, l. 6; see also p. 13, l. 5). More important were the functions of the Censor, who had to be a man between thirty and fifty, and who perhaps, as a rule, represented the lay element[10], giving instruction "to the many" (p. 13, l. 7) which he even imparts to the Priest (p. 13, ll. 5—6). He is to be first consulted in the case of admission of new members wishing to join the Sect, and to examine them, and to give them their place in it (p. 13, ll. 11—12). Offences committed by members of the Sect are reported to him, and penitents are apparently to apply to him for readmission (p. 9, l. 18 seq., and p. 15, l. 7 seq.). Every litigation and controversy is also brought before him (p. 13, ll. 14, 15)[11], and together with the Judges, he administers the monthly offerings of the Congregation, out of which the needy and the aged are to be supported

---

[9] No representation from the proselytes is mentioned there.

[10] This is the impression one receives from p. 13, ll. 5, 6, where the Censor is put in contradistinction to the Priest. See above, p. xiii, note 6, for the tendency of the Sect to have the lay element represented in all their important offices.

[11] See p. 15, l. 13, where the text, however, is defective.

(p. 14, l. 13 seq.).   We must assume that a governing body consisting of ten Judges was only required in the case of larger settlements.   Their jurisdiction was very extensive, they having the power to inflict capital punishment and banishment on the members of the Sect, besides determining the regular civil cases (p. 9, l. 10; p. 10, l. 1; p. 12, l. 4), but at least a Priest and a Censor were considered a necessity as soon as the population counted at least ten members.   If the Priest is not "tried," a Levite takes his place (p. 13, l. 3).

In this manner the Sect organized itself in various cities (p. 12, l. 19) or camps (p. 7, l. 6; p. 14, l. 3), forming there congregations or assemblies (p. 11, l. 23; p. 12, l. 6; p. 13, l. 11; p. 14, l. 10).   One city, however, seems to have been set apart as the City of the Sanctuary, the inhabitants of which were submitted to a rigorous observance of certain laws connected with Levitical purity (p. 12, ll. 1, 2).   Perhaps it was in this Sanctuary that the altar was placed in which regular sacrifices were brought (p. 11, l. 17), whilst the other settlements were only provided with a house of worship, which also had to be avoided by the unclean (p. 11, l. 22).

Thus far, the history and the constitution of the Sect as suggested by our MS.   We come now to its teachings.   That the Sect accepted the Canon of the Old Testament needs no further proof.   This is clear enough both from its tenets and practices, regulated after the injunctions of the Scriptures as understood by the Sect.   In the Halacha as well as in the Hagada we have constant citations from and allusions to almost all the parts of the Scriptures. One of the most important tenets of the Sect bearing upon the Messianic belief is largely based on a passage from the Prophets (p. 3, l. 21), who are further cited in the polemics against its opponents (p. 4, l. 13 seq.; p. 5, l. 13; p. 7, l. 14, etc.).   For the practice, of course, it is the Pentateuch which is considered the main authority, cited under the term of Torah, תורה or תורת משה or ספר התורה (see, for instance, p. 5, l. 2; p. 7, l. 7; p. 15, l. 2; p. 16, l. 5; p. 20, l. 13), and forming the particular object of interpretation; though in contradistinction to the Rabbinic usage, the Sect occasionally also derives norms for the practice from the prophetic writings (p. 9, ll. 9—10, text and notes).

But besides the collection of the Books forming the Canon of the Old Testament, the Sect seems also to have considered as sacred certain "external writings," forming a part of the *Pseudepigrapha*.   This can be said with certainty of the Book of Jubilees, which is once quoted by its full name as the *Book of the Divisions of the Seasons* (p. 16, l. 3 ספר מחלקות העתים), but to which reference is more frequently made without giving the name (see Index sub Book of Jubilees).   The same may also be maintained with fair certainty of the Testaments of the Twelve Patriarchs, to a portion of which, the Testament of Levi (p. 4, l. 15), at least, we have a fairly distinct reference, whilst there are also other allusions to it (see Index). Besides these books still extant, though not exactly in the same shape as they have come down to us, the Sect must have also been in possession of some *Pseudepigrapha* now lost. This is evident from the reference to Yochaneh and his brother, who opposed Moses on the occasion of Israel's first redemption (p. 5, ll. 17—18, text and notes). In another place we have an allusion to "the Word which Jeremiah has spoken to Baruch, the son of Neriah, and Gehazi, the servant of Elisha" (p. 8, ll. 20, 21), which suggests the existence of Pseudepigraphic works ascribed to these Biblical personages and considered authoritative by the Sect. Perhaps some canonical importance was also given to the ספר ההגו (p. 10, l. 6, and p. 13, l. 2), the nature of which is not quite clear. It does not seem to be identical with the Pentateuch, as this latter is, as pointed out above, cited under the regular title of תורה (see above, p. xv). Together with the ספר ההגו are also mentioned the Foundations of the Covenant, בספר ההגו ויסודי הברית (p. 10, l. 6). This might suggest that the Sect was in possession of some sort of a manual containing the tenets of the Sect, and perhaps also a regular set of rules of discipline for the initiation of novices and penitents.

The loyalty to the Prophets on the one hand, and the recognition of the Book of Jubilees and other *Pseudepigrapha* as authoritative writings, mark the Sect with special features distinguishing it both from the majority of Jews (as represented by the Pharisees), and from the Samaritans, the most ancient Sect in Israel; the former being hostile to all the books not forming a part of our present Canon, and the latter rejecting even the authority of the Prophets.

Another point of supreme importance separating them both from Jew as well as Samaritan is the regulation of the calendar. The Sect looks upon itself as the remnant unto which God revealed "the hidden things in which all Israel erred: His Holy Sabbaths and His glorious festivals, the testimony of His righteousness and the ways of His truth and the desires of His will which a man shall do and live by them" (p. 3, ll. 13—16; cf. p. 6, ll. 18—19). It need hardly be pointed out that this passage is a mere paraphrase of the passage in the Book of Jubilees: "And all the children of Israel will forget, and will not find the path of the years, and will forget the new moons, and seasons, and Sabbaths, and they will go wrong as to all the order of the years[12]." The "hidden things" are, in the Book of Jubilees, disclosed to the Sect by a special revelation[13], but the calendar of this Pseudepigraphic work differs in the most important essentials both from that of the Pharisees and from that of the Samaritans (see below, p. xx).

It is, however, the Pharisees, in particular, against whom the polemics of

---

[12] See Jub. **6** 34 seq., to the end of the chapter.   [13] See Jub. **6** 3.
See also Ch. **23** 19.

the Sect are directed. They are, as it seems, dubbed as "the builder of the wall," or "fence," referring probably to their motto, "Make a fence to the Torah" (p. 4, l. 19; p. 8, l. 18, and p. 19, l. 31, text and notes). The accusations the Sect brings against their antagonists are both of a general and of a specific nature. They are denounced in our Text as transgressors of the Covenant, removing statutes and given to persecution of the righteous, and despising the upright whom they turn over to the sword, against whose soul they gather (p. 1, ll. 20, 21)[14]. They are the children of destruction, and, at least implicitly, they are accused of appropriating moneys belonging to the Sanctuary, robbing the poor, making the widows their prey, and murdering the orphans (p. 6, ll. 15, 16).

The adduced reproaches are of a general nature, forming in the main a mere paraphrase of certain Scriptural verses applied by the Sect without much discrimination to their opponents (notes to p. 1, l. 20; p. 6, l. 16, etc.). There is also to be taken into account that the parallel passages as offered in p. 8, ll. 5—9, suggest that these accusations can hardly be applied in their entirety to the Pharisees. For we have there also the complaint that their antagonist "cast off restraint with an high hand to walk in the ways of the wicked." But as is clear from the context these "wicked" can be none else but the Greeks[15]. The denunciation must accordingly refer to the Hellenistic Party, in part, at least, unless there are some words missing in our Text. But we have, as already indicated, accusations of a very specific nature, and these leave no doubt that the object of the Sect's general abuse was mainly the Pharisees. The first of these accusations is polygamy, the opponents of the Sect being ensnared by two (wives) described in our text as "fornication" (p. 4, ll. 20, 21). It is in this connection that David (who married eighteen wives) is ruled out of court as one ignorant of the contents of the Law, which was only discovered with the rise of Zadok (p. 5, ll. 2, 3, 5).

This prohibition, as it must be specially pointed out, extends also to divorce, or rather to marrying a second wife, as long as the first wife is alive though she had been divorced[16]. This is followed by another accusation that

[14] The "man of scoffing who dropped to Israel waters of deceitfulness" (or lies) (p. 1, ll. 14, 15; p. 4, l. 10, note 10 and p. 8, l. 14) and is the cause of all these evils, is perhaps identical with the Commanding One of p. 4, ll. 19, 20, of whom the same metaphor (מטיף) is used, and is, as apparent from the context, responsible not for new revelations but for false interpretation of the Law. Is he the head of the men of scoffing of p. 20, l. 11, who are the special opponents of the New Covenant?

[15] See p. 8, ll. 9—11, ראש מלכי יון, unless we should assume that in his preference for a Scriptural term the writer used the word יון for Rome (which latter does not occur in the Bible) without any regard to accuracy.

[16] See notes to p. 4, ll. 20, 21. Cf. also p. 7, l. 1; p. 8, ll. 6, 7. About the prohibition of polygamy among the Samaritans, see Kirchheim, p. 20. Cf. Montgomery, p. 43. According to the evidence of R. Eleazar b. Tobiah in his *Lekach Tob* to Deut. 21 5 (p. 35 b, ed. Wilna), the Karaites also forbade marriage with two women (cf. Poznanski, *Revue*, 45, p. 186). About the Zadokites, see below, p. xix.

S. (Frags. A & B)   c

their opponents "defile" the Sanctuary, inasmuch as they do not separate according to the Law, and neglect (according to the interpretation of the Sect) certain laws concerning נדה (p. 5, ll. 6, 7). Then a protest follows against the permission to marry one's niece, accompanied by an argument proving it to belong to the forbidden degrees (p. 5, ll. 7—11). But, both the case of נדה and not less this case of עריות belong to the group of laws forming the subject of the most heated controversies between the Samaritans and the Karaites on the one side, and the Pharisees (or Rabbinic Judaism) on the other[17]. The point at issue in the law of נדה is not given by our author, but in that of עריות he agrees with the Samaritans and Karaites, and we may conclude that this is also the case with נדה. Likewise, the laws concerning the Sabbath, that play such an important part with the Sect, agree in the main with those given in the Book of Jubilees, to which also the Samaritan and the Karaitic codes offer some important parallels, but they differ in many respects from the Pharisaic practice[18]. The few dietary laws, again, as well as laws relating to Levitical purity contained in this Text, show a strong divergence from the Pharisaic custom[19]; and the same may be remarked of the laws bearing upon the annulling of vows which the Sect seems to forbid altogether[20].

The annals of Jewish history contain no record of a Sect agreeing in all points with the one depicted in the preceding pages. But sufficient traces and traits seem to have been left of it in the accounts of the earlier sects to justify us in advancing an hypothesis towards its identity. I am thinking of the Sect of the Zadokites to which reference is to be found in the early Karaitic writings. Thus, we are told by Kirkisani in his *Book of Lights and the High Beacons* (written about 637), "Zädok was the first who exposed the Rabbanites and contradicted them publicly. He revealed a part of the truth and composed books in which he frequently denounced the Rabbanites and criticised them. But he adduced no proof for anything he said, merely saying it by way of statement, except in one thing, namely, in his prohibition against marrying the daughter of the brother, and the daughter of the sister. For he adduced as proof their being analogous to the paternal and maternal aunt[21]." Now, this description of the Zadok book well fits our Text which, in its Hagada, is largely polemical, whilst its Halacha affords little else than mere statements. A real argument and refutation of the opposite opinion we have only, as stated by Kirkisani, in the case of prohibiting the marriage with one's niece, which struck Kirkisani the more, as use is made there of the

---

[17] See notes to p. 5, ll. 6—11.
[18] See notes to p. 11, ll. 1, 2, 9, 13—15, 16, 17.
[19] See notes to p. 12, ll. 11—18.
[20] See notes to p. 16, ll. 6—13, but the text is so defective in that place that the meaning must be considered doubtful.
[21] See Kirkisani, p. 283.

interpretary rule of Analogy or היקש with which the Karaites operate so much in their marriage laws[22].

Of the laws peculiar to the Zadokites, only two are recorded by Kirkisani. The one is that they "absolutely forbade divorce, which the Scriptures permitted[23]." In the chapter, again, treating of Jesus, and his followers, the Nazarenes, he remarks, "Jesus forbade divorce as the Zadokites forbade it[24]." A similar remark he has about Obadiah of Ispahan (or Abu-Isa), who "forbade divorce as the Zadokites and the Nazarenes forbade it[25]."

Hadasi's evidence is to the same effect, namely, that Obadiah of Ispahan (or Abu-Isa), like the Zadokites, forbade divorce in all cases; which, he declares, is not in agreement with the word of God. In a similar manner, he expresses himself in another place, where he censures the religion of the Zadokites for the same prohibition as being against the Scriptures[26]. But as pointed out above, this is just the view of the Sect which regarded a second marriage during the lifetime of the first husband, even after divorce, as fornication. (See above, p. xvii.)

The second law which Kirkisani attributes to the Zadokites and to which he likewise objects is in connection with the calendar. "They (the Zadokites) also fixed all the months at thirty days each. It is possible that they relied in this on the story of Noah. Again, they excluded the day of the Sabbath from the sum of the days of the feast of Passover, so as to make them seven days besides the Sabbath. In the same way also with the feast of Tabernacles[27]." Hadasi practically repeats the same fact without adding anything fresh to it[28].

What is meant by the story of Noah, we learn from another place in Kirkisani, and from Japheth's Commentary to Gen. **1** 14, and Lev. **25** 5. According to this testimony the Zadokites or Zadok made reference to the account of the deluge which lasted 150 days (Gen. **8** 3), beginning with the 17th of the second month (Gen. **7** 11) and ending on the 17th of the seventh month (Gen. **8** 4), thus covering five months. This proves that each month counted thirty days[29]. The same argument is indicated in the paraphrase which the Book of Jubilees gives of Gen. **8** 3, "And the water prevailed on the face of the earth *five months*—one hundred and

[22] See p. 5, ll. 8—11. The only other place where the Sect adduces something like an argument in an Halachic question, is p. 4, l. 21 and p. 5, l. 1, but in this point the Karaites differed as much from our Sect as the Rabbanites, as we shall see presently, whilst Kirkisani only speaks of the criticism of the Rabbanites.

[23] See Kirkisani, p. 304.

[24] See Kirkisani, p. 305.

[25] See Kirkisani, p. 311. See also Gratz's *Ge-schichte der Juden*, vol. v. pp. 156, 405.

[26] See Hadasi, *Alphabeta*, 97, 98. Cf. Geiger's *Zeitschrift*, 1836, p. 99.

[27] See Kirkisani, p. 304.

[28] See *Alphabeta*, 97, 98. Cf. Poznanski, *J. Q. R.* X. p. 265, note 1.

[29] See Kirkisani, ibid. With reference to Japheth, see Poznanski, *Revue*, vol. XLIV. p. 177, and *J. Q. R.* x. p. 265, note 1. Cf. also Ibn Ezra to Gen. **8** 3.

c 2

fifty days[30]." Now, the fixing of the calendar is just one of the most important points in which this schism showed itself. The Sect (as we have seen, p. xv) accepted the calendar given by the Book of Jubilees, which at once separated them both from Jew and Samaritan. But as we learn from these documents, the difference consisted chiefly in the fact that the Book of Jubilees accepted the solar year of twelve months, of thirty days each, and four intercalary days[31]. It is true that our Fragment contains no distinct reference either to the thirty days or to the argument from the story of Noah. But we must never forget that our Text consists, as explained above, only of extracts from a larger work (see above, p. x), and it is easily possible that Kirkisani was in possession of this larger work, whilst the scribe of our text, in his careless manner, thought it sufficient to indicate, in a general way, the existence of serious differences in the calendar between the Sect and its opponents, but omitted the details as known from the Book of Jubilees. It is also possible that our copyist relegated these details to the Halachic part, represented in our MS. only by a fragment, just as he did with the laws relating to the Sabbath, or to the annulling of vows[32], whilst Kirkisani was in the possession of a complete copy. On the other hand, when a certain Karaite, Hasan ben Mashiach, in his controversy against R. Saadya (with regard to the calendar) attested that "the writings of the Zadokites are known among people, but they contain nothing of what that man (Saadya) mentioned; that there are in the writings of the Zadokites (various) things in which they differed from the Rabbanites in the Second Temple, with regard to sacrifices, etc., but there is not even a single letter like that which the Fayyoumite reported[33]," we may assume that

[30] See Jub. 5 27.

[31] See above, p. xvi. This would agree with Beer's interpretation of the calendar of the Jubilees, in his *Das Buch der Jubiläen* (Leipzig, 1856). See Jub., the whole of ch. 6 text and notes, and references given there to the various explanations of the calendar of the author of the Book of Jubilees; to which is only to be added Epstein's discussion of this subject in his *Eldad ha-Dani*, pp. 155—161, but which is practically only a *résumé* of his article in the *Revue* referred to by Dr Charles. Epstein's suggestion that the Book of Jubilees has two kinds of years, an ecclesiastical year and a civil year, settles, it is true, many a difficulty in the text of the Book as it has come down to us. But it is not impossible that the original reading which was in possession of the Sect differed greatly from the present text. We have only to assume that in the case of Shabuoth, the Sect did not press the fifteenth of the month, taking it to mean the middle of the month or near it. Assuming the ממחרת השבת

(Lev. 23 11—15, see Jub. 15 1, text and notes) to mean the whole feast of Passover, and ignoring the Sabbath of the Passover which the Zadokites, as we have seen, do not count, the sheaf-waving would take place on the 23rd, and the feast of Shabuoth would thus (allowing in accordance with Beer 30 days for both Nissan and Iyar) fall on the 12th of Sivan, which agrees with the Falashic tradition.

[32] See, for instance, p. 6, l. 18, and cf. p. 10, l. 14 to end of p. 11. Cf. also p. 7, l. 7 and p. 16, l. 6 seq.

[33] See Poznanski, *Revue*, vol. XLIV. pp. 176, 177. Cf. also his *Karaite Literary Opponents of Saadaya Gaon*, pp. 15, 16. See also Hilgenfeld, *Ketzergeschichte*, p. 160, note 271, and reference given there to Geiger. How confused and contradictory the notions about the Zadokite calendar were, is also clear from another passage of an earlier Karaite who thought that they began the month on the 15th after the New Moon, when the moon is in its full strength. See Poznanski, *Revue*, vol. XLIV. p. 172.

he had a copy something similar to ours in which the calendar differences were given only in a general way, while the Halachic part had more extracts relating to sacrifice than ours.   The divergence between the testimony as to the nature of the Zadok books known to writers in the tenth century may thus be easily attributed to the difference in the texts used by the different scholars of that period.   Our Text may thus, with good reason, be defined as containing extracts from a Zadok book, representing features contained in the copies of these authorities, but as it forms only extracts, these features are sometimes partly obscured ; whilst other features may be entirely eliminated.   But this does not in any way contend against the likelihood of their being of Zadokite origin.

This likelihood is raised, in a measure, to a degree of certainty when we consider the fact that it is the Zadokites from which the Sect derived its spiritual pedigree.   It is to a Zadok to which the Sect ascribes the merit of having rediscovered the Law, in which act he is favourably contrasted with David, who was ignorant of it (p. 5, l. 5; cf. above, p. xiii).   Who this Zadok was, of the many persons bearing this name in the Bible, it is impossible to say. At any rate, the impression is that he was a Biblical personage[34].   But it is not only to the remote past to which the Sect appeals ; the Zadokites or rather the Sons of Zadok, according to the Sect, form the " sure house of Israel," and are apparently connected with them who "held fast to the commandments of God," and who were in possession of the hidden things—of the calendar (p. 3, ll. 12 seq., 19 and 26).   They are, indeed, those who remained loyal to the Sanctuary, the very chosen ones of Israel, called by name, that arose at the end of the days, and who apparently kept a Station מעמד, and were connected with the government of the Sect (p. 4, ll. 1—5; cf. also p. 2, l. 9, text and notes).   A book emanating from such a sect might plausibly be regarded as the writings of the Zadokites, or as a Zadok book.

The term Zadokites naturally suggests the Sadducees ; but the present state of knowledge of the latter's doctrines and practices does not offer enough points of resemblance to justify the identification of them with our Sect[35].   At present it seems to me that the only ancient Sect which comes here into consideration is the Dosithean, for our Sect has left so many

[34] Perhaps we have here some reminiscence of the well-known Hagada given by Rashi and Kimchi in their commentary to 2 Kings **22** 8.   According to this, King Ahaz during his reign burnt the Torah, but they saved one copy which they hid between the rubble of the walls of the Temple, which was discovered by the High Priest Hilkiah during the reign of King Josiah when they were occupied with the repair of the walls.

[35] It need hardly be pointed out that there are both in the Hagada and in the Halacha of our Sect features which strikingly recall the famous hypothesis of Geiger regarding the Sadducees and the Old Halacha.   But this hypothesis is still so undeveloped in its details, that it seems better to leave the subject in abeyance.   It is a further and larger question whether we have to deal with a sort of counter-tradition or with an interpretation claiming to go back to primitive Judaism.

marked traces on the accounts which have come down to us about the Dositheans that we may conclude that they were in some way an offshoot from the schism which is the subject of our inquiry.   The accounts of the Dosithean sect are, as is well known, contradictory and confusing.   They vary in date, in the characterization of the sect, and in the description of its origin.   There is no need to reproduce them here, or to give the various attempts which have been made to explain them, or to reconcile their various contradictions.   Yet almost all these accounts, contradictory as they may be in other respects, offer the one or the other traces of the characteristics of our Sect, which suggest, if not an identity with, at least the descent from our Sect, which should be noted here[36].

Thus, the testimony of several early accounts of the Dosithean sect connects in some way or another the Dosithean schism with that of the Sadducees, or puts it at least chronologically very close to the latter.   This feature reminds us strongly of our Sect, which derived its spiritual pedigree, as we have seen, from the Zadokites.   Some accounts go even to the length of making Zadok a disciple of Dositheus, which we may take as a mere overstatement of the high antiquity of the Sect[37].   If Abul-Fath goes as far as to speak of a sect called Dustan, which arose in the time of Alexander the Great[38], it may mean that the Sect claimed to have its origin in a parent sect dating from the Greek period preceding the Maccabean reign.   This would fairly correspond with the claims of our Sect, which places the first appearance of its founder 390 years after the desolation of the Land by Nebuchadnezzar, which would bring us, as I have pointed out, to within a generation of Simon the Just, who flourished about 290 B.C.   Such a date could easily be brought, it may be remarked in passing, into connection with the Zadok of the "Aboth d'Rabbi Nathan" who, according to Jewish tradition, was the disciple of Antigonus of Soko, the disciple of Simon the Just, and the originator of the Saducean heresy[39].   I must, however, remark that I have my doubts about the integrity of the Text relating to this date.   For our calculation would necessitate the assumption that the author of our Text knew more of the Persian chronology than either the great majority of the Jews or the Samaritans, which is not likely.   As pointed out in the notes to our Text, it is probable that we have to read (p. 1, l. 6) ארבע instead of שלוש (490) corresponding with the

---

[36] For a general view of these accounts, see Hilgenfeld, *Ketzergeschichte*, pp. 155—161 (also Index, sub Dositheus), Nutt, *Fragments of A Samaritan Targum*, pp. 47—52, and Montgomery, *The Samaritans*, pp. 252—264. See also Kraus, article *Dositheus*, in the Jewish Encyclopedia, vol. IV., and reference given there.

[37] See Philaster (*Corpus Haereseologici*, i., ed.

Oehler), I. 4, 5. Cf. Pseudo-Tertullian, I., text and notes. See also Epiphanius, I. 79. Abul-Fath also places one Dosithean Sect before the Sadducees.

[38] See Abul-Fath, p. 82. Cf. Montgomery, p. 254.

[39] See " Sayings of the Jewish Fathers," Taylor, I. 2, 3, and ibid. *Excursus*, III. p. 111. See also above, p. xii.

seventy weeks of years of Dan. **9** 2, 24. This cycle of years, however, as we know, is never exact, and may be adapted by any apocalyptic writer to any event in history which struck him as the great crisis in the history of the nation or even of his Sect. Such a crisis evidently took place when the Sect escaped to the North and sought refuge in Damascus (p. 4, l. 2, and p. 7, ll. 13, 14). But no such occurrence is recorded in Jewish history[40]. We are practically left without any definite date. But at any rate, the claims of our Sect were for a very high antiquity, which further receives support from the reference in our Text, on p. 8, l. 11, to the head of the Kings of Javan, though our Text, in its present condition, shows Roman influences[41]. It is thus not to be wondered at if the Dositheans, as an offshoot of our Sect, made the same pretensions, and even exaggerated them.

Another point of contact between our Sect and the Dositheans is the calendar, both fixing thirty days for every month of the year[42]. The testimony of Abul-Fath is most emphatic on this point when he says, "They (the Dositheans) abolished the reckonings of their astronomical tables. All their months consist of exactly thirty days. They abolished the true festivals and removed the commandments of the fasts and the afflictions[43]." When Abul-Fath proceeds to say that they count the fifty days from the morrow after the Passover, as the Jews do, the similarity with the Jews probably consisted in this, that they interpreted the ממחרת השבת (Lev. **23** 11, 15) to mean the Feast (in contradistinction to the Sadducees who took that word to mean the Sabbath); but, on the other hand, they differed from the Jews in that they understood by it the last day of the Feast, or the seventh day of the Passover (see above, p. xx, note 31). Abul-Fath further bears evidence to the strictness of the Dositheans in their observance of the Sabbath, a fact which is also recorded with more or less variation by some Fathers of the Church. This is a feature which we observe also in our Sect, though the details given by Abul-Fath and the Fathers are not the same, and it may be that they have been misunderstood by the former[44]. The statement of Epiphanius is more general, when he says, "In the

[40] One can only think of the conjecture of Juynboll, in his *Commentarii in historiam gentis Samaritanae*, Leyden, 1846, according to which a number of Samaritans might have emigrated to Damascus, the capital of Antiochus Cyzicenus, their ally in the wars with John Hyrcan, in which they were defeated, which took place somewhere between 128 and 106 B.C. Kirchheim, p. 9, gives this as a fact, but practically there is no authority for it whatever, except this guess by Juynboll.

[41] For instance, the office of the Censor, occurring frequently in our Text. (See p. 9, l. 18, and elsewhere.) Such an office, entirely unknown to Judaism, could have been only borrowed from the Romans. We must also remark that these denunciations of the Pharisees could hardly relate to the Greek times. As far as historical evidence goes, the Pharisees could only have made their power felt at a much later date.

[42] See above, p. xix, as regards our Sect. With regard to the Dosithean Sect, see Pseudo-Clements, *Recognitions*, II. 8. Cf. Hilgenfeld, pp. 37, 160. See also Abul-Fath, p. 82.

[43] See Abul-Fath, p. 82. Cf. Montgomery, p. 254.

[44] See Abul-Fath, ibid. Cf. our Text, p. 10, l. 22 to p. 11, l. 17, text and notes. See also Epiphanius, ibid., and Origen, *De Principiis*, IV. 17. In his statement there that they remained over the Sabbath in the same position until the evening, he probably

same way they observe Circumcision and the Sabbath," by which he probably means their rigour in observing it[45]. When he further says, that "they have no intercourse with all people because they detest all mankind," we may readily recognize here the law of our Sect requiring the washing of the clothes when they were brought by a Gentile (because of contamination), and the prohibition of staying over the Sabbath in the vicinity of Gentiles[46]. His statement that the Dositheans had their own forms of government is also borne out by any number of passages in our text in which the government of the Sect forms a special feature[47]. His statement, again, that they abstain from eating living creatures may have some connection with the law in our Text on p. 12, l. 11, which may perhaps be understood to imply that the Sect forbade honey, regarding it as אבר מן החי (a limb cut off from a living animal), which would agree with the testimony of Abul-Fath that they forbade the eating of eggs, except those which were found in a slaughtered fowl[48]. More difficult is it to know what Epiphanius exactly meant when he said that "some of them abstain from a second marriage, but others never marry." The text is not quite certain at this point. But may we not perceive in it, at least, an echo in some way of the law of the Sect prohibiting a second marriage as long as the first wife is still alive[49]?

What is more remarkable is that even in the dogmatic teachings of the Dosithean Sect, to which most writers attribute a somewhat gnostic aspect, placing the Sect practically outside the confines of Judaism, traces may be found strongly reminiscent of our Sect. Epiphanius is probably right when, against almost all the others, he maintains that the Dositheans believed in resurrection[50]. The statement by most Fathers of the Church that the Dositheans denied the Prophets is probably only due to the confusion with the Samaritans. On the other hand, the assertion of Photius that Dositheus was particularly hostile to Judah, one of the twelve patriarchs, and that the Dositheans declared their founder to be the Messiah, is in harmony with the tendency of our Sect and the claims for their founder[51]. Sharastani's account that they recognized in Dostan the Star, and declared him as the Only One (which is the Messiah), recalls also the claims of our Sect who speak of their founder as the Star, and apply to him the name of the Only Teacher[52]. It may

confused it with another Sect. But see also Abul-Fath, 151 (Montgomery, 257), where we have some similar statement regarding the adherents of Dusis, that if they travelled at all on the Sabbath, they did not take their hands out of their garments. See Wreschner, p. 15.

[45] Epiphanius, ibid.

[46] See Epiphanius, ibid., and see our Text, p. 11, ll. 3, 4, 14, 15.

[47] Epiphanius, ibid. See above, p. xv.

[48] See Epiphanius, ibid., and Abul-Fath, ibid.

[49] See Epiphanius, ibid., and note 5. Cf. above, p. xvii, about our Sect.

[50] See Epiphanius, ibid. See also Abul-Fath, 151 (cf. Montgomery, p. 257).

[51] See Photius, *Bibliotheca*, code 230. Cf. also Hilgenfeld, p. 157, note 262, and Montgomery, p. 255, about Origen. Cf. above, p. xiii, about our Sect.

[52] See Sharastani, pp. 258, 259. Cf. Montgomery, pp. 259, 260. See also Abul-Fath, p. 251, about the peculiar term *Vechdu* (יחיד).

further be suggested that it is not impossible that the term the "Standing One" (ἑστώς, or *stans*) to be met in patristic literature in the accounts of Dositheus or Simon Magus, has its origin in the Men of the Station with whom we meet in our Text, and who were apparently looked upon as the leaders of the Sect[53].

We may further remark here that the Falashas, whose connection with the Dositheans had already been suggested by Beer, show also certain features strongly reminiscent of our Sect[54]. To the feature of the calendar, reference has already been made above[55]. To this may be added the fact which we learn now from the *Te-Ezaza Sanbat* of the strong similarity of the Sabbath laws with those given in the Book of Jubilees, and hence also with those expounded in our Text[56]. The law, again, occurring in our Text, of submitting cloths brought by a Gentile to a special purification has a parallel in the testimony of several travellers, according to which the Falashas change their dress and take a bath after having come into contact with a Christian or a Mohammedan[57]. We know also that the Falasha law prohibited the marriage of a niece, threatening all the terrors of Hell for its transgression, which affords another point of similarity with the laws of our Sect[58]. Another point of agreement worth mentioning here is the tradition regarding Zadok's rediscovery of the Law, which may, as suggested above, be responsible for the claim of the Falashas that it was Azariah, the son of Zadok, who brought with him the scroll of the Law to Abyssinia[59]. The term, again, בית השתחות, is strongly reminiscent of the Falashas' *Mesgeed*, and may perhaps be ascribed to the influence of some Falasha scribe. But on the other hand, it should not be forgotten that the Falashas hope for the restoration of Zion and Jerusalem, and their veneration for the House of David is strongly in contrast with the tendency of our Sect.

We may, then, formulate our hypothesis that our text is constituted of fragments forming extracts from a Zadok book, known to us chiefly from the writings of Kirkisani. The Sect which it represented, did not however pass for any length of time under the name of Zadokites, but was soon in

---

[53] See, for instance, *Recognitions of Clement*, Bk. I. chap. 72; Bk. II. chap. 7 and chap. 11. (Cf. Hilgenfeld, p. 37); Clementine Homilies II. chaps. 22, 24; Homily XVIII. chap. 13; Hippolytus, *Refutation*, Bk. VI. chap. 12. Cf. our Text, p. 2, l. 9, text and notes.

[54] See Beer, p. 56 seq.

[55] See p. xx, note 31.

[56] See *Tĕ-Ézâza Sanbat*, J. Halévy, Paris, 1902, pp. 142, 143, and see above, p. xviii, n. 18, the reference to the Sabbath laws in Jub. and in our text.

[57] See p. 11, ll. 3—4, and *Journal in Abyssinia*, by Samuel Cabot, London, 1834, pp. 174, 363. See also the *Falashas*, J. M. Flad, London, 1869, p. 55.

[58] See the Baruch of the Falashas, edited by J. Halévy, in the same collection, p. 203, and cf. above, pp. xvii and xviii. Altogether, this whole collection is still in need of a thorough critical examination and comparison with the Pseudepigraphic literature.

[59] See above, p. xxi. With regard to these claims, see Bruce, *Travels*, London, 1805, vol. II. pp. 399, 407. See also Flad, p. 73.

S. (Frags. A & B)　　　　　　　　　　　　　　　*d*

some way amalgamated with and perhaps also absorbed by the Dosithean Sect, and made more proselytes among the Samaritans than among the Jews, with which former sect it had many points of similarity. In the course of time, however, the Dosithean Sect also disappeared, and we have only some traces left of them in the lingering sect of the Falashas, with whom they probably came into close contact at an early period of their (the Falashas') existence, and to whom they handed down a good many of their practices. The only real difficulty in the way of this hypothesis is, that according to our Text the Sect had its original seat in Damascus, north of Palestine, and it is difficult to see how they reached the Dositheans, and subsequently the Falashas, who had their main seats in the south of Palestine, or Egypt. But this could be explained by assuming special missionary efforts on the part of the Zadokites by sending their emissaries to Egypt, a country which was especially favourable to such an enterprise because of the existence of the Onias Temple there[60]. The severance of the Egyptian Jews from the Palestinian influence (though they did not entirely give up their loyalty to the Jerusalem Sanctuary), prepared the ground for the doctrines of such a Sect as the Zadokites in which all allegiance to Judah and Jerusalem was rejected, and in which the descendants of the House of Zadok (of whom indeed Onias himself was one) represented both the Priest and the Messiah.

This is the only workable hypothesis I am able to offer at present. But whatever its destiny—for the condition of our Text precludes certainty and invites difference of opinion—one result which I am about to state seems to me to be beyond any doubt. And this is that it is among the sects severed from the general body of Judaism in which we have to look for the origin of such Pseudepigraphic works as the Book of Jubilees, the Book of Enoch, the Testaments of the Twelve Patriarchs, and similar productions,—and *not* in Pharisaic Judaism.

This fact was recognized more than half a century ago by Beer, who thus expressed himself with regard to the Book of Jubilees :—" Its whole type is a peculiar one, and is apparently based on a sectarian foundation." But this is also the characteristic which may be applied to the Book of Enoch and the Testaments of the Twelve Patriarchs, which are so closely related to one another, all of which grew up on sectarian soil[61]. And surely this is the only possible view which could be formed of this class of writings by any scholar who has ever made a proper study of Rabbinic literature, such as the Mishna, the Talmud, and the "great Midrashim." Passing from these genuine Rabbinic

---

[60] See Frankel's hypothesis in the *Monatsschrift*, v. p. 390, about the place of the rise of the Book of Jubilees.

[61] See Beer, p. 56. See also Epstein, p. 199, with reference to the Book of Enoch and the Book of Jubilees.

works to the Pseudepigraphic class of literature, he feels transported to another world—from a world of interpretation and argument to a world of fiction.   It is not any longer the living voice of the school to which he is listening, but the dead imaginings of some writer impersonating the heroes of remote antiquity.   The Rabbinic literature indeed occasionally gives either in the way of overstatement or bona-fide as authority for a law or an ordinance or a moral precept the name of a patriarch or prophet. Such cases, however, are exceptional, and are rooted chiefly in tradition[62].   On the other hand, with the writer of the *Pseudepigrapha*, the exception is the rule.   He is a regular book maker, in which the masquerade feature is developed into a fine art, whilst, as a schismatic, he is not satisfied to form a link in the chain of tradition, but endeavours to appear himself as the source of tradition.   His revelations are not in harmony with custom and usage, and must therefore be dated back to the Biblical or patriarchal times.   This is a form of authorship absolutely unknown to "official Judaism" of the early centuries, if by "official Judaism" is understood Pharisaism which formed the large bulk of the nation, which identified itself with the Synagogue, which taught in the schools, and largely also controlled the service in the Temple. Parallel passages, it is true, to some of the contents of the *Pseudepigrapha* are to be found in Rabbinic literature.   But these are chiefly offered by the Chapters of R. Eliezer and other works of a similar nature, all of them dating from a comparatively late period.   Indeed, they are themselves a sort of *Pseudepigrapha* of unknown origin, only that their heroes are mostly Rabbinic heroes, such as R. Eliezer b. Hyrcanus, R. Akiba, R. Ishmael, etc., instead of Biblical heroes.   They differ from the old productions, both in style and in tendency, and they are not above the suspicion of having already made use both of Christian and even of Mohammedan sources[63].

It was only of late years that different kinds of Pharisaism were discovered[64], each of them represented by the one or the other Pseudepigraphic works.   We even went so far as to perceive in the Testaments of the Twelve Patriarchs a Midrash, portions of which were read to the suspected woman under the sanction of the High Court of Justice[65].   This hardly needs

[62] See, for instance, Mishna, *Eduyyoth*, 8. 7, where R. Joshua says, "I received it from R. Jochanan b. Zakkai, who heard it from his master, and his master from his master, a law unto Moses from Mount Sinai," that Elijah's mission before the advent of the Messiah will only be in a certain given way.

[63] Even the book, סדר אליהו רבה, attributed to the Prophet Elijah, does not eliminate the features of interpretation and tradition.   In many portions, it is nothing else but a running commentary in the regular style of the Midrash to the texts from the Bible (cf. Friedmann's Introduction, p. 132); whilst the term חכמים is frequently turning up as authority for certain statements.   Sometimes, even the names of the Rabbis are given (Friedmann, ibid., pp. 59, 60).

[64] See Dr Charles, *Book of Jubilees*, p. lix.; *Testaments of the Twelve Patriarchs*, p. 52.   Cf. W. Baldensperger, *Die Messianisch-Apokalyptischen Hoffnungen des Judenthums*, p. 42, note 1.

[65] See Dr K. Kohler, *J. Q. R.*, v. p. 400 seq., and Dr Charles, *Testaments*, p. xvi.   This is quite consistent with another theory of Dr Kohler that the "Mishnaic system is the code of life of a Chasidim

d 2

refutation. As far, at least, as the Rabbinic literature is concerned, there is not the slightest indication justifying such a statement. The general impression we receive from the Rabbinic literature, which remains, after all, the only authoritative source for the teachings of the Pharisees, is that they had a deep aversion to all "external writings," though not all the Rabbis were equally severe in their judgment upon it as, for instance, was R. Akiba. Hence, it is not likely that they would have indulged in the production of a literature towards which they all maintained a more or less hostile attitude. And this impression is now confirmed by our Text. For whatever difficulties the present unsatisfactory state of our MS. may place in the way of the student, and whatever doubts may prevail as to the meaning of this or that passage, one thing is certain, that we have to deal here with a Sect decidedly hostile to the bulk of the Jews as represented by the Pharisees. It is a Sect equipped with additional sacred books of its own, a calendar of its own, and a set of laws of its own, bearing upon various commandments of the Scriptures. It is at variance with the nation at large in its interpretation of the past, abusing its heroes, as in the case of David (p. 5, ll. 2—5), and the princes of Judah (p. 4, l. 11; p. 7, ll. 13, 14; p. 8, l. 3), nor does it share its hopes and aspirations for the future, the Messiah expected by the Sect being an offspring from Aaron. The Covenant of the Forefathers is an expression turning up again and again (p. 1, l. 4; p. 4, l. 9; p. 6, l. 2; p. 8, l. 18 [= p. 19, ll. 30, 31])[66], but it is the Sect apparently on whom both the duties and the privileges devolve at a later period. They who builded the Fence (thus trying to be saved by their own merits), failed to understand the significance of God's love of the Fathers, and the import of His oath to them[67], wherefore God hated them, whilst the Covenant of the Fathers belongs to the others (the members of the Sect). Indeed, these latter are the "sons" of the Book of Jubilees, who convict

---

colony" (*J. Q. R.* v. p. 406, note 1), which need not be discussed here. With regard to the Testaments, however, I will only refer here to Bacher, *Agada der Tannaiten*, 2 ed., p. 457, where the real explanation of the בכתובים הראשונים is given. It is to be further remarked that *Jer. Sotah*, 16 *d*, omits these words. Personally, I have little doubt that בכתובים הראשונים is a corruption of לאבות הראשונים, this term being also applied to the heads of the tribes and other men of early times. (Cf. *Mechilta* 48*a*, and *Aboth d' R. Nathan*, 13 *b*.) Hence, his urging the מאבותם (Job 15 18). This view receives strong support from the version of the *Midrash Haggadol* ואומרים לפניה דברים שאינה כדאי לשמען היא וכל משפחת בית אביה כגון מעשה ראובן בבלהה ומעשה יהודה בתמר ומעשה אמנון באחותו שנ' אשר חכמ' ינדו ולא כי"ח

מאב"ו מה שכר נטלו על כך להם לבדם ניתנה הארץ. See also *Midrash Haggadol* to Gen. p. 681. Cf. also Maimonides, *Hilchoth Sotah*, 3. 2. Perhaps I may remark here that Dr Charles' statement that even the Talmud (*Kiddushin*, 66 *a*) describes him (John Hyrcanus) as a second David (ibid., lii.), is incorrect. There is nothing of the kind there, the name David not occurring at all, and the impression is rather that the Pharisees did resent his wearing two crowns.

[66] It is noteworthy that reference to the ברית in one way or another occurs not less than 35 times in this short text.

[67] See p. 8, ll. 13, 14, 15, though the text is not quite correct in this place.

their fathers and their elders of forsaking the Covenant[68], or as those who "have forgotten commandment and covenant, and feasts, and months and Sabbaths and jubilees, and all judgments[69],"—that is, the men who differed in the interpretation of the meaning of the Covenant and the rules for the "feasts and months and Sabbaths and jubilees and all judgments" from the principles laid down in the additional sacred book, the Book of Jubilees. And it is among them, again, that those books arose which gave authority to the New Covenant. Having ruled out their fathers from the Covenant, they must date back their teachings to the *forefathers* and to the patriarchs and other Biblical personages. Certainly their Book of Jubilees, as well as their Testaments of the Twelve Patriarchs, and their Book of Enoch, did not agree in all particulars with the texts which have come down to us. The Book of Jubilees, for instance, must have contained more Halacha than it contains at present. Nor can all these passages, either in the Book of Jubilees or in the Testaments of the Twelve Patriarchs favourable to Judah have formed a part of the original works as known to the founders of the Sect. All such passages are probably a later addition by succeeding generations, who must have entirely recast the contents of the Testaments of the Twelve Patriarchs. But through whatever changes and interpolations this class of *Pseudepigrapha* may have passed—and certain of them may have been undertaken with the purpose of reconciling their teachings with those of the nation at large—their sectarian character always remained prominent, especially in their Halachic parts. Naturally all this class of *Pseudepigrapha* is of supreme importance for the history of Christianity, which undoubtedly was the consummation of all sectarian endeavour preceding it, and must have absorbed all the hostile elements arrayed against official Judaism; but for this very reason it cannot be considered as a factor in the development of Pharisaic Judaism. Altogether, I have the feeling that the "higher theology" is a little too hasty in its reconstruction of Pharisaic Judaism, relying too much on a few isolated Hagadic passages which in one way or another crept into Rabbinic literature, and entirely ignoring the Halacha. Lagarde somewhere makes the remark that the treatment of the Pentateuch must never be approached without a thorough knowledge of the Halacha, either in questions bearing upon higher criticism or in those touching upon textual criticism. How much more is this the case with Pharisaism. The only authoritative source for it is and will always remain the Talmud, and the "great Midrashim," in their Hagadic and not less in their Halachic parts.

[68] Jub. **23** 16. [69] Jub. **23** 19.

xxx

FRAGMENTS OF A ZADOKITE WORK

TEXT A.

¶ I

1 Now, therefore, hearken unto me, ye all who know righteousness[1] and meditate
2 upon the work of | God[2]. For He has a controversy with all flesh[3] and He will
3 execute judgment[4] upon all who despise Him. | For because of their treason that
4 they forsook Him, He hid His face[5] from Israel and from His sanctuary | and
   delivered them unto the sword[6]. But when He remembered the covenant of the
5 forefathers[7] He left a remnant | to Israel and gave them not over unto exter-
6 mination. And at the end of the wrath[8], three hundred | and ninety years after
   He had delivered them into the hand of Nebuchadnezzar[9], the King of Babylon, |
7 He remembered them, and made bud from Israel and Aaron a root of a plant[10]
8 to inherit | His land, and to rejoice in the good of His earth. And they
9 meditated over their sin and they knew that | they were guilty men, and they
10 were like the blind *groping in the way[11] | twenty years[12]. And God considered
11 their deeds[13], for they sought Him with a perfect heart[14] | and He raised for
    them a[15] teacher of righteousness[16] to make them walk in the way of His heart.
12 And He made known | to later generations what He has wrought[17] in a *former
13 generation[18] in an assembly of treacherous men[19]. | They are those who turned
    out of the way[20]. This is the time concerning which it has been written: "As
14 a backsliding heifer | so did Israel slide back[21]," when there arose the man of
15 scoffing[22] who dropped to Israel | waters of deceitfulness[23] and caused them to
    wander in the wilderness where there is no way[24], to bow down the loftiness of
16 eternity[25], to turn away | from the paths of righteousness and to remove the bound

¶ I

[1] See Isa. **51** 7.

[2] See Job **37** 14.

[3] See Hos. **4** 1. See also Jer. **25** 31.

[4] See Gen. **18** 25 etc.

[5] Ps. **10** 11.

[6] See Jer. **25** 31.

[7] See Lev. **26** 45.

[8] Heb. l. 5 ובקץ חרון. Heb. p. 5, l. 20, offers the parallel ובקץ חרבן הארץ.

[9] Such a number is known from Ezek. **4** 5, cf. Jewish Commentators a. l., but it is more probable that we should read ארבע instead of שלוש (490) corresponding with the seventy weeks of years of Dan. **9** 2, 24, playing such an important part in the Pseudepigraphic literature familiar to our author. See Test. Levi, **16** 1, **17** 2.

[10] Heb. l. 7 שורש מטעת. Cf. Isa. **60** 21 נצר מטעי. The following לירוש את ארצו suggests that the words were taken from Isa. Accordingly, we should read נצר מטעו. Cf. also Zech. **6** 12, and Enoch **1** 16, and Test. Judah, **24** 5.

[11] See Isa. **59** 10 and Deut. **28** 29, which parallels indicate that we should read Heb. l. 9, מגששים instead of וכימנששים, the וכי' having probably come in through the כעורים.

[12] See below Heb. p. 20, l. 5, speaking of forty years. But I am not quite certain whether they refer to the same occurrence.

[13] See Ps. **33** 15.

[14] See 1 Chron. **29** 9.

[15] See Jud. **3** 15 etc.

[16] See Hos. **10** 12.

[17] See Ps. **78** 6.

[18] Reading Heb. l. 12 ראשון instead of אחרון, which is a clerical error come in through the אחרונים in the same line. It is also possible that the whole phrase is a mere dittography of the בדורות אחרונים, the copyist also thinking of Ps. **78** 6.

[19] See Jer. **9** 1 עצרת ב'.

[20] See Exod. **33** 8 etc. Cf. below Heb. p. 2, l. 6, and p. 8, l. 4.

[21] See Hos. **4** 16.

[22] See Isa. **28** 14. Cf. Text B, p. 20, l. 11.

[23] See Micah **2** 6, 11 (cf. Prov. **22** 3 לחם כז') that is the false prophet. Cf. below Heb. p. 4, ll. 19 and 20; and p. 8, l. 14; and p. 20, l. 15.

[24] See Ps. **107** 40.

[25] גבהות ע'. See Isa. **2** 17. Perhaps we have in גבהות a corruption from גבעות. Cf. Gen. **49** 26 "the everlasting hills."

XXXI

17 which the forefathers have set in their inheritance[26]. So as | to make cleave
unto them the curses of the covenant[27], to deliver them to the sword that shall
18 execute the vengeance | of the covenant[28]. Because that they searched in smooth
19 things[29] and chose deceits, and looked forward | to the breaches[30]. And they chose
20 the goods of the throat[31] and justified the wicked and condemned the just[32] | and
*transgressed the covenant[33] and broke the statute and[34] gathered themselves together
21 against the soul of the righteous[35] man. And all that walked | uprightly their soul
abhorred[36] and they pursued them with the sword and *rejoiced at the* war of
|| Page 2 the people[37]. Therefore, was kindled the wrath || of God against their congregation[38]
to make desolate their multitude, and their deeds* were unclean[39] before Him. |

¶ II 2   And now, hearken unto me ye all who entered into the covenant[1] and I will
3 reveal to you[2] concerning the ways | of the wicked. God loves knowledge. Wisdom
4 and counsel[3] He placed before Him | prudence[4] and knowledge, they minister
5 to Him. Long-suffering[5] is with Him and an abundance of forgiveness | to atone for
those who return from sin[6], and power and might and great wrath in flames of
6 fire[7]. | Therein are all the angels of destruction[8] for them who turned out of the
7 way and despised the statute[9], so that there should be no remnant | nor escaping[10]
for them. For, before the world was, God chose them not, and ere they were
8 established He knew | their deeds, and He contemned the generations of blood[11]
9 and hid His face from the earth | to *exterminate[12] them till they were consumed[13].
And He knew* the years of the station[14] and the number and the explanation
10 of their ends[15], for all | the *things that be everlasting and are to happen[16], to

---

[26] See Deut. **19** 14. Cf. below, Heb. p. 5, l. 20.

[27] See Deut. **28** 21, and **29** 21.

[28] See Lev. **26** 25.

[29] See Isa. **30** 10 דברו לנו חלקות.

[30] Heb. ll. 18, 19 ויצפו לפרצות. Perhaps corruption
of ויפרצו פרצות "broke breaches" in the sense of
licentiousness and lawlessness. Cf. Rab. Dict. s. v.

[31] Heb. l. 19 הצואר. Perhaps a corruption of העובר
"perishable" "passing away." Cf. *J. Q. R.* vol. 16,
p. 479, the expression עולם עובר in a Samaritan writing
dating from the 12th century.

[32] See Prov. **17** 15.

[33] Heb. l. 20. Reading ויעברו ב' for ויעבירו. Cf.
Joshua **7** 15.

[34] See Ezek. **47** 7.   [35] See Ps. **94** 21.

[36] Cf. Ps. **107** 18.

[37] Heb. l. 21 ויסיסו לריב עם. Perhaps corruption of
וישישו ל' ע' "They rejoiced at the war." Another alter-
native is ויסיתו meaning, "they goaded the people into
war."

[38] See Ps. **106** 40.   [39] See Ezek. **36** 17.

¶ II

[1] Heb. l. 2 באי ברית for בברית ב'. Cf. Jer. **34** 10
and below, Heb. p. 12, l. 10; p. 15, l. 5 etc. By this
probably is meant the "New Covenant." Cf. below,
Heb. p. 6, l. 19.

[2] Heb. l. 2 ואגלה אזנכם. More probable is that
אזנכם is a corruption of עיניכם, as below, l. 14. See
1 Sam. **20** 2 and **22** 8.

[3] Heb. l. 3 ותושיה.

[4] Heb. l. 4 ערמה. Cf. *Beth* Hammidrash (Jellinek)
v. 174 about the Gates of ערמה which God opens for
Metatron. See also Prov. **8** 12.

[5] Exod. **34** 6 etc.

[6] See Isa. **59** 20.

[7] Heb. l. 5 חֵמָה. Perhaps we should read חַמָּה
"heat" as suggested by the context "flames of fire."
ולהבי Heb. ibid. is probably a corruption of להבות.
Cf. Ps. **29** 7.

[8] Heb. l. 6 חבל. The term מ' חבלה frequently in
Rab. literature. Cf. Rab. Dict. s. חבל and s. מלאך.

[9] See Micah **3** 9.

[10] See Ez. **9** 14.

[11] Heb. l. 8 מדם. Perhaps it is a corruption of
מקדם "of yore" or the former generations.

[12] Assuming that the מי in the Heb. text which gives
no sense is a remainder of להשמידם.

[13] See Deut. **2** 15, Jer. **24** 10.

[14] Heb. e.g. מעמד. See below, Heb. p. 4, l. 5.
Meaning obscure. Heb. p. 20, l. 5, would imply that
station means as much as the position of the member in
the inner council of the Sect, and their activity as governors
or heads among the men of the "perfection of holiness."

[15] Heb. l. 9 ופרוש קציתם. Heb. p. 4, l. 5, however,
suggests the emendation ומספר צרותיהם, "the number
of their sufferings." See, however, Heb. p. 16, l. 2.

[16] Heb. l. 10 הוי עולמים ונהיית. Meaning obscure.
I take the הוי as a participle of הוה. Cf. Jastrow and

11 that which will come to their ends[17], for all the years of eternity. | And in all of
them He raised for Himself men called by name[18], in order to leave a remnant
12 to the earth[19] and to fill | the face of the world with their children[20]. And through
13 His Anointed[21] He made them know His Holy Spirit, and he | is true[22], and the
*explanation of their names[23], and them He hated He made go astray. |

¶ III 14   Now, therefore, children, hearken unto me[1] and I will open your eyes to see
15 and to meditate over the deeds | of God, and to choose what He desireth and
16 despise what He hateth. To walk uprightly[2] | in all His ways and not to seek
after *the thoughts of the imagination[3] guilt and after the *eyes of fornication[4].
17 For many | were led astray by them, and mighty men of valour stumbled by them
18 from beforetime and hitherto. Because they walked in the stubbornness | of their
heart[5] fell the *Watchers[6] of the heaven. By them[7] were they caught because they
19 kept not the commandment of God. | And their children whose height was like
the height of the cedars[8] and whose bodies were like mountains* likewise fell[9]. |
20 All flesh that was on dry land *also perished[10], and they were as though they had not
21 been[11]. Because they did their | own will and kept not the commandment of their
Maker until His wrath was kindled against them[12]. ||

║ Page 3   By it* went astray the sons of Noah and *their families[1], and because
2 of it they were rooted out[2]. | Abraham did not walk in it and he *became
3 friend[3] because he kept the commandment of God and chose not | the will of his
own spirit. And he delivered (it) to Isaac and to Jacob[4], and they observed (it)[5]
4 and were recorded as friends | of God[6] and men of the covenant for ever[7]. By
5 them the sons of Jacob went astray and they were punished* according[8] to | their

Kohut s. v. For ונהיית read ונהיות. Cf. below, p. 13,
l. 8 Heb. Cf. also Ecclus. Heb. **42** 19.

[17] Heb. ibid. עד מה יבוא. I hardly need say that
these translations are only tentative.

[18] Cf. Num. **16** 2 קראי [מעד אנשי] שם in accordance
with which our text is perhaps to be emended. See
also below, Heb. p. 4, l. 4.

[19] See Ezek. **14** 21.

[20] See Isa. **27** 6.

[21] Heb. l. 20 משיחו. See also Heb. p. 12, l. 23;
p. 14, l. 19; p. 19, l. 10; p. 20, l. 1.

[22] Heb. lines 12, 13 והוא אמת, referring probably to
the רוח in opposition to the רוח שקר of Belial. Cf.
Jub. **1** 20, 21.

[23] Heb. l. 13 ובפרוש שמו שמותיהם. The parallel,
however, offered by Heb. p. 4, ll. 4, 5, makes it clear that
the שמו here is a dittography; whilst instead of ובפרוש,
we should read ופרוש. Meaning not quite clear to me.

¶ III

[1] See Prov. **8** 32.

[2] See Ps. **101** 6.

[3] Heb. l. 16 במחשבות יצר. See Gen. **6** 5 יצר
מחשבות. Perhaps יצר is here as much as יצר הרע.

[4] Heb. ibid. עני, corruption of עיני. Cf. Num. **15**
39. Cf. Sifre 35ᵃ ואחרי עיניכם זו זנות. See also
Test. Issachar, **7** 2; 2 Peter **2** 14.

[5] Cf. Jer. **13** 10.

[6] Heb. l. 18 עירי corruption of עירי the "Watchers."
Cf. Enoch **1** 5; **7** 2; Jub. **4** 16; Test. Reuben, **5** 6;
and Test. Naphtali, **3** 3, 5, text and notes.

S. (Frags. A & B)

[7] Heb. l. 18 בה which the scribe often wrote for בם.

[8] See Amos **2** 9.

[9] Heb. l. 19 כי נפלו which is probably a corruption
of גם כן נ'. See also the following note.

[10] Reading in the Hebrew כל בשר אשר היה בחרבה
גוע [גם כן]. Cf. Gen. **7** 22 and 23. Cf. also Jub. **4** 24.

[11] See Obad. 15, Job **10** 19.

[12] See Isa. **5** 23, etc.

¶ IV

[1] Heb. l. 1 ומשפחותיהם probably suggested by Gen.
10 32 נח בני משפחות. But the reading is doubtful,
the MS. being torn and the letters in brackets missing.
The sin to which he refers is perhaps the eating of blood
(cf. Jub. **6** 18 and below, l. 6), assuming that some
sentence is missing in which reference to this sin was
made. It is also possible that the בה at the beginning of
this paragraph (p. 3, l. 1 "in it") is a corruption of ברם.
Of course, תעי, the second word in this line is a mere
clerical error for תעו.

[2] Heb. ibid. בה הם נכרתים. Cf. Lev. **7** 27;
Jub. **6** 12; that is, liable to the punishment of כרת.

[3] "Became friend" Heb. l. 2 ויעשה אוהב which
reading however is very doubtful as indicated by the
brackets. Cf. Jub. **19** 9, and N.T. James **2** 23.

[4] See Jub. **21** 18 where Abraham commands Isaac to
refrain from eating blood. See also Jub. **6** 19.

[5] Heb. וישמרו omitting אותה (המצוה). Cf. Jub.
6 19, text and notes "a b omit 'it'."

[6] See Jub. **19** 9 and **30** 21, cf. Singer, p. 151.

[7] See Gen. **14** 13.

[8] Reading Heb. l. 4 לפי instead of לפני.

e

(65)

error. And their children in Egypt walked in the stubbornness of their heart to

6 take counsel against | the commandments of God and every man doing* that which

7 was right in his own[9] eyes and they ate blood[10]. Therefore He exterminated | their males in the desert* when He spake* to them in the desert in Kadesh, Go up and possess* the *land[11]. *And they provoked* His spirit[12], and hearkened not|

8 unto the voice of their Maker[13], the commandments of their teachers[14], and murmured

9 in their tents[15]. Therefore the wrath of God was kindled | against their congregation[16], and their children perished by it, and their kings were exterminated by it, and their

10 mighty men perished by it | and their land *was made desolate*[17] by* it. By it

11 were guilty[18] the first that entered into the covenant, and they were delivered | unto the sword[19]. Because they forsook the covenant of God and chose their* own will

12 and sought after the stubbornness | of their heart[20], every man doing according to his pleasure[21].

¶ V 13   But with them that held fast to[1] the commandments of God, | who were left among

14 them, God confirmed His covenant with Israel for ever, revealing | unto them the hidden things in which all Israel erred: His holy Sabbaths and His glorious

15 festivals, | the testimony of His righteousness and the ways of His truth and the

16 desires of His will which a man shall do | and live by them[2]. He opened before

17 them[3] and they digged a well of many waters, | and he that despises them shall not live[4]. But they *wallowed[5] in the transgression of man[6] and in the ways of

18 the unclean woman. | And they said that it belongs to us[7]. But God in the *abundance[8] of His wonder made atonement for their sins[9] and forgave their trans-

19 gression. | And He built them a sure house in Israel[10], the like of which never arose

20 beforetime and | hitherto. They who hold fast to Him are for the life of eternity,

21 and all glory of man is for them; as | God confirmed it to them through Ezekiel,

‖ Page 4 the prophet, saying: "The priests and the Levites and the sons ‖ of Zadok that

2 kept the charge of His sanctuary when the children of Israel went astray | from *them they shall bring near unto me fat and blood[11]."

---

[9] See Jud. **17** 6.

[10] See Jub. **4** 6.

[11] The Heb. text (ll. 6 and 7 ורשו את...ויכרת) is very corrupt. But the parallel passages in Num. **14** 29, 43, Deut. **1** 40—46, **9** 23, 24 and Ps. **106** 33 suggest the following correction ויכרת זכורם וכאשר דבר להם במדבר] קדש עלו ורשו את הארץ after which our translation was made.

[12] Heb. l. 7 רוחם ולא etc. which gives no sense, but the references given in the former note suggest וימרו את רוחו. It is also possible that the missing words are ויבחרו ברצון רוחם "and chose the will of their own spirit." Cf. above, ll. 2 and 3.

[13] See Isa. **22** 11.

[14] Heb. l. 8 יוריהם. Cf. below, Heb. p. 6, l. 11, and p. 20, l. 14.

[15] Heb. l. 8 וירגנו וג'. See Ps. **106** 25.

[16] See Ps. **106** 40. Cf. above, p. 1, l. 21, and below, Heb. p. 8, l. 13.

[17] Reading Hebrew l. 10 נָשַׁמָה for שממה. Cf. Jer. **12** 11, and Lev. **26** 33.

[18] Heb. l. 12 חבו. See Rab. Dict. s. v. חוב.

[19] See above, Heb. p. 1, l. 17.

[20] See above, Heb. p. 2, l. 16.

[21] See Esther **1** 8.

¶ V

[1] Heb. l. 12 ובמחזיקים במצות וג'. Cf. Isa. **56** 4, seq. Cf. below, Heb. p. 20, l. 27. See also Test. Naphtali, **3** 1.

[2] See Lev. **18** 5. The whole passage evidently refers to calendar differences. Cf. Jub. **1** 14; **6** 34, 37 and **23** 19. It is however not clear what is meant by the "Holy Sabbaths" (שבתות קדשו). Cf. below, Heb. p. 6, l. 18 and p. 20, ll. 30 and 31. Perhaps it refers to certain laws regarding the observance of the Sabbath. Cf. Singer, pp. 191 and 198. See Introduction, pp. xvi and xviii.

[3] Heb. l. 16 לפניהם פ'. Perhaps corruption of עיניהם פ' "He opened their eyes." Cf. 2 Kings **6** 20 etc.

[4] More fully is the simile of the well developed below. Heb. p. 6, l. 2, seq.

[5] Heb. l. 17 התגוללו. Cf. Heb. below, p. 8, l. 5.

[6] Heb. ibid. בפשע אנוש. Prov. **29** 6 ב' איש.

[7] Perhaps allusion to Ezek. **11** 15, and **33** 24.

[8] Heb. l. 17 ברוי corruption of ברוב.

[9] Heb. ibid. כפר בעד עונם which suggests כפר בעדם. Cf. Lev. **16** 6 etc. See also below, Heb. p. 4, l. 10.

[10] Cf. 1 Sam. **2** 35 etc.

[11] Ezek. **44** 15 והכהנים הלוים בני צדוק אשר שמרו

¶ VI 3   The priests are the captivity[1] of Israel | who have gone forth out of the land
of Judah and they who have joined them[2]. And the sons of Zadok are the chosen |

4 of Israel called by names[3] that arose at the end of the days[4]. Behold the explanation |

5 of their names according to their generations, the end of their station and the number

6 of their sufferings and the years | of their sojourns[5] and the explanation of their

7 deeds. The holy they alter which God made atonement | for them[6]. And they
justified the righteous and condemned the wicked[7]. And all they who come after

8 them | to do according to the interpretation of the Law in which the forefathers were

9 *instructed[8] until the *completing[9] | of the end of these years. In accordance with

10 the covenant which God has confirmed to the forefathers to make atonement | for
their sins, so shall God make atonement for them[10]. And after the completing of the

11 end in accordance with the number of these years | *one shall not join the house of

12 Judah[11], but every man shall stand up against his | net[12]. The wall is built, the decree

13 is far removed[13]. And during all these years there will be | Belial[14] let loose against Israel

14 as God hath spoken through Isaiah, the prophet, the son | of Amoz, saying: Fear
and the net and the snare are upon thee, O inhabitant of the land[15]. Its explanation

15–16 is[16] | : three nets of Belial concerning which Levi the son of Jacob hath spoken[17] | by *

17 which he ensnared Israel[18] and *directed their faces to the three kinds | of righteousness.

את משמרת מקדשי בתעות בני ישראל מעלי המה יקרבו
אלי לשרתני ועמדו לפני להקריב לי חלב ודם נאם אדני ה'.
Our Heb. l. 21 and p. 4, ll. 1, 2 text reproduced by the
translation reads הכהנים והלוים ובני צדוק אשר שמרו
את משמרת מקדשו בתעות בני ישראל מעליהם יגישו לי
חלב ודם. The differences are striking and some of
these may be ascribed to the carelessness of the scribe,
but it is not impossible that the differences in the first
three words were made intentionally to indicate that his
priests and Levites were not identical with the sons of
Zadok. This is at least the impression one receives from
the comment given in the lines that follow.

¶ VI

[1] Heb. l. 2 שבי. Cf. Heb. p. 6, l. 5; p. 8, l. 16
(text B, l. 29) which word I read שְׁבִי "captivity." The
word, however, can also be read שָׁבֵי "repentants." Cf.
p. 19, ll. 15, 16. But p. 6, l. 5, connecting the שבי with
the immigration from the land of Judah, speaks in favour
of "captivity."

[2] Heb. l. 3 והנלוים עמהם representing the לוים of
Ezekiel.

[3] See above, Heb. p. 2, l. 11.

[4] Cf. Gen. 49 1, Dan. 10 14 etc.

[5] Heb. l. 6 התגוררם. It may also mean wanderings.
Cf. above, Heb. p. 2, ll. 9—12. As above reference is
contained here to the history of the sect, the names of its
leaders, the sufferings during their wanderings before they
settled and their various activities. But unfortunately all
these details were omitted by the scribe.

[6] Heb. ll. 9, 10 הקודש שונים...בעדם of which I
give a literal translation, but it renders no sense. The
text is evidently corrupt and before the הקודש some
words are evidently missing. It is, however, possible,
that we should emend הקודש שונים into הראשונים. Cf.
below, ll. 9, 10, though even with this emendation the
sense is not quite clear. Another possibility is that the

הקודש שונים is a corruption of המקדש שומרים, "they
keep the charge of the sanctuary," which is one of the
functions of the sons of Zadok.

[7] See above, Heb. p. 1, l. 19.

[8] Heb. התוסרו used by this writer in the sense of
instruction. Cf. Heb. p. 7, l. 5. See also Heb. Dict.
See, however, p. 20, l. 31, which probably means "were
chastised."

[9] Heb. l. 8 שלים corruption of שלום, cf. below, l. 10.

[10] The meaning of these last two sentences is entirely
obscure. All we can see is that he contrasts his congregation with its priests, its Levites and the sons of Zadok
with the wicked men who followed the איש הלצון
(Heb. p. 1, l. 14) who are further accused of having
justified the wicked and condemned the righteous (Heb.
p. 1, l. 19). They are not entirely free from sin but
they are redeemed by the fact that they follow the
explanation of the Law as was understood by the
forefathers (ראשונים), that is Noah and the Patriarchs
(in the Book of Jubilees). Hence they obtain pardon,
as their forefathers did.

[11] Heb. l. 11 אין להשתתפה עוד על בית יהודה. Cf.
Isa. 14 1.

[12] Heb. כי אם לעמוד איש על מצודו (ll. 10, 11) that
is to watch over the net lest he be caught.

[13] See paraphrase of Micah 7 11 but the application is
not clear to me.

[14] See Jub. 1 20.

[15] Isa. 24 17.

[16] Reading Heb. l. 14. Heb. פ׳׳רו, meaning as much
as פרשו. Cf. Heb. and Rab. Dictionaries, s. פשר.

[17] Heb. l. 15 אשר עליהם אמר לוי בן יעקב. Perhaps
some words are missing here. In any case we have here
a distinct reference to the Testament of Levi, see below
note 18.

[18] Heb. ibid. l. 16 אשר הוא תפש בהם בישראל taking
the הוא to refer to בליעל. Cf. Jub. 1 20. It is however

e 2

---

(67)

18 The first is fornication, the second is *wealth[19], the third | is the *pollution of the sanctuary[20]. He that fleeth from this will be ensnared by that, and he that escapeth

19 the one will be ensnared | by the other[21]. They that builded the *wall[22] who walked after the *commanding one[23].

¶ VII 20   The commanding one is he who prophesies* | concerning which he said, "For

21 a surety they do drop words[1]." They are ensnared by two: by fornication[2], taking | two wives during their lifetimes[3], *but the foundation of the creation[4] is, "Male and female

‖ Page 5 created He them[5]." ‖ And they who came into the Ark, "Two and two went into the

2 Ark[6]." As to the prince[7] it is written, | "He shall not multiply wives unto himself[8]."

3 *But David read not in the Book of the Law that was sealed, which | was in the Ark.

4 For it was not opened in Israel from the day of the Death of Eleazar | and Joshua[9], and

5 the Elders who worshipped Ashtareth[10]. And it was hidden | and was *not discovered[11] until Zadok arose. But they *concealed[12] the deeds of David save only the blood

6 of Uriah[13] | and God abandoned them to him. They also contaminate the sanctuary

7 as* they | separate not[14] according to the Law and lie with her who sees the blood

8 of her issue[15]. They take | unto them a wife[16] the daughter of their brother and the

---

possible that the author was thinking of Ezek. **14** 4, 5 ומכשול עונו ישים נגד פניו...למען תפש את בית ישראל בלבם. To place before man the "stumbling-blocks of his iniquities" is thus a means of leading him back to righteousness. הוא would thus refer to Levi and תפש would mean by which he (Levi) "took" Israel (in their hearts).

[19] Reading Heb. l. 17 הון instead of הין. Cf. Heb. p. 6, l. 15 and p. 8, l. 5. See Jub. **23** 21.

[20] Heb. p. 4, l. 10. Reading Heb. l. 18 טמאת המ' instead of טמא. Some sort of a parallel may be found to this passage in Test. Levi, **14** 5—8, cf. ibid. **9** 9 (see also p. 229) and Jub. **30** 15, though the parallel is neither complete nor distinct enough. But it is possible that our author had a more complete text. See also Jub. **7**. 21 text and notes with reference regarding the "three things" "owing" to which "the deluge came upon the earth": fornication, uncleanness (=טומאה?) and iniquity (גזל or חמס?).

[21] See Isa. **24** 18, and Jer. **48** 44.

[22] Heb. l. 19 בוני החוץ before which expression, some words must be missing. חוץ is a corruption חַיץ cf. Ezek. **13** 10. The writer also probably thought of Lamen. **2** 14. We have here as well as below, p. 8, l. 12, an attack on Pharisees whom he derides as fence or wall builders to protect the law whilst in truth they are the worst offenders. Possibly this denunciation is in some way connected with the accusation of Test. Levi, **14** 4, "teaching commandments contrary to the will of God."

[23] See Hos. **5** 11. הצו to יטיפון is only a disturbing parenthesis.

¶ VII

[1] See Micah **6** 6, 11. Cf. above, p. 1, l. 14; below, p. 8, l. 1 and p. 19, l. 25.

[2] Heb. l. 20 בשתים בזנות וג'. The בשתים is an anticipation of שתי נשים in the following line which the author considered as זנות. It is followed in p. 5 (l. 6) by

---

an explanation of טומאה whilst the explanation of הון is apparently missing, being given only in general terms on p. 6, l. 15, seq.

[3] Heb. l. 21 בחייהם. The argument is evidently not only directed against polygamy, but also against divorce which certain Jewish sects forbade. Bachrach, in his *Yoreach Lemoadim*, p. 49*a*, perceives in the wording of Jub. **3** 7 (see text and notes about the versions), also a prohibition against divorce, which, however, is questionable. See also Introduction, pp. xvii and xix.

[4] Heb. l. 21 הבריאה which term for creation is rather late.

[5] Gen. **1** ·27, cf. Matt. **21** 3. Aboth d'R. Nathan p. 5*a* uses the same argument of Adam against polygamy but does not give the verse.

[6] See Gen. **7** 9.

[7] Heb. l. 1 הנשיא.

[8] Deut. **17** 20.

[9] Heb. l. 4 ויהושע ויושע which is a mere dittography.

[10] See Jud. **2** 13.

[11] Reading Heb. ll. 4, 5 ויטמן ולא נגלה instead of ויטמון נגלה. Another possibility is that נגלה is a corruption of מגלה and is here=ספר. To which Zadok reference is made here is difficult to say. It must in any case be a Biblical personage. See Introduction, p. xxi.

[12] Heb. l. 5 ויעלו, which I take to be a corruption of ויעלימו.

[13] See 1 Kings **15** 5, of which our author evidently does not approve.

[14] Reading l. 7 מבדילים for מבדיל.

[15] Heb. ibid. הרואה את דם וג' which is the regular Rabbinic term for menstruation. For differences between Rabbinites and Samaritans and the Karaites, see Vreschner, *Die Samaritanische Tradition*, p. 30 seq. and the references given there to Geiger and others.

[16] Reading Heb. l. 8 אשה instead of איש.

9 daughter of their sisters[17]. But Moses said, "Thou shalt not | approach the sister of thy
10 mother: she is thy mother's near kin[18]," and the law of incest[19] for males | is written,
and like them[20] are the females; and if the daughter of the brother uncovers the
11 nakedness of the brother | of her father* he[21] is a near kin. They also contaminated
12 their holy spirit[22] and with a tongue | of reproaches they opened the mouth against
the statutes of the covenant of God, saying, They are not proper. But abomination |
13 they speak concerning them. They all kindled[23] a fire and set in flames the sparks[24].
14 The weaving | of spiders are their weavings and the eggs of adders are their eggs[25].
15 He who comes near them | shall not be innocent. Like *a thing accursed shall his
16 house be guilty[26]* unless he was* forced[27]. Beforetimes[28] God *observed | their deeds
and His wrath was kindled because of their devices. For it is a people of no under-
17 standing[29]. | They are a nation void of counsel[30], because there is no understanding in
18 them[31]. For beforetimes rose[32] | Moses and Aaron through the prince of the Urim[33],
19 *when[34] Belial raised Yochaneh and | his brother[35] in his device when Israel was
delivered for the first time[36]. |

¶VIII 20   And at the end of the destruction of the land there arose those who removed the
21 bound[1] and led astray Israel. | And the land became desolate because they have spoken
|| Page 6 rebellion[2] against the commandments of God through Moses and also || against His
2 holy Anointed one[3], and they prophesied a lie to turn away Israel from after | God.

---

[17] Reading Heb. ibid. אחותיהם for אחותו. It is also possible that we ought to read אחיו for אחיהם in which case it would correspond with אחותו.

[18] Heb. ll. 8, 9 אל אחות אמך לא תקרב שאר אמך היא but the nearest parallel Lev. **18** 13 reads ערות אחות אמך לא תגלה כי שאר אמך היא.

[19] Heb. l. 10 העריות which is a Rabbinic term. Cf. Rab. Dict. s.v.

[20] Heb. l. 10 וכהם as much as וכמוהם.

[21] Reading Heb. l. 11 והוא for והיא. The argument turns up often in Karaitic books if he must not marry his aunt she must not marry her uncle. Cf. Kircheim p. 28 with reference to the Samaritans. See also Hadasi, *Eshkol Hakkofer*, p. 117 c, and *Likkute Kadmonioth*, ed. Harkavy, pp. 97 and 100. See also Poznanski, *Kaufman Gedenkbuch*, 172, seq.

[22] Heb. l. 11 רוח קדשיהם. See below, p. 7, l. 7. See Dr Gaster's edition of the Will of Naphtali, P.S.B.A., 1894, p. 117, אשרי אדם אשר לא יטנף את רוח אלהים הקדושה, Wertheimer, בתי מדרשות II. p. 14, אשרי אדם שלא יטמא רוח אלהים שבקרבו.

[23] Heb. l. 13 קדחו which I corrected after Isa. **50** 11, קרחי.

[24] Heb. ibid. ומבערי זיקות. Isa. ibid. ומאזרי זיקות.

[25] See Isa. **59** 4, 5.

[26] Heb. l. 15 כהר ביתו יאשם which I take as a corruption of כחרם ב' י'. Possibly כהררים=כהר (see Jer. **17** 6) whilst יאשם=יֵשַׁם "to be desolate" (see Hos. **14** 1). See also below, l. 21. Job **27** 18 suggests כעש ב' יאשם, but none of these explanations is satisfactory.

[27] That is to say, that in case of compulsion, he is exempt from punishment. Heb. ibid. כי אם נלחץ. I

hardly need repeat here that the explanation of such corrupt texts is merely tentative.

[28] The Heb. equivalent Ibid. למילפנים (l. 17 מלפנים) is preceded by the words כי אם which I omitted as a mere dittography.

[29] See Isa. **27** 11.   [30] Deut. **32** 28.

[31] See Deut. ibid. ואין בהם תבונה.

[32] Heb. l. 17 עמד. Possibly it is a corruption of עזר "helped." The connection of the following lines with the preceding is not clear to me.

[33] Heb. l. 18 שר האורים. Perhaps it is a corruption of שר הפנים "the prince of the Presence" who helped Moses against the devices of Belial (or Mastema), cf. Jub. **48** 2 and 9. Cf. especially ibid. *v.* 4, "And I delivered thee out of his (Mastema's) hand"; the deliverer, apparently, is the angel of the Presence, who dictates to Moses the contents of the Book of Jubilees. See Jub. **1** 27; **2** 1.

[34] Heb. ibid. ויקם which I took to mean here as much as כאשר הקים.

[35] The brother is Mamre. We have evidently here a reference to the well-known Jannes and Jambries legend. See the literature in Schürer, *Geschichte des Jüdischen Volkes*, III., 1898, pp. 292—294. Cf. also *Realencyklopädie für protestantische Theologie und Kirche*, 3rd edition, Vol. VIII., p. 587.

[36] Heb. l. 29 את. Perhaps corruption of עת. See N.T. 2 Tim. **3** 8.

¶ VIII

[1] Cf. Heb. above, p. 1, l. 16. See also ibid. l. 5, text and notes.

[2] See Deut. **13** 6. See also below, Heb. p. 12, l. 3.

[3] Heb. l. 1 במשיחו הקודש as much as ב' הקדוש. Cf. above, Heb. p. 2, l. 12.

But God remembered the covenant with the forefathers[4]. And He took from Aaron*
3 men of understanding and from Israel | wise men and made them* understand[5], and
4 they digged the well[6]. "The princes digged the well; they digged it, | the nobles of
the people, by the lawgiver[7]." The well is the Law, and they who digged it are the |
5 captivity[8] of Israel who have gone forth out of the land of Judah[9] and sojourned in the
6 land of Damascus[10], | all of whom God called princes. For they sought Him and their
7 bough was not turned back | in the mouth of one[11]. And the Lawgiver is he who
8 interprets the Law concerning whom | Isaiah said, "He bringeth forth an instrument for
9 his work[12]." And the nobles of the people are they | who came to dig the well by the
10 precepts[13] which the Lawgiver ordained | to walk in *them[14] for all end of the wicked-
11 ness[15]. And they shall reach *nothing beside them[16] until there will arise[17] | the teacher
of righteousness[18] in the end of the days. And all they who were brought[19] into
12 the covenant | they shall not enter into the Sanctuary to kindle His altar, and
13 be shutting | the door, concerning whom God said, "Who is there among you who
14 would shut the doors[20], neither do you kindle my altar | for naught[21]." If[22] they
will not observe to do[23] according to the interpretation of the Law, until the end
15 of the wickedness[24], and to separate | from the children of destruction[25], and to
separate from the wealth of wickedness which is contaminated by a vow and
16 curse[26], | and *from[27] the wealth of the sanctuary, and rob the poor of his people
17 (so that) widows be their prey, | and they murder the fatherless and [28]to distinguish
18 between clean and unclean[29] and to make known between | the holy and the
profane, and to observe the Sabbath according to its interpretation and the feasts |

[4] See Lev. **26** 45. See also above, p. 1, l. 4, and below, p. 8, l. 17.

[5] Heb. l. 3 וישמעם corruption of וישמיעם. The word may also be read וישביעם "he made them take an oath."

[6] See above, Heb. p. 3, l. 16.

[7] Heb. l. 4 במחוקק. Cf. Num. **21** 18, or by the direction of the Lawgiver.

[8] Heb. l. 5 שבי. See above, Heb. p. 4, l. 2, text and notes.

[9] Cf. above, Heb. p. 4, ll. 2, 3.

[10] See below, Heb. l. 19.

[11] Heb. ll. 6, 7 ולא הושבה פארתם בפי אחד, of which the last twelve words are a literal translation but give no sense. Perhaps we should read ו' השברה פ' בפרי אחד. Cf. Ezek. **31** 12. The meaning would be that their searching in or interpreting of the Law had not the effect of breaking the bough by a single fruit, that is did not result in any heresy. Cf. the Rabbinic phrase קצץ בנטיעות and see Rab. Dict. s. נטיעה and s. קצץ.

[12] Isa. **54** 16.

[13] Heb. l. 9 חוקים=במחוקקות. More probable is that we had here במשענות כאשר. Cf. Num. **21** 18.

[14] Reading in Heb. l. 10 בהם for במה. This word can also be read כמה.

[15] Heb. ibid. בכל קץ הרשיע. The last word I took to be a corruption of הרשע. Cf. Ezek. **21** 30. Cf. below, Heb. p. 12, l. 23; 15, l. 7 and p. 20, l. 23. It seems that sometimes the term means as much as the beginning of repentance, but in other places it has to be taken as meaning till the end of the wickedness in general preceding the advent of the Teacher of Righteousness.

[16] Heb. ibid. וזולתם that is any new things not included in בהם as dictated by the Lawgiver shall not be reached before the end of the days. Cf. also Prov. **2** 19. The Teacher of Righteousness is expected to rise again, when he will appear in the same capacity, or in that of the Anointed (cf. p. 12, l. 23 and p. 20, ll. 1 and 32).

[17] See Ezra **2** 63 and Nehem. **7** 65.

[18] See above, Heb. p. 1, l. 11 and p. 3, l. 8.

[19] Heb. l. 11 הובאו, instead of באו. Cf. above, Heb. p. 2, l. 2, text and notes. Special rules of conduct as well as ritual observances are, as it seems, prescribed for the members of the Sect wishing to enjoy the privilege of entering the sanctuary; otherwise, the doors are shut before them.

[20] Mal. **1** 10 מי גם בכם ויסגור דלתים whilst our text, Heb. l. 13, omits גם and reads by mistake דלתו.

[21] Mal. ibid.

[22] Here, as it seems, begins the set of rules to which the men of the Covenant were pledged, given mostly in a negative way. The diction is very awkward, and there may be some words missing.

[23] See Deut. **12**a.

[24] Cf. above, note 15.

[25] Cf. Jub. **15** 26, a metaphor which may have been suggested by Isaiah **1** 4.

[26] See Heb. l. 15 בנדר וחרם which may also mean that they shall take a vow etc. to be separated from etc.

[27] Reading Heb. l. 16 ומהון instead of ובהון. Cf. above, p. 4, l. 17, and cf. also Test. Levi, **14** 5.

[28] See Isa. **10** 2 and Ps. **94** 6.

[29] See Lev. **11** 47. Cf. Jub. **6** 37.

19 and the day of fast[30]* according to the command[31] of them who entered in to the
20 New Covenant[32] in the land of Damascus. | To raise their offerings according to their
21 interpretation[33], to love every one his neighbour | as himself[34], and to strengthen the hand
‖ Page 7 of the poor and the needy and the stranger[35], and to seek every one the peace ‖ of
his neighbour.   And no man shall commit treason against his nearest of kin,
2 separating himself from *fornication[36] | according to the Law[37].   To admonish every
3 one his neighbour according to the Law[38], and not to bear a grudge | from day to
day[39], and to separate from all the contaminations according to their laws[40].   And
4 no man shall defile | his holy spirit[41], *(even) as God did separate them[42].   All
5 they who walk | in these things in the perfection of holiness[43] according to all the
*instructions[44], the covenant of God

TEXT A	TEXT B = Page 19 in the Hebrew
6 *stands fast to them[45] | to preserve them for a thousand generations.	*stands fast to them to preserve them for* thousands of *generations*[1]. *As it is written[2], " He keepeth the covenant and mercy | with them who love 2 Him[3] and keep His[4] commandments for a thousand generations."
¶ IX And if they settle in camps in accordance 7 with the *usage[1] of the land and take | wives	*But if they settle in camps according to the* ¶ IX *laws | of the land* which *were[5] from old and take 3 wives* in accordance with the usage of the Law
and beget children they shall walk according to 8 the Law, and according to | the *foundations[2] according to the usage of the Law as He had spoken, "between man and his wife and between 9 father | and his son[3]." But upon all them that	*and beget children | they* *shall walk[6] according to 4 the Law and according to the foundations according- ing to the usage of the Law | as He had spoken 5 "between man and his wife and between father and his son." But upon all them that despise | the 6*

[30] That is the Day of Atonement.

[31] Heb. l. 19 . . במצא, some letter missing in the MS. which I read כמצות.

[32] See Jer. **31** 30. Cf. also N. T. 1 Cor. **11** 25; Heb. **8** 8.

[33] Referring probably to differences in the question of tithes. Cf. Jub. **32** 11.

[34] See Lev. **19** 18. Cf. also Jub. **7** 2, **36** 4—8; Test. Simon, **4** 7; Issachar, **5** 2, **7** 6; Dan. **4** 3; Gad, **4** 2; Benjamin, **2** 3; N.T. John **13** 34, **15** 12; Romans **12** 10. Cf. Schürer, III. p. 347, note 91 (3rd ed.).

[35] See Ezek. **16** 49.

[36] Reading Heb. l. 7 הזנות, instead of הזונות. Cf. above, p. 2, l. 16, and p. 4, l. 20.

[37] That is according to the law of the Sect forbidding polygamy and marriage after divorce. See above, p. 4, ll. 20, 21, text and notes.

[38] See Lev. **19** 17. Cf. below, p. 9, l. 2.

[39] See Lev. ibid. See N.T. Romans **12** 19.

[40] See Ezra **6** 21.

[41] See above, Heb. p. 5, l. 11.

[42] Heb. l. 4 להם. The הבדיל refers to the thing טמא. Cf. Lev. **20** 25.

[43] Heb. l. 5 בתמים קדש. Cf. below, Heb. p. 20, ll. 2, 5.

[44] Heb. l. 5 יסורו, corruption of יסורים, in the sense of instructions. Cf. above, p. 4, l. 8. See, however, below, Heb. l. 8, the possibility of יסודים.

TEXT A

[45] Heb. l. 5 נאמנות. Cf. below, Heb. p. 14, l. 2. Cf. Ps. **89** 29 suggesting the emendation נאמנת.

¶ IX

[1] Heb. l. 6 כסרך meaning custom, usage. See Rab. Dict. s. סרך and סירכא. Cf. below, p. 10, l. 4, etc.

[2] Reading with Text B היסורים instead of היסורים, though the latter meaning "instructions" is not im- possible.

[3] See Num. **30** 17 which however read בין אב לבתו. Cf. below, p. 16, l. 10, seq., which is really a continuation of the same law, breaking up in this place abruptly.

TEXT B

[1] See Heb. p. 7, l. 6. The italics throughout denote agreement between Text A and Text B.

[2] Heb. l. 1 ככתוב=ככ. Cf. Josh. **8** 31 etc.

[3] Heb. l. 2 לאהב. The line over the word is probably a sign of abbreviation (לאהביו). Cf. Deut. **7** 9.

[4] Reading with Deut. ibid. מצותיו for מצותי, which is also indicated by the line over the word.

¶ IX

[5] Reading Heb. l. 3 היו for היה.

[6] Heb. l. 4 ויתהלכו.

TEXT A

despise[4]...when God will bring a visitation upon the land will be returned the desert of

10 the wicked; | when there will come to pass the word which is written in the words of Isaiah

11 the son of Amoz the prophet | who said, *"He will bring[5] upon thee and upon thy people and

12 upon thy father's house days that | have* not[6] come from the day[7] that Ephraim departed from Judah." When the two houses of Israel[8]

13 separated | Ephraim* turned away[9] from Judah, and those who turned back were delivered to

14 the sword and those who held fast[10] | escaped into the land of the North. As He said, "And I will cause to go into captivity[11] Siccuth your

15 King | and Chiyun your images[12], from the tents of Damascus[13]." The books of the Law are the

16 Tent | of the King, as He said, "And I will raise up the tent of David that is fallen[14]." The King |

17 is the congregation and Chiyun the images[15] are

18 the books of the Prophets | whose words Israel has despised[16], and the Star[17] is he who explained

19 the Law | who came to Damascus, as it is written, "There came forth a Star out of Jacob and a

20 sceptre shall rise | out of Israel[18]." The Sceptre

TEXT B

commandments and the statutes *will be returned the desert of the wicked; when God will bring a visitation upon the land,* | *when there will* 7 *come to pass the word which is written* by the hand of Zechariah, *the prophet,* "O sword, awake, against | my shepherd and against the 8 man that is my fellow, says God[7], smite the shepherd and the sheep shall be scattered, | and I will turn mine hand upon the little 9 ones." And they that watch him are the poor of the flock[8]. | *These shall escape at the* 10 *end of the visitation[9], and they that* remain *will be delivered to the sword,* when there will come the Anointed | * from Aaron and Israel[10]. 11 As it was at the end of the first visitation concerning which * He[11] spoke | through Ezekiel 12 to mark a mark upon the foreheads of them

[4] Supply from Text B "the commandments and the statutes."

[5] Heb. l. 11 יבוא whilst Isa. **7** 17 from which this verse is taken has יביא ה׳ which is reproduced in our translation.

[6] Supplying from Isa. ibid. לא before באו in Heb. l. 11.

[7] Heb. l. 12 מיום, Isa. ibid. למיום.

[8] See Isa. **8** 15.

[9] Reading Heb. l. 13 סר instead of שר.

[10] Heb. ibid. והמחזיקים. Cf. above, Heb. p. 3, l. 12, and below, p. 8, l. 2, according to which we should supply at least באלה.

[11] Heb. l. 14 והגליתי, but Amos **5** 26 from where the verse is taken has ונשאתם "And you have borne."

[12] Here we must supply from Amos, ibid. כוכב אלהיכם אשר עשיתם לכם. "The Star of your god which ye made to yourselves" as is evident from Heb. l. 18 below.

[13] Heb. l. 15 מאהלי דמשק, but Amos, ibid. מהלאה לדמשק "beyond Damascus."

[14] Amos **9** 11, but there it reads ביום ההוא אקים instead of והקימותי, Heb. l. 16.

[15] Heb. l. 17 וכינוי הצלמים וביון הצלמים of which the first two words are a clerical error corrected by the scribe himself.

[16] See Test. Levi, **16** 2.

[17] See above, note 12.

[18] Num. **24** 17. Cf. Test. Levi, **17** 3 and reference in the notes.

[7] Heb. l. 8 אל, whilst Zechariah **13** 7, from where this entire verse is taken, has in this place ה׳ צבאות.

[8] See Zechariah **11** 7.

[9] See Text A, l. 21.

[10] Reading Heb. l. 11 מאהרןומישראל instead of אהרן וישראל. Cf. below, Heb. p. 20, l. 1.

[11] Reading Heb. l. 11 הוא for יחזקאל which is a mere clerical error come in through the יחזקאל in the next line.

TEXT A

is the prince of all the congregation, and when
21 he will rise " he will destroy | all the children of
Seth[19]." These escaped[20] at the end of the first
|| Page 8 visitation[21], || and those who removed back
were delivered to the sword[22]. And this also
will be the judgment of all of them who have
2 entered into his covenant who | will not hold
fast to these[23] to visit them *with[24] destruction
through the hand of Belial. This is the day |
3 on which God shall visit[25]. The princes of
Judah were *like them that remove the bound.
Upon them I will pour out my wrath like
4 water[26]. | For they became diseased incurably[27]
and they *crushed them[28]. *They are all rebels[29],
5 because they turned not out of the way | of the
traitors and they *wallowed[30] in the ways of
harlots and in the wealth of wickedness[31] and
6 (in) revenge and every man bearing grudge | to
his brother and every man hating his neighbour[32]. And they *committed treason[33] every
7 man against his next of kin | and were joined to
unchastity[34] and *sold themselves to wealth and
gain*[35], every man of them did that which
8 was right in his own eyes[36]. | And they chose

TEXT B

that sigh and cry[12], | but they that remain will 13
be *delivered to the sword* that avengeth the
vengeance of the covenant[13]. *And this also will
be the judgment of all of them who have entered* | into 14
the covenant who will not hold fast to these statutes
*to visit them with destruction through the hand of
Belial.* | *This is the day on which God shall visit,* 15
as He has spoken, " *The princes of Judah were
like them that remove* | *the bound. Upon them I* 16
will pour out *my wrath*[14] *like water.* Because
they entered[15] into the covenant of repentance |
and *yet *they turned not out of the way of the* 17
traitors and they dealt wantonly in *the ways of
harlot*ry *and in the wealth of wickedness* | *and in* 18
*revenge and every man bearing grudge to his
brother, and every man hating his neighbour. And
they *committed treason*[16] *every man* | *against his* 19
next of kin and were joined to unchastity and they
were mighty[17] *for wealth and gain, and every
man* | *of them did that which was right in his* 20
own eyes, and chose the stubbornness of his heart,

---

[19] Num. ibid.
[20] Heb. l. 21 מלטו for נמלטו. See Text B, l. 10.
[21] Heb. הראשן for הראשונה.
[22] See above, p. 1, l. 17.
[23] Supply from Text B, "to these statutes."
[24] Heb. l. 3 לכלה "to destruction."
[25] Supply here from Text B, "as he has spoken."
[26] Our text, Heb. l. 4 is defective and corrupt, omitting
the words כמסיני גבול after יהודה and reading אשר
עליהם אשפוך כמים עברתי for תשפוך עליהם עברה.
The translation is after Hos. 5 10 and Text B.
[27] Reading Heb. l. 4 לאין מרפא. Cf. 1 Chron. 21 18.
See also Hos. 5 13.
[28] Heb. ibid. וידקמום. Perhaps a corruption of
וירכאום.
[29] Reading Heb. ibid. כולמו instead of כל.
[30] Heb. l. 5 ויתגוללו. Cf. above, Heb. p. 3, l. 17.
[31] See above, Heb. p. 6, l. 15.
[32] See above, Heb. p. 7, l. 2.
[33] Reading Heb. l. 6 וימעלו instead of ויתעלמו. Cf.
above, Heb. p. 7, l. 1. It is also possible that it is a
corruption of ויתעלסו. Cf. Prov. 6 18.
[34] Heb. l. 7 ויגשו לזמה.
[35] Heb. l. 7 ויתנכרו להין which I took to be a corruption of ויתמכרו להון. See however Text B.
[36] Cf. above, Heb. p. 3, l. 6.
  S. (Frags. A & B)

[12] See Ezek. 9 4.
[13] See Lev. 26 25.
[14] Reading Heb. l. 16 עברתי (for עברה). See Hos.
5 10 from where this verse is taken.
[15] The meaning is, "*though* they entered."
[16] Reading Heb. l. 18 וימעלו for ויתעלמו. Cf. note
29, Text A.
[17] Heb. l. 19 ויתגברו. Cf. Isa. 5 22.

TEXT A

every man in the stubbornness of his heart[37] and they separated not from the people[38]. And

9 they cast off restraint with an high hand | to walk in the way of the wicked ; concerning whom God said, "Their wine is the poison of dragons |

10 and the head of asps that is cruel[39]." The dragons are the kings of the nations and their

11 wine is | their ways, and the head of the asps is the head of the kings of Javan[40], who came

12 to execute vengeance upon them. | But upon all these things they meditated not who builded the *wall[41] and daubed it with untempered

13 mortar.   For | one confused of spirit[42] and who dropped lies prophesied to them[43] that the wrath of God was kindled against all His congrega-

14 tion[44] | and what Moses said, "Not for thy righteousness or for the uprightness of thine

15 heart dost thou go to inherit | these nations[45], but because He loved thy fathers and because

16 He would keep the oath[46]." | And so is the law for the captivity[47] of Israel who turned out of the way of the people[48]. Through the love of God

17 of | the forefathers who *aroused the people toward Him[49], He loved them that came after

18 them.   For to them | is the covenant of the fathers, but in his hatred[50] of them who builded the[51] *wall His wrath was kindled. And like unto

TEXT B

and they separated not from the people | and 21 *their sins. And they cast off restraint with an high hand to walk in the ways of the wicked ; concerning whom | God said, ' Their wine is the* 22 *poison of dragons, and the head of asps that is cruel.' The dragons | are the kings of the nations* 23 *and the wine is their ways, and the head of asps is the head | of the kings of Javan who came to execute* 24 *vengeance upon them. But upon all these things they meditated not who builded | the wall and* 25 *daubed it with untempered mortar. For the* *man walking in wind[18] and weighing storms the prophet of* *man[19] | to lie that the wrath of God* 26 *was kindled against all his congregation, and what Moses said | to Israel, ' Not for thy right-* 27 *eousness or for the uprightness of thine heart dost thou go to inherit these nations, | but because He* 28 *loved thy fathers and because He would keep the oath.' So | is the law for the captivity of Israel* 29 *who[20] turned out of the way of the people. Through the love of God of the forefathers | who* 30 *aroused the people toward[21] God* *and he loved them that came after them, for to them |* *is the covenant of the fathers. But* God *hates and* 31 despises *them who builded the wall and His wrath was kindled* against them and against all | *who* 32

---

[37] See above, Heb. p. 3, l. 5.

[38] Supply here from Text B " and their sins."

[39] Deut. **32** 33.

[40] Heb. l. 11 יון = Greece, relating either to Alexander or Antiochus?

[41] Reading החייץ instead of החוץ. Cf. above, Heb. p. 4, l. 19, text and notes.

[42] Heb. l. 13 מבוהל which reading is however doubtful.

[43] See above, Heb. p. 1, l. 14.

[44] Perhaps there are missing at the beginning of Heb. l. 14 ולא זכרו אשר. They remembered not what Moses etc.

[45] See Deut. **9** 5 omitting however here after את the words ארצם כי ברשעת.

[46] Cf. Deut. **7** 8 which however reads כי מאהבת ה' אתכם ומשמרו. This looks almost as an intentional alteration of the text.

[47] See above, p. 4, l. 2, text and notes.

[48] ולא נזרו מעם l. 8.

[49] Heb. l. 17 הועירו. Supplying from Text B העם.

[50] Reading l. 18 ובשונאו instead of ובשונאי and supplying בם after אפו.

[51] Reading החייץ for החוץ. See above, p. 4, l. 19, text and notes.

[18] Heb. l. 25 הולך רוח. Cf. Micah **2** 11.

[19] Heb. ibid. מטיף אדם. Micah ibid. however has מ' העם.

[20] Supplying Heb. l. 29 אשר before סרו.

[21] Heb. l. 30 העירו. Perhaps the writer took it from יעד "to gather after," but which can also be read העירו. The על gives no meaning in either way. Possibly העירו is right, in which case we should have to translate the passage, " who bore witness against the people (and) for God."

TEXT A

19 this judgment | it will be for everyone who despises the commandments of God, and He for-
sook them and they turned away in the stubborn-
20 ness of their heart. | This is the word which Jeremiah has spoken to Baruch the son of
21 Neriah, and Elisha | to his servant Gehazi. All the men who entered into the New Covenant in the land of Damascus[52].

[52] See above, p. 6, l. 19. Here is a break in the MS.

TEXT B

walk after them. *And like unto this judgment
it will be for every one who despises the command-
ments of God,* | *and He forsook them and they* 33
turned away in the stubbornness of their heart.
So are *all the men who entered in to the New
Covenant* | *in the land of Damascus* but they turned 34
and committed treason and turned away from
the spring of living waters. | * 'They *shall not 35
be[22] counted in the assembly of people, and in
its writing[23] *they shall not be written.' From
the day when there was gathered in[24] || the only || Page 20
teacher until there will arise the Anointed from
Aaron and from Israel[25]. And this is also the Law |
for all that entered into the congregation of men 2
of perfection of holiness[26], but he will * cease[27]
accomplishing the statutes that are upright. | He 3
is the man who is melted in the furnace. When
his deeds will appear[28] he shall be expelled from
the congregation | as though his lot had not 4
fallen among them that are taught by God[29].
According to his treason they shall record him[30]
* with the men | of * perversion[31] until he will 5
come back to stay in the station of the men of
perfect holiness. | And when his deeds shall 6
appear according to the interpretation of the
Law in which walk | the men of perfection of 7
holiness, no man shall * profit[32] him in wealth
and labour, | for the saints of the Most High have 8
cursed him. And like this judgment shall be to
everyone who despises both among them who

[22] Heb. l. 35 לא יחשבו. Of the לא, only very faint traces remain.

[23] Heb. ibid. ובכתבו. The paper is torn and faded in this place but the reading is fairly certain. Cf. Ez. 13 9, from where this verse is taken.

[24] Heb. ibid. האסף meaning "died." This word is followed by יור and מורה which are both cancelled.

[25] See Heb. above, p. 19, ll. 10, 11.

[26] Heb. l. 2 תמים הקדש. Cf. above, Heb. p. 7, l. 5.

[27] Heb. ibid. יקוץ which I took as coming from קצץ. It may of course be derived from קוץ "to abhor," "to despise," but the first seems to me to be more probable.

[28] Heb. l. 3 בהופע. Cf. below, l. 6. I think however that in both these cases it is a corruption of בהורע "deteriorate." The בהופע may have come in from below, l. 25.

[29] See Isa. 54 13.

[30] Heb. l. 4 יזכירווהו, which was probably followed by עם.

[31] Heb. l. 5 מעות. See Heb. Dict. s. עות.

[32] Heb. l. 7 יאות. See Heb. and Rab. Dict. s. אות. Here it means probably to "associate."

f 2

Text B

were before | and among them who came after[33], 9
who placed idols upon their hearts and walked in
the stubbornness | of their hearts. They have 10
no share in the house of the Law. Like the
judgment of their neighbours who returned | with 11
the men of scoffing[34] they shall be judged. For
they uttered error against the statutes of right-
eousness and despised | the covenant and the 12
pledge of faith which they have affirmed in the
land of Damascus; and this is the New Covenant[35]. |
And there shall not be unto them or unto their 13
families a share in the house of the Law. And
from the day | when there was gathered in the 14
only teacher[36] until all the men of the war were
wasted who walked | with the man of lies about 15
forty years[37]. And at the end of these there will
be kindled | the wrath of God against Israel as 16
He said, 'There is no King, and no prince[38],'
*and no Judge, and none | rebuking in righteous- 17
ness[39]. And they who turn from sin...[40] who
observed the covenant of God......man |......his 18
brother He will support their steps in the way of
God. 'And God hearkened | and heard and a 19
book of remembrance was written before Him
for them that fear God and think | upon His 20
name[41]'......until there will be brought up[42]
salvation and righteousness for them who fear[43]
God. Then shall ye return and discern between
the righteous | and wicked, between them that 21
served Him[44] and them that served Him not."

[33] Heb. ll. 8, 9 לכל המאם בראשונים ובאחרונים.
The meaning is not quite clear whether the despiser is
one of the בראשונים etc. or the ראשונים etc. were the
object of his contempt.

[34] Heb. l. 11 אנשי הלצון. Cf. Heb. p. 1, l. 14.

[35] Cf. above, Heb. p. 6, l. 19 and p. 8, l. 21.

[36] Heb. l. 14 יוריה. Cf. above, Heb. p. 3, l. 8 and
p. 6, l. 11.

[37] Heb. l. 15 כשנים ארבעים. See above, Heb. p. 1,
l. 10 שנים עשרים.

[38] See Hos. **3** 4.

[39] This quotation כאשר אמר וכו' (Heb. ll. 15, 16)
must rest on some confusion by the scribe of Biblical
verses such as Isa. **11** 4 and Hosea **3** 4.

[40] After the word פשע Heb. l. 15 we have a trace of
a י which may have been the beginning of יעקב. Cf.
Is. **59** 21 (ביעקב).

[41] See Mal. **3** 16.

[42] Heb. l. 20 יעלה.

[43] Heb. ibid. ושבתם וראיתם, etc. The largest part
of this line is faded, but the reading as given in the text
is fairly certain. Cf. Mal. **3** 18.

[44] Heb. l. 21 עבד. Traces of letters follow which

TEXT B

" And showeth mercy * unto thousands[45] of them
that love Him | and unto them that observe 22
* His commandments[46] for a thousand generations," from the * house of Peleg[47] that have
gone out from the city of the sanctuary. | And 23
they confided in God at the end of the treason
of Israel and they polluted the Sanctuary and
they came back unto God. | The * prince of the 24
people[48] with few words[49]...according to His spirit
they shall be judged...in the counsel | of holi- 25
ness. And all they who broke through the
bound of the Law of those who entered into the
covenant when there will shine forth | the glory 26
of God to Israel they will be cut off from among
the camp and with them all they who do
wickedly[50] | of Judah in the days of its trial[51]. But 27
all they who hold steadfast to these laws to go
out | and to come in according to the Law and 28
listen to the voice of the teacher and shall confess
before God...we | are guilty, we and our fathers 29
because they walked contrary[52] unto the laws of
the covenant | and true is thy judgment against 30
us. And they will not lift the hand against
His holy statutes, His righteous judgment | and 31
the testimony[53] of His truth. And they will be
chastised by the first judgments in which | the 32
children of the men of the only one were
judged. And they will listen to the voice of
the teacher of righteousness. And they will not
* answer[54] | the statutes of righteousness when 33
they hear them. They will rejoice and be glad

may be taken as a ו. They may also be taken as a ל,
which would be the remainder of אל. See Mal. ibid.

[45] See Exod. **20** 6 which the scribe partly confused
with Deut. **7** 9. See above, Heb. p. 19, l. 17. After
חסד Heb. l. 21 there is space for לאלפים.

[46] Heb. l. 21 ולשמריו, omitting by mistake the word
מצותיו.

[47] Heb. l. 22 מבית פלג, reading doubtful. Before
these words a space of nearly two words appears blank,
but no traces of letters are visible.

[48] Heb. l. 24 נסיך, but only the נ and the ך are certain.

[49] Heb. l. 24 בדברים מעט, but the reading is
doubtful.

[50] Heb. l. 27 מרשיעי, probably as much as רשעי.

[51] Heb. l. 27 מצרפותיו.

[52] See Lev. **26** 21.

[53] Heb. l. 31 ועדוות. Cf. above, Heb. p. 3, l. 15.

[54] Heb. l. 32 ישיבו "answer" or rather "contradict."

TEXT B

and their hearts will exult[55] and they will show themselves mighty | against all the children of 34 the world, and God will make atonement for them and they will see[56] His salvation for they put their trust in His holy name.

[55] Reading Heb. l. 33 ויעלו for ויעזו.
[56] Heb. l. 54 ור being a remainder of וראו.

¶ X ‖ Page 9   Any man who will destroy a man[1]* in accordance with the statutes of the
2 gentiles* so that he is to be *put to death[2], | *it is concerning him[3] that He said, "Thou shalt not avenge nor bear any grudge against the children of thy people[4]." And
3 every man of them who hath *entered[5] | into the Covenant who shall bring a* charge[6]
4 against his neighbour which is not* proved[7] before witnesses | and* shall beat[8] him in his fierce wrath or *speak against him *to his elders so as to insult him, is taking
5 vengeance and bearing grudge; | but it is only written, "He [9]will take vengeance of
6 his adversaries and He is bearing grudge against His enemies." | If he held his peace from day to day [10]but in his fierce wrath he spake against him in a matter
7 concerning death[11] | his* sin is upon him[12] because he did not fulfil the commandment
8 of God who said to him, "Thou shalt surely rebuke | thy neighbour[13] and not suffer
9 sin upon him." As to the oath concerning which | He said "thy hand shall not help
10 thee[14]," if a man will make *another *man swear in the open field[15] |—that is not* in the presence of[16] the judges or their word[17]—his hand has helped him. And he who
11 has lost | (anything), and it is not known who has stolen it from the* Tent[18] of
12 the camp in which the thing has been stolen, its owner shall* proclaim[19] | it by the oath of cursing[20], and whoso hears, if he knows and utters it not, he shall be
13 guilty[21]. | In any* recompense made[22] for that which has no owners he who makes

¶ X

[1] Heb. l. 1 יחרים אדם מאדם. The מאדם I took to be a dittography. The expression was probably suggested by Lev. **27** 29 כל חרם אשר יחרם מן האדם.

[2] Heb. ibid. להמית that is according to the laws of the גוים. I take this law to contain a prohibition against acknowledging the jurisdiction of the gentiles (ערכאות של גוים) which is also forbidden by Rabbinic law. Cf. Maimonides, *Mishneh Torah, Hilcoth Sanhedrin*, ch. 26, § 7, text and reference given by the commentators.

[3] Heb. ibid. הוא followed by ואשר, Heb. l. 2 which I read אשר.

[4] See Lev. **27** 28. Cf. above, Heb. p. 7, l. 2.

[5] Reading Heb. l. 2 מבא instead of מביאי.

[6] Heb. l. 3 דבר. Cf. Deut. **22** 20. See also Heb. Dict. s. v.

[7] Heb. ibid. בהוכח. Cf. below, l. 18. Cf. Test. Gad, **4** 2, 5, to which our text seems to be a partial parallel.

[8] Heb. l. 4 והביאו, corruption of והכהו.

[9] The verse in Nahum **1** 2 reproduced here reads נוקם ה׳ לצריו, our scribe avoiding the Tetragrammaton.

[10] Cf. Num. **30** 15.

[11] Heb. l. 6 בדבר מות meaning perhaps that he accuses him of a capital offence. It is however possible we should read here אמת for מות, that is even if it be true.

[12] Reading Heb. l. 7 עונו בו for ענה בה.

[13] Heb. l. 8 רעך, but Lev. **19** 7 reproduced here has עמיתך.

[14] See 1 Sam. **25** 26 and 31, where the הושע ידך לך is considered an act of violence amounting to bloodshed. Cf. *Baba Kama*, 27 b, and *Tur, Choshen Mishpath*, S 4, where the principle of עביד אינש דינא לנפשיה.

[15] See Lev. **14** 7 etc.

[16] Reading Heb. l. 10 לפני instead of לפנים.

[17] Heb. ibid. מאמרם that is the decision of the judges.

[18] Reading Heb. l. 11 ממועד (=אהל מעד) instead of ממאד.

[19] Reading ibid. ישמיע instead of ישביע and taking בעליו ibid. as the subject. For a somewhat similar institution in Rabbinic Judaism see *Baba Mezia* 28 b.

[20] Cf. Num. **5** 21.

[21] See Lev. **5** 1.

[22] That is, for a מעל.

14 the recompense[23] shall confess to the priest, | and it shall all belong to him, besides the ram of the guilt offering. And so everything lost that was found and has no |

15–16 owners it shall belong to the priests, for he who* found it[24] knows not its law. | If its owners were not found they shall keep it in trust. If a man acts treacherously |

17 against any law and his neighbour sees it and he is only one—if it be a charge of

18 death he shall make it known* | in his presence to the Censor, proving[25] it to him.

19 And the Censor shall write it down with his hand ; until he will do it | again before one, *and then he shall come back and make it known to the Censor. If he will

20 be caught again before | another, his sentence shall be finished[26]. And if they are two

21 and they witness* against | him in another thing[27] the man shall be only excluded

22 from the Purity[28], if they are trustworthy. | And on the day on which the man sees it he shall make it known to the Censor. And according* to the statute...[29] two |

23 trustworthy witnesses, and through one* witness to exclude* from the Purity. And

| Page 10 there shall rise no || * witness[30] before the judges to kill at his mouth[31] whose days

2 were not fulfilled to pass | among them that are numbered[32]* and who fears* not[33]

3 God. No man shall be* believed as a witness against his neighbour | who transgresses a word of the commandment with a high hand until he was worthy to repent[34]. |

¶ XI 4   And this is the usage[1] of the judges of the congregation[2]. Ten men selected[3] |

5 of the congregation according to the *age[4] ; four of the tribe of Levi and Aaron

6 and six of Israel | learned in the Book of *the Hagu[5] and in the foundations of the

7 covenant, from five | and twenty years old even unto sixty years old[6]. But none shall

8 be appointed after he be | from sixty years old and above to judge the congregation.

9 For through the unfaithfulness of man | his days* diminished[7], and when the wrath of

---

[23] Heb. l. 14 המושב participle *hifil* of שוב. Perhaps it is a corruption of המשיב. Supplying, of course, האשם. Cf. for the law Num. **5** 8 of which our text looks almost like a paraphrase.

[24] Heb. l. 15 מוצאיה for מוצאה.

[25] Heb. l. 18 בהוכיח למבקר. Cf. above, l. 3. The office of the מבקר a sort of censor or inquisitor is unknown otherwise.

[26] Heb. l. 20 שלם משפטו. This third אחר or אחד (l. 20) is apparently the third witness.

[27] Heb. l. 21 דבר אחר, in contradistinction of דבר מות (?). The meaning of this law and the one that follows is not clear to me. It would seem as if in the case of death our Text insists upon three witnesses, whilst in other cases, punished only by the exclusion from the טהרה, two witnesses are sufficient ; whilst the words, "and through one witness to exclude from the Purity," in l. 23, perhaps refer back to the case of death, that the evidence even of one witness has the result of exclusion from the Purity.

[28] Heb. ibid. הטהרה meaning perhaps the Camp or the congregation. Cf. Heb. p. 12, ll. 5, 6.

[29] Heb. l. 22 ועל החוק. The latter word I first read החון by mistake. The MS. is faded and the middle of the next word is partly torn away, only a י being visible at the beginning. The remaining letters are כלו. I can only suggest that it is a remainder of יקבלו "they shall accept," but there is no trace of the leg of the Kof.

[30] Reading Heb. l. 1 עיד or עד for עוד. Cf. Deut. **19** 15.

[31] See Deut. **17** 6.

[32] That is, who have not reached the age of twenty-five. Cf. Exod. **30** 13 and 14. Cf. below, l. 6.

[33] Supplying before ירא Heb. l. 2, the word ולא.

[34] Heb. l. 3 עד זכו לשוב "to do repentance." Cf. also Num. **15** 30 ביד רמה "presumptuously."

¶ XI

[1] Heb. l. 4 סרך. Cf. above, Heb. p. 7, l. 6.

[2] This word העדה, Heb. l. 4, is followed by עד which I took as mere dittography.

[3] Heb. l. 5 ברורים. Cf. *Jer. Kiddushin*, 66a, הברורין שבאחיך with reference to the appointment of officers.

[4] Heb. l. 5 העת. It may also mean "for the time being."

[5] Heb. l. 6 בספר ההגו. Cf. Ps. **49** 4 והגות, "meditation." What is understood by this הגו, whether a special book of the sect or the regular Scriptures I am unable to say.

[6] Cf. Num. **8** 24 and Lev. **27** 7.

[7] Reading Heb. l. 9 ימיו for ימו.

God* was kindled[8] against the inhabitants of the earth, he said to remove[9] their |

10 minds before they shall complete their days[10].

¶ XII 11   As to be cleansed in water. No | man shall wash in filthy waters or not sufficient[1]

12 for *immersion[2] of a man. | None shall cleanse himself in the *waters[3] of a vessel.

13 And every pool in a rock in which there is not sufficient | water for* immersion which an unclean person has touched, its waters shall be contaminated *like[4] the waters of the vessel. |

¶ XIII 14   As to the Sabbath to keep it according to its law, no man shall do work on the sixth

15–16 day | from the time in which the globe of the sun[1] | is removed from the gate in its

17 *fulness[2], for it is He who said, "Keep the | Sabbath day to sanctify it[3]." And on the

18 day of the Sabbath no man shall utter a word | of *folly[4]. And surely none shall demand any debt of his neighbour[5]. None shall judge on matters of property, and gain[6]. |

19 None shall speak on matters of work and labour to be done on the following morning[7]. |

20–21 No man shall walk in the field to do the work of *his affairs[8] | on *the day[9] of the

22 Sabbath. None shall walk outside his city* more[10] than a thousand[11] cubits. | No man

23 shall eat on the day of the Sabbath but of that which is prepared[12] or perishing* | in

‖ Page 11 the field[13]. None shall eat or drink but *from that which was* in the camp[14]. ‖ *But if he was[15] on the way and went down to wash he may drink where he stands, but

---

[8] Reading Heb. ibid. ובחרות for ובחרון.

[9] Heb. ibid. לסור as much as להסיר.

[10] Cf. Jub. **23** 11.

¶ XII

[1] Heb. l. 11 ומעוטים מדי. Cf. the following line.

[2] Heb. ibid. מרעיל which I took as a corruption of מטביל. Cf. *Erubin* 4*b*, and reference given there, שכל גופו עולה בהן.

[3] Reading Heb. l. 12 במי for במה. This law seems to be directed against מים שאובים "drawn water," which also according to the Rabbinic law is unfit for immersion. Cf. Maimonides, *Hilcoth Mikwaoth*, ch. 4, § 3.

[4] Reading Heb. l. 13 כמימי for במימי.

¶ XIII

[1] Heb. l. 15 גלגל השמש. In Rabbinic ג' חמה see Rabb. Dict. s. גלגל. See particularly Jer. *Berachoth* 2*b* התחיל גלגל חמה לשקוע זהו בין השמשות.

[2] Reading Heb. l. 16 במלואו for מלואו. Perhaps we should emend בבואו "at its setting."

[3] Deut. **5** 12. Perhaps it is the word שמור which is urged deriving from it what is known in Rabbinic literature as תוספת, that is the time added to a holy day before it actually begins. See *Rosh Hashauah*, 9*a* and cf. Rabb. Dict. s. תוספת. See Hadasi, *Alphabeta*, and *Gan Eden* by the Karaite, Aaron the Elder, 37*a*, and Bashiatsi, p. 40 seq., and 45*d*.

[4] Heb. ll. 17, 18 דבר נבל meaning probably the same as דברי חול, that is matters of a secular nature which must not be discussed on the Sabbath. The Rabbis

derive this prohibition from Isa. **58** 13. Cf. *Shabbath*, 150*a*. See also Maimonides, *Mishneh Torah*, *Hilchoth Shabbath*, ch. 24.

[5] Heb. l. 18 ורק אל ישה ברעהו כל. Cf. Deut. **15** 2.

[6] Heb. l. 18 הון ובצע. See *Mishne Beza* v. 2.

[7] Heb. l. 19 למשכים. Cf. Mishne *Bikkurim* III. 2. Cf. Rabb. Dict. s. שכם.

[8] Reading Heb. l. 20 חפציו or חפצו. This probably only means to plan the work for the following day. Cf. the references given in note 4.

[9] Supplying at the beginning of Heb. l. 21 the word ביום.

[10] Heb. ibid. על, but is preceded by a word looking somewhat like אד. Perhaps it is a corruption of אך, but it is more likely to be a mere clerical error, the scribe having first written by mistake אד, and correcting himself afterwards by the proper word על.

[11] Heb. l. 21 אלף. No such "Sabbath limit" however is known. Probably it is a mere clerical error for אלפים. Cf. Heb. p. 11, l. 6. See also Jub. **50** 8, text and note.

[12] Heb. l. 22 המוכן, that is destined or prepared for this purpose from the eve of the Sabbath or the feast. Cf. *Mishne Beza* I. 2. See also Rabb. Dict. s. כון. Cf. Jub. **50** 9 and **2** 29.

[13] "The field." Of the Heb. equivalent בשדה l. 23, only the ה is certain, whilst there is also a faint trace of the ד.

[14] Supplying Heb. l. 23, אשר, after the אם.

[15] Supplying at the beginning of Heb. p. 11 ואם היה, though the possibility is not excluded that we have here a lacuna in the MS.

2 he shall not draw | into any vessel[16]. No man shall send the son of the stranger[17] to
3 do his affairs on the day of the Sabbath. | No man shall put on garments that are
4 filthy or were brought by a gentile unless | they were washed in water or rubbed off
5 with frankincense[18]. No man shall *mingle[19] of his own will | on the Sabbath. No
6 man shall walk after the animal to feed it outside of his city more than | two thousand
7 cubits[20]. None shall lift his hand to beat it with his fist. If | it be stubborn he
  shall not remove it out of his house[21]. No man shall carry anything from the house |
8 to the outside or from the outside into the house and if he be in the* gate[22] he shall
9 *not carry out | anything of it or bring[23] in anything into it. None shall* open[24]
10 the cover of a vessel that is pasted on the Sabbath. No man shall carry | on him
  spices[25] to go out and *come in on[26] the Sabbath. None shall[27] move in the
11 house* on the day of the Sabbath[28] | rock or earth. No nurse shall bear the suckling
12 child[29] to go out and to come in on the Sabbath[30]. | No man shall *provoke[31] his man-
13 servant or his maidservant or his* hireling[32] on the day of the Sabbath. | No man
14 shall deliver an animal on the day of the Sabbath[33]. And if it falls into a pit | or
  ditch, he shall not raise it on the Sabbath[34]. No man shall *rest[35] in a place near |
15 to the gentiles on the day of the Sabbath. No man shall profane[36] the Sabbath for
16 the sake of wealth and gain. | And if any person[37] falls into a *gathering of water
17 or into a place | of[38]...he shall not bring him up[39] by a ladder or a cord or

---

[16] The meaning of these laws is to be found in the interpretation of Exod. **16** 29, Jub. **50** 8 and **2** 29. Cf. Singer, p. 199 and Charles' notes to Jub. ibid. Cf. also Hadasi, *Alphabeta*, 147.

[17] Heb. l. 2 בן הנכר. See Isa. **56** 6.

[18] This law does not refer exactly to the Sabbath, but to all the days of the week on account of contamination (טומאה). See Introduction, p. xxv.

[19] Heb. l. 4 יתערב. Meaning obscure. Perhaps it is a corruption of ירעב, which would mean as much as to be hungry, or to starve oneself, thus containing a prohibition against fasting on the Sabbath. Possibly, it is a direct corruption of יתענה. Cf. Jub. **50** 12.

[20] See above, note 11.

[21] Cf. Jub. ch. **2** 29, text and notes.

[22] Reading Heb. l. 8 מבוי for מובה. Cf. Rabb. Dict. s. מבוי and מבוא. About this law in general, cf. Jub. **2** 29, 30 and **50** 8.

[23] Reading Heb. ll. 8—9, יוציא—יביא, instead of יוצא—יבא.

[24] Reading Heb. l. 9 יפתח for פתח. Cf. Hadasi, *Alphabeta*, 148. The Rabbinic law is very mild in this respect. See *Shabbath*, 146 a, and Maimonides, *Hilchoth Shabbath*, ch. 23, § 2. See also Jost, III. p. 303.

[25] Heb. l. 10 סמנים, more correct סממנים. Cf. Rab. Dict. s. סממן and סמן. Cf. Mishneh, *Shabbath* vi. 6. Tosefta, ibid. v. 10 and T. B. *Shabbath* 65 a where a similar law is to be found.

[26] Reading Heb. ibid. ולבוא, though in the MS. the ו is a little short and looks like ולביא.

[27] Heb. ibid. יטול. Cf. Rab. Dict. s. נטל and טלטל (טול). The latter is more common in such connection.

[28] Reading Heb. ibid. יום השבת for מושבת.

[29] Cf. Num. **11** 13.

[30] Cf. Mishneh, *Shabbath*, XVIII. 2, and Maimonides, *Hilcoth Shabbath*, ch. 18, par. 16.

[31] Heb. l. 12 ימרא.

[32] Reading Heb. ibid. שכירו for שוכרו.

[33] See Mishneh, *Shabbath* XVIII. 3 where we have such a law with regard to the festivals (יום טוב). Cf. *Tur Orach Chayim*, par. 339.

[34] Reading Heb. l. 14 תפול for תפיל. The Rabbinic law is less strict. See *Shabbath*, 129 b, and Maimonides, *Hilcoth Shabbath*, ch. 25, par. 25.

[35] Reading ibid. l. 14 ישבות for ישבית, that is, not to stay over the Sabbath in a gentile vicinity. Cf. Wreschner, pp. 14—15, for a similar law of the Samaritans and the Karaites.

[36] Heb. l. 15 יחל, perhaps a corruption of יחלל. Perhaps we have to understand by it the prohibition of buying and selling on the Sabbath. Cf. Jub. **50** 8.

[37] Heb. l. 16 נפש אדם.

[38] Heb. l. 16 אל מים מקום מים ואל מקום. The first מים is cancelled in the MS. מקום is undoubtedly a corruption of מקוה, cf. Lev. **11** 36, which emendation is reproduced in the translation. After the second מקום some word is missing.

[39] Assuming that Heb. l. 17 reads יַעֲלָה, and thus refers to the נפש in the preceding line. For the Rabbinic law in this respect, see *Yoma*, 84 b, and Maimonides, *Hilcoth Shabbath*, ch. 2, par. 7. It is more probable that some words are missing at the end of the preceding line, and that l. 17 is the beginning of a new law.

S. (Frags. A & B)   *g*

18 instrument. No man shall bring anything on the altar on the Sabbath, | save the burnt-offering of the Sabbath, for so it is written, "Save your Sabbaths[40]."

¶ XIV 19   No man shall send | to the altar burnt-offering or meat-offering or frankincense 20 or wood through the hand of a man contaminated by any | of the uncleannesses[1], 21 allowing him[2] to contaminate the altar, for it is written, "The sacrifice | of the wicked is abomination, but the prayer of the *righteous is like an offering of 22 delight[3]." And everyone who comes into | the house of *worship[4] he shall not enter when he is contaminated *without[5] washing. And when the trumpets of the Congre- 23 gation sound | it shall be (done) before or after[6], and they shall not disturb the whole

‖ Page 12 service *on the Sabbath[7] ‖ it is holy. No man shall lie with a woman in the city 2 of the Sanctuary to contaminate | the city of the Sanctuary by their uncleanness[8]. 3 Any man over whom the spirits of Belial will have dominion | and he will speak rebellion[9], he shall be judged according to the law of the " Ob and Yiddeoni." And 4 he who will err | to profane the Sabbath and the Feasts shall not be put to death ; 5 but[10] it is upon the sons of man | *to watch him[11] *whether[12] he will be healed of 6 it. And they shall watch him seven years and then | he shall come into the Congregation. None shall stretch out his hand to shed the blood of any man 7 from among the gentiles | for the sake of wealth and gain[13]. Nor shall he take 8 anything of their property in order[14] that they blaspheme not, | unless by the counsel 9 of the *Congregation[15] of Israel. No man shall sell an animal | or bird that is 10 clean to the gentiles in order that they sacrifice them not[16]. Nor shall he | sell them anything of his threshing-floor or his winepress in all his *property[17]. Nor shall he 11 sell them his manservant or maidservant | who entered with him into the covenant of 12 Abraham[18]. No man shall make himself abominable[19] | with any living creature or

---

[40] Perhaps he is referring to Lev. **23** 38 מלבד שבתות ה interpreting it to mean "save the Sabbath of the Lord" on which the burnt offering and the meat offering etc. recorded in the preceding verse are forbidden. Of course the correct translation is " *beside* the Sabbaths of the Lord." More probable it is that we have here a reference to Jub. **50** 10, " and rest thereon from all labour......save burning frankincense and bringing oblations and sacrifices ......for Sabbaths," which the scribe in some way confused with the preceding law and wrote אל יעל, instead of אל יעש and then omitted several words which might easily be supplied from Jub.

¶ XIV

[1] Reading l. 20 הטומאות for הטמאות.

[2] Heb. ibid. להרשותו. See Rabb. Dict. s. רשה or רשי.

[3] Prov. **15** 8, but the second clause of the verse reads there ותפלת ישרים רצונו " The prayer of the upright is his delight." The reading ותפלת צדקם כמנחת רצון as our text has it (Heb. ll. 20, 21) is undoubtedly corrupt and points to a confusion with Prov. **15** 29.

[4] Heb. l. 22 בית השתחות lit. the house of prostration, cf. the Arabic مسجد. Cf. Levy's *Wörterbuch über die Targumim* II. 141 about בית סגידו and בית סנידהון, but it is never applied to a *Jewish* place of worship. The term is strongly suggestive of the Falashas' *Mesgeed*.

[5] Supplying ibid. after טמא the word בלי or בלא, cf. above l. 4. But it is also possible that it means as much as a טמא who is in need of כבוס. Cf. Lev. **11** 14 and **15** 10. See also 2 Chron. **23** 19.

[6] Heb. l. 23 יתקדם או יתאחר which may also mean be it earlier or later.

[7] Heb. ibid. השבת but only the ת is traceable whilst the other letters are torn off. The meaning of the law is entirely obscure to me.

[8] Heb. l. 2 בנדתם.

[9] See Deut. **13** 6.

[10] Heb. l. 4 כי.

[11] Heb. l. 15 משמרו. Perhaps a corruption of לשמרו.

[12] Reading אם for ואם.

[13] The meaning of this law is that he is only permitted to kill a gentile when it is a case of self-protection.

[14] Heb. l. 7 בעבור.

[15] Heb. l. 8 חבור, cf. Rab. Dict. s. חבר(עיר).

[16] That is to their idols. Some similar laws are to be found in Mishneh, *Aboda Zarah* I. 8, and 9. Cf. also the Gemara to these Mishnas.

[17] Heb. l. 10 בכל מאדו. Perhaps we should read מאודם "for all their property" that is for any money. See Rab. Dict. s. מאד.

[18] For a similar Rabbinic law see Mishneh, *Gittin* IV. 6.

[19] Cf. Lev. **11** 43.

13 creeping thing, to eat of them the beehives[20], even[21] any living creature | that moveth
14 in the waters[22]. Nor shall the fish be eaten unless they *were split | alive and
their blood was shed[23]. But all the locusts after their kind shall come into fire
15 or into water | whilst they are still living, for this is the manner of their creation[24].
16 And all wood and stones | and dust which will be polluted by the uncleanness of
17 man *shall be polluted like them[25]*. According to | their uncleanness shall be
unclean he who toucheth them. And every instrument, nail, or pillar in the wall |
18 which will be with the dead in the house shall be unclean, *like the uncleanness[26] of
an instrument of work[27]. |

¶ XV 19   And *this is the usage[1] of the settlement of the cities of Israel, according[2] to
20 these judgments to separate between | the clean and unclean[3] and to make known
21 *the difference between the holy and the profane[4]. And these are the statutes | *to
instruct[5] to walk in them the whole nation[6] *according to the law[7]...*every
22 time[8]. And in this law[9] | shall walk the whole seed of Israel and they shall not be

---

[20] Heb. l. 12 לאכל מהם מעגלי הדבורים. The מהם
is probably a mere clerical error, whilst the מעגלי הדבורים
means as much as the Rabbinic כוורת דבורים, cf.
Jastrow s. כוורת. I do not remember any sect that
forbade honey, though there was the consideration that
it comes from an unclean insect, cf. *Bechoroth* 7 *b*.
Perhaps it refers to particles of the bees which are mixed
up with the honey. Rabbinic Judaism had no scruples
in this respect and allowed the honey as it came from the
bee-hives (see *Shulchan Aruch, Joreh Deah* § 81), whilst
the Karaites protested and insisted on a preparation of
the honey (through filtering) so as to separate these
particles. Cf. Salmon b. Jerucham's denunciation of this
less stringent usage of the Rabbanites מזבובים ועד
יתושים ודבורים· התירו לבלע בחורים ואמרו לא זה
משרצי אדמה בדבורים ושכחו השרץ ואחור
נסגנים וסרים. (MS). Cf. *Eshkol Hakkofer Alphabeta*,
236. See however, Introduction, p. xxiv.

[21] Heb. l. 12 עד. It is not impossible that this is a
shortened quotation from Lev. **11** 43—46 which began
ככתוב אל (*v.* 43) to *v.* 46.

[22] Cf. Lev. **11** 46.

[23] Reading and supplying Heb. l. 14 דמם ונשפך.
The ונשפך is almost certain though the פ is torn off
whilst there are also definite traces of the דמם. This
agrees in part with the view of the older Karaites and
Samaritans, who forbade the eating of fish that died in the
water or were found dead on the shore. Cf. Wreschner,
p. 51. The splitting of the fish had, according to this
writer, to be done by one of the Sect, as the אסיפה,
according to some Samaritans and Karaites, had to be
done by a Jew. Emphasis has also to be put on the
ונשפך דמם. The law is directed against the Rabbinic
opinion permitting the eating of the blood of fish. See
Sifra 39 *a* and *Kerithoth* 20 *b*.

[24] See Wreschner ibid. p. 52, about the mode of killing
the locusts in water. As to meaning of the last words,
"for this is the manner of their creation." See *Chullin*,
27 *b*, where we have a homily to the effect that cattle

have to be killed in a certain way because they were
created out of the dry land (earth); fish, again, require
no killing, being created out of the water; whilst birds,
which were created out of alluvial mud (a combination of
water and earth) occupy also, with regard to their ritual
killing, a middle place between cattle and fish. The
notion was thus that the mode of killing is in some way
connected with the element out of which the animal in
question was created. We may thus assume that in the
composition of the locust, according to our author, the
elements of water and fire are to be found, hence they
shall be killed by water or by fire. According to the
Rabbinic law, the locust requires no killing at all. See
Maimonides, *Mishneh Torah, Hilchoth Shechitah*, ch. I. 1,
and *Tur Joreh Deah*, § 13.

[25] Reading Heb. l. 16 יגואלו כמוהם for לנאולי שמו
בהם referring to the האדם בטמאת. The ו of the שמו
may also be taken as a final ן.

[26] Reading Heb. l. 18 כטמאת for בטמאת.

[27] Heb. l. 18 כלי מעשה. Cf. Num. **31** 51. Both
this law and the one preceding it are in contradiction
to the Rabbinic law, exempting all these things from
טומאה. Cf. *Mishneh Kelim* XII. 3 and Maimonides,
Hilchoth Kelim, ch. X. 1.

¶ XV

[1] Heb. l. 19 סרך. Supplying at the beginning of the
line the word וזה as below, l. 22 and elsewhere.

[2] Supplying Heb. l. 19 פי after על.

[3] Lev. **11** 47.

[4] Cf. Lev. **10** 10. See also Num. **35** 24.

[5] Reading Heb. l. 21 להשביל for למשכיל, though
למשביל (for the wise man) is not absolutely wrong.

[6] Heb. ibid. כלהו.

[7] Reading Heb. ibid. כמשפט for למשפט.

[8] Heb. ibid. ועת. Of the preceding word some
traces remain which may be taken as עת.

[9] Heb. ibid. וכמשפט meaning as much as ובמשפט.
Cf. p. 6, l. 10, (בהם) להתהלך במה.

g 2

23 cursed. And this is the usage of the settlement | ......*congregation[10]......in the end

‖ Page 13 of the wickedness and until there will arise the Anointed *from Aaron[11]. ‖ * and

2 Israel—till ten men at least[12] by thousands and hundreds and fifties | and tens[13]. And when there will arise ten, the man who is a priest learned in the Book of the

3 Hagu[14] shall not[15] depart. According | unto his word shall they all be ruled[16]. And

4 if he is not tried[17] in all these but a man of the Levites is tried | in these, then the lot shall be cast[18] that all those who enter into the camp shall go out and come in

5 according to his word[19]. And if | there be a decision regarding the law of leprosy *which[20] a man will have, then shall come the priest and stand in the camp, and

6 the Censor[21] shall instruct him | in the explanation of the law. And if it *increased[22],

7 he shall shut him up for unto them | is the judgment[23].

¶ XVI And this is the usage of the Censor of the camp. He shall instruct the

8 many in the deeds | of God, and shall make them understand *His mighty wonders[1], and shall narrate before them the *happenings of eternity[2] *in the Law of

9 God*[3], | and shall have mercy with them as a father with his children, and shall

10 *forgive all their rebellions*[4]. Like a shepherd with his flock[5] | he shall loose all

11 the bonds of their knots[6]......[7] oppressed and crushed *in his congregation*[8]. | And everyone who shall join his congregation, he shall count him according to his

12 *deeds[9] his *understanding[10], his might, his strength and his property. | And they shall record him in his place in accordance with his *assignment[11] through the lot in

13 the camp[12]. But no man of the children of the camp shall rule | to bring a man into

---

[10] The MS. is both faded and torn in this place. The תהל.. which is taken as קהל in the translation is very doubtful. Before בקץ traces of לה may be seen.

[11] Reading Heb. p. 12, l. 23, and p. 13, l. 1, משוח מאהרן ומישראל for מ'אהרן וישראל. Cf. Heb. p. 19, ll. 10, 11, and p. 20, l. 1, text and notes. In my first reading of the MS., I assumed that there is a lacuna in the MS. between p. 12 and p. 13, as indicated by the asterisks at the bottom of p. 12. But further study convinced me of the continuity of the text, as it proceeds on p. 13, to give interpreting details to the סרך מושב on p. 12, remaining in force till the advent of the Messiah. Cf. p. 6, l. 10, which is an exact parallel, only that there he calls the "Messiah," the Teacher of Righteousness, l. 11.

[12] Heb. l. 1 למועט, the מושב consisting of ten men at least.

[13] Heb. ibid. ומיאיות.

[14] See Heb. above, p. 10, l. 6.

[15] Heb. l. 2 אל ימש. Cf. Exod. 33 11.

[16] Heb. l. 3 ישקו. Cf. Gen. 41 40.

[17] Heb. ibid. בחון.

[18] Cf. Josh. 19 1 etc. Here it seems to be a mere phrase = it shall be decided.

[19] Cf. Num. 27 21 etc. Apparently if there is a priest (כהן) he comes first.

[20] Supplying Heb. l. 5 before יהיה the word אשר.

[21] See above, Heb. p. 9, l. 17 etc.

[22] Reading Heb. l. 6 פשה instead of פתי. But it is also possible that פָּתִי (fool, ignorant) is correct. The meaning would be that even in the case when the priest is an ignorant man and has to be instructed by the Censor, the act of shutting up the leper had to be done by the priest. Cf. *Sifra*, 60 b, and *Mishneh Negaim* III. 1, for a similar law.

[23] Cf. Hos. 5 1.

¶ XVI

[1] Reading Heb. l. 18 פלאו for פלאי.

[2] Heb. l. 8 נהיות עולם. Cf. Heb. above, p. 2, l. 10.

[3] Reading Heb. ibid. בתרת יה for בפרתיה. Perhaps this word is a corruption of בפרטיה "details." See Rab. Dict. s. פרט.

[4] The MS. is torn and probably also corrupt in this place. The translation assumes the reading and emendation in Heb. l. 9 וישא לכל מרדותם (for מרחובם).

[5] See Isa. 40 11.

[6] See Isa. 58 7 which suggests the emendation of רשעותיהם (wickedness) instead of קשריהם in Heb. l. 10.

[7] The MS. is torn in this line (10) as indicated by the dots. The traces left suggest also some such words לעתי ז', or למתי זדים.

[8] Reading Heb. ibid. בעדתו for בעדתי. Cf. also Deut. 28 33.

[9] Heb. l. 11 למעשיו supplying the ע which is torn away.

[10] Heb. ibid. ושכלו as much as ושכלו.

[11] Heb. l. 12 יהותו which I took to be a corruption from יצאו. See above, l. 4. It is also possible that the word is a corruption of יחוסו "genealogy," "pedigree." Cf. Rab. Dict. s. יחום.

[12] Supplying Heb. ibid. after the ה the letters מחנה, or עדה "congregation."

14 the congregation *without the[13] word of the Censor of the camp. | Nor shall any man
of them who entered into the covenant[14] deal with[15] the sons of the *strangers[16]
15 *unless | hand to hand[17]. No man shall perform a *thing as[18] buying and selling[19]
16 *unless he has spoken[20] | to the Censor of the camp and he shall do[21].....and not...
17-18 .... | and so to him who expels[22] and he.................... | afflict[23] him and in
19 the love......he shall not incline[24]......... |they, [25]and he who is not connected with.........|
20-21 And this is the settlement of the camps.   All......|shall not succeed to settle in the
|| Page 14 22 land[26] |...||that have not come from the day that Ephraim
2 departed from Judah[27]. And all they who walk in these | the covenant of God *is
steadfast to them[28] to save them[29] from all the snares of the pit, for suddenly...[30] |
¶XVII 3 *And this is the usage[1] of the settlement of all the camps. They shall be
4 counted all by their names, the Priests first, | the Levites second, the children of
Israel third[2], and the proselyte fourth[3]. And they shall be recorded by their
5 names | one after another, the Priests first, the Levites second, the children of Israel
6 third, and the proselyte fourth. And so they shall be seated and so they shall ask
7 for everything[4]. And the Priest who will count | *the many[5] shall be from thirty
8 years old and upwards until sixty years old[6] learned in the book...[7] | in all the
laws of the Torah to *speak them[8] according to their rules. And the Censor who is |
9 over all the camps shall be from thirty years old and upwards until fifty years

[13] Supplying Heb. l. 13 after העדה the word מבלי.
The MS. is here torn.

[14] See Heb. above, p. 2, l. 2. It is not unlikely
that the אל here is a mere dittography. Heb. l. 14
באי ברית.

[15] Heb. l. 14 באי ברית אל אל. I took the second אל
to be a mere dittography. Cf. above, Heb. p. 2, l. 2,
and elsewhere. This is followed by אל ישאל, but the
trace of the ל is very uncertain, and on closer examination
I found it to be a ו, thus reading אל ישא ואל יתן meaning
"to deal," "to have money transactions." Cf. Rab.
Dict. s. נשא.

[16] Heb. l. 14 בני השחר which gives no meaning, and
which I emended ב' הנכר. Cf. above, Heb. p. 11, l. 2.
Before the בני some short word is torn off which may have
been את or עם. After השחר is also room for another
short word, probably כי.

[17] Heb. l. 15 כף לכף. See Prov. 16 5 יד ליד.
Cf. also Epstein, pp. 68, 74, note 5. The תקיעת כף is
one of the various ways of affirming a money transaction.
Yet the meaning remains unclear to me.

[18] Supplying Heb. ibid. after איש the word דבר of
which traces are fairly visible.

[19] Supplying the letters למוקח] ולממוכר.

[20] Supply Heb. ibid. the end of the line אמר of which
some faint traces are visible.

[21] Heb. l. 16 ועשה, before which the letters נה still
remain, which points to מחנה.

[22] Heb. l. 17 למנרש. Perhaps it reads למגרש "open
place." The two other words remaining in this line offer
no clue.

[23] Heb. l. 18 ענוהו, the reading of which is very
doubtful, most of this line being torn off, and what

remains is very faded. After the word ובאהבת we have
the letters חם.

[24] Heb. ibid. יטה, reading uncertain; and so is the
following ..הב.. which may perhaps also be taken as
בהם or ..יהם.

[25] Heb. l. 19 הם, but some faint traces of a possible
ש are visible before the הם.

[26] Only a few letters giving no words remain of l. 22,
whilst l. 23 is entirely missing.

[27] See Isa. 7 17. Cf. above, Heb. p. 7, l. 11.

[28] Cf. Heb. above, p. 7, l. 5.

[29] Heb. l. 2 להנצילם instead of להצילם.

[30] At the end of the line we have the letters ונע (which
are certain), followed by traces of letters, the first of which
may be a נ, but also perhaps פ. Perhaps we have here
some corrupt quotation from Mal. 3 1 ופנה פתאים.

¶ XVII

[1] Reading Heb. l. 3 וזה סרך for וסרך.

[2] Heb. l. 4 שלשתם, below, l. 6 שלושתם.

[3] Heb. ibid. והגר רביע.

[4] Heb. l. 6 וכן ישאלו לכל, which however may also
mean they shall be asked (יִשָׁאֵלוּ), that is whilst sitting in
counsel when they are asked for their opinion.

[5] Reading l. 6 את for שא.

[6] See Lev. 47 3 and Num. 4 3, but our numbers
correspond with neither of these precedents.

[7] The MS. is here torn off. Perhaps we should
supply ההגו as above, Heb. p. 10, l. 6.

[8] Reading לדברם though only the roof of the ד
remains now. Perhaps the meaning of this word is "to
guide them." See Rab. Dict. s.v. דבר.

10 old[9] *married[10] in all | counsel of men, and in every tongue[11]......According to his
11 word shall come in they who enter the Congregation | every man his share[12]. And
   everything concerning which any man shall have to speak he shall speak to the
12 Censor, | with regard to any controversy or suit[13].

¶ XVIII   And this is the usage of the many to prepare[1] all their needs. The amount |
13 of their offerings *are[2] for every moon[3]...And they shall give it into the hands of
14 the Censor and the judges. | From it they shall give for the *poor[4] and from it[5]
   they shall strengthen the *hand[6] of the poor and the needy. And to the aged man
15 who | ......to the man who *wanders[7] and to him who was *captured[8] by a strange
16 people, and to the virgin who[9] | ....*he who has[10] none seeking after him[11] all
17 the labour[12]...and not................. | And this is the explanation of the settlement......
18—19 .... | And this is the explanation of the judgments which.............. | Aaron
20 and Israel[13] and he will forgive our sins................... | in money[14] and he knows......|
21—22 ....punishment six days and he that speaketh....................... | against

¶ XIX Moses[15]..................... |

|| Page 15 ||............[1] and also with *Aleph Lamed* and also with *Aleph Daleth*[2], but an oath
2 of the *covenant[3].............. | by the curses of the covenant. But the Law of Moses[4]

---

[9] See above, note 6.

[10] Heb. l. 9 בעול which I read בָּעוּל. According to this the sect would insist upon the marriage of the מבקר as the Rabbis did with regard to the high priest. Possibly it is a mere dittography of the following בכל. It is also possible that it is a corruption of בא. It would then be connected with the בסוד אנשים of the next line, "coming into every assembly of men." Cf. Gen. **49** 6.

[11] The MS. is here torn and only the letters reproduced in the text remain. The ר of רמ has the Babylonian vowel רֹ.

[12] Heb. l. 11 איש בתרו. See Gen. **15** 10.

[13] See 2 Sam. **15** 4.

¶ XVIII

[1] Heb. l. 11 להכין.

[2] Heb. l. 12 תרומתן הם. But the reading is very doubtful, and the faded letters look also like שני ימים "two days." It would then perhaps mean that the earnings of two days in every month should be set apart for certain communal purposes.

[3] The MS. has here הם...ט as reproduced in the Heb. text, ibid. the middle letters being torn off. המשפט ("the law," "rule") is the word which suggests itself.

[4] The MS. is torn and faded in this place as indicated in the Heb. text, l. 14 עם...בער which may perhaps be corrected into בער עניים. It may also be a corruption of כהנים (priests).

[5] Heb. ibid. מני; but there are also traces of a מ after the ו. I thus read וממנו for וממני.

[6] Reading Heb. ibid. ביד for בה. Cf. Ezek. **16** 49.

[7] The MS. is mutilated here. I first read ינע, as reproduced in Heb. l. 15, but on closer examination I find that it may be read ינוע "who is wandering," that is, homeless.

[8] Reading and supplying Heb. l. 15 ולאשר ישָׁבָה.

[9] Scarcely legible traces are left here of letters ן לה ג which could be construed into אין לה גואל "who has no near kinsman." Cf. Ruth **3** 9 and 12.

[10] Heb. l. 16 אשר of which word however only the ר remains.

[11] Heb. l. 16 אין לו דורש. Cf. Jer. **30** 17.

[12] Only very faint traces remain here in the MS. representing perhaps עבד "slave."

[13] Probably we had here משוח מאהרן וג'. Cf. below, Heb. p. 18, l. 1.

[14] Heb. l. 20 בממון the preceding letters are very uncertain.

[15] Heb. l. 22 במשה which however is uncertain as it may also be read במשפט. There were also on this line traces of שף. Line 23 is entirely missing.

¶ XIX

[1] Here perhaps some leaf or leaves are missing in the MS. The first word of this page (Heb. p. 15, l. 1) is faded and the last letter is discernible ע which suggests ישבע "he shall take an oath."

[2] Heb. l. 1 וגם באלף ולמד וגם באלף ודלת. That is אל of אלהים and אד of אדני. Cf. Mishneh, *Shebuoth* IV. 13 באלף דלי"ת...משביע אני עליכם. Cf. also T. B. *Shebuoth* 35 a and *Masecheth Soferin*, ed. Joel Müller, pp. vii and 58.

[3] Reading and supplying with fair certainty, Heb. ibid. שבועת הבורית. The line probably finished with או "or the curses," etc. Even in its present defective state what remains of the text allows us to assume that we have here a law that one shall take no oath either by the full name (the Tetragrammaton) or by any other name of God, such as *Elohim* or *Adonai*. The Samaritans, according to the well-known statement in *Jer. Sanhedrin*, 28 b, were in the habit of taking the oath by the Tetragrammaton. Cf. Kirchheim, *Karme Shomron*, p. 26. Our Sect only allowed the oath by the covenant.

[4] Does this mean to swear by the Law? Cf. *Shebuoth* 38 b; שבועה בספר תורה; but there it does not mean to swear by the Law but to keep the scroll.

3 he shall not mention[5], for[6]... | And if he swears and transgresses he will profane the
4 Name[7]. And if by the curses of the Covenant...... | the Judges. And if he trans-
5 gressed he is guilty and he shall confess and shall return and shall not bear... | [8]death.
And he who enters into the covenant for the whole of Israel a statute for ever
6 with their children *that[9]... | to pass among them that are numbered[10] by the oath of
7 the covenant they shall confirm it upon them. And this is also | the law in every
end of the wickedness[11], for everyone who returns from his corrupt way. On the
8 day of his speaking | with the Censor of the many they shall count him by the oath
9 of the covenant that Moses established | with Israel. The covenant[12]......*Moses
10 with all heart[13]... | soul everything be found to be done in them[14].... And no man
11 shall make known to him[15] the | laws until he will stand before the Censor[16]......be *per-
12 suaded[17] by him when he examines him. | And when he will confirm it upon him to
13 return to the Law of Moses with all his heart and all his soul | ......of him if[18].........
and everything which was revealed of the Law with regard to a controversy[19]...... |
14–15 ....in him[20]......the Censor him and shall command him......... | until[21]......*killed
16–17 him[22]......and the madman and all.............. | till.....................| *daughter[23]......|
‖ Page 16 .... ‖ covenant with you and with the whole of Israel. Therefore
2 the man shall confirm it upon *himself[24] to return to | the Law of Moses for in it
everything is *exactly explained[25].

¶ XX 3   As to the explanation of their ends[1] *for a remembrance[2] | to Israel of all
these, behold, it is exactly explained in the Book of the Divisions of the Seasons[3] |

[5] Reading Heb. l. 2 יזכיר for יזכור.

[6] After כי "for" the MS. is badly faded, but traces of letters בזה מפי ..ה—, but everything must be considered as very uncertain.

[7] Heb. l. 3 וחלל השם that is by his transgressing the oath he is profaning the Name. Cf. Lev. **19** 12. At the end of the line probably the words יובא לפני are missing.

[8] Probably some such word as עון is to be supplied here. Cf. Lev. **17** 16. This law as given in the text seems to be a corrupt condensation of Lev. **5** 4, 5 and 23.

[9] Heb. l. 5 אשר though very little trace remains of the ר. Traces of letters indicated by the dots look somewhat like י.מ.ע. Perhaps we had here יולדו.

[10] See Exod. **30** 13. The meaning of the law seems to be that their children shall take an oath by the covenant when mustered in the congregation, that is at the age of thirty as above, Heb. p. 14, ll. 3 and 6.

[11] Heb. l. 7 קץ הרשע, that is in the case of repentance. Cf. above, Heb. p. 6, ll. 10 and 14.

[12] Heb. l. 9 את הברית. These words are followed by לש suggesting לשמוע "to obey." The ל that comes next may be the remainder of לתורת followed by משה.

[13] Heb. ibid. לב which is followed by the trace of a ו forming probably the remainder of ובכל. See below, l. 12.

[14] Heb. l. 10 בם which may be a corruption of בה "in it," that is, in the Torah. The MS. is torn in this place only traces of illegible letters remaining, of which nothing is decipherable except the י.

[15] Heb. ibid. ידיעהו.

[16] The word following Heb. l. 11 indicated by dots read probably אשר "who."

[17] Heb. ibid. יתפתה the reading of which however is very doubtful. The word looks somewhat like יחפוזר. The paper is torn in the middle of the word. Perhaps, it read יחפוש בו "he shall inquire into him," that is, into the novice or penitent.

[18] Heb. l. 13 אם. The ר following it is very doubtful. The left traces look also somewhat like ..נ. or ים.

[19] Heb. ibid. לריב. Cf. above, p. 14, l. 12.

[20] Heb. l. 14 בו. The word is preceded by the trace of a ך and followed by traces of י.

[21] Heb. l. 15 עד which I first took as בד. Then come some very faint traces of עמד or יומו or מים.

[22] Heb. ibid. המתו which is however very doubtful. The left traces may also read המתו or הממקו. All the remaining single letters are very doubtful.

[23] Heb. l. 17 בת, which is however very doubtful, whilst it might also be the ending of any number of words like שבת, etc. The last six lines are entirely missing.

[24] Reading Heb. l. 1 נפשך for נפשו.

[25] Heb. l. 2 מדוקדק. See Rab. Dict. s. דוק and דק.

¶ XX

[1] Heb. l. 2 ופרוש קציהם. Cf. above, Heb. p. 2, l. 9.

[2] Reading l. 2 לזכרון for לעורון.

[3] Heb. מחלקות העתים ליוב' ובשב'. By this undoubtedly the Book of Jubilees is meant, though no such full title of this Pseudepigraphic work is thus far known. See Charles, *Introduction*, p. xiv seq. See also the Prologue to the book, p. 1.

4 according to their jubilees and their weeks. And on the day on which the man
5 will confirm upon himself to return | to the Law of Moses the angel of Mastema[4]
6 will turn away from behind him if he will fulfil his word. | Therefore Abraham was
circumcised on the day of his knowing *it[5]. As to what He said, "that which is
7 gone out of thy lips | thou shalt keep[6]" to confirm, every oath of a bond[7] by which
8 a man will confirm upon himself | to perform a commandment of the Law till the
9 *price of death[8] he shall not redeem it[9]. Every thing which |...[10] a man upon himself[11]...
10 ....till price of death he shall not confirm it[12]...... | the oath of the woman
11 which *Moses said [13]to disallow her oath[14]. No man | shall disallow an oath which
12 *no man knew*[15]. It is to be fulfilled. As to disallowing[16] | if it is to transgress the
covenant *then he shall disallow it and not confirm it. And so is also the law for
13 her father. | As to the law of *offerings[17], no man shall vow anything for the altar
14 under compulsion[18]. Nor | shall the *priests[19] take anything from the Israelites[20]
15 ......a man *dedicate the food[21]........ | this is what he said, "They hunt every man
16 his brother with a net*[22]." Nor | shall devote.........of all.......⹁..........his possession |
17–19 holy.......................shall be punished... | he who takes a vow........................... | to
the judge[23]............................

---

[4] Heb. l. 5 מלאך המשטמה. Cf. Jub. **10** 8, text and notes.

[5] Heb. l. 6 ביום דעתו, that is, the importance of this law and its inherent virtue consists in man's being saved from the power of Mastema and other demons. Cf. Jub. **15** 26, 32.

[6] Deut. **23** 24.

[7] Cf. Num. **30** 3.

[8] Heb. l. 8 עד מחיר מות, meaning perhaps, "the risk of death."

[9] Heb. ibid. אל יפדהו. Perhaps we should read יפרהו ("he shall not make it void") for יפדהו. See also below, note 11.

[10] There is before the איש Heb. l. 9 the trace of a ם which suggests יקים "confirm."

[11] Heb. ibid. נפשו, followed by a ל. Before the עד we have distinct traces of רה, but between the ל and the רה there is enough space to supply לסור מן התוזרה to "turn away from the Law." We might now explain these laws in the following way. First, that a man is bound to keep his vow pledging him to a particular commandment of the Law, even at the risk of death, having no powers of annulling it; second, that a man is bound not to keep his vow even at the risk of his life, if this vow was intended to abolish a commandment of the Law. The second עד מחיר מות may be a mere dittography, coming from the preceding line.

[12] The missing word in this place at the beginning of Heb. l. 10 must have been על (Heb. p. 10, l. 14 etc.) or בדבר "as to."

[13] Supplying ibid. אמור מ[שה.

[14] See Num. **30** 6, 8, 9.

[15] Heb. l. 11 supplying the dots לא וי[ד]רו[ע א]דם, which however is very doubtful. There is a trace of a נ after the ע of ידע.

[16] That is as to the concession which the Scriptures make to the father and to the husband, in this respect they refer only to cases where the vow involves a breach of the Law.

[17] Heb. l. 13 הנדרב[ו]ת. The roof of the ב is still fairly discernible.

[18] Heb. ibid. אנום.

[19] Reading and supplying Heb. at the beginning of l. 14 [והכ]הנים.

[20] Probably here was some word like בחזקה "by force." After this there is room for a small word like ולא.

[21] Heb. ibid. יקדש איש מאכל. If we put ולא before it as suggested in the preceding note, then we should translate "nor shall a man devote."

[22] Corrected and restored Heb. ibid. after Micah **7** 2, איש את אחיהו יצודו חרם. The meaning of the law is not clear to me.

[23] The last lines are entirely missing, whilst from the preceding four lines, only a few words remain.

CORRECTIONS TO THE HEBREW TEXT

TEXT A.

Heb. p. 1, l. 2   רִב for רִיב.

     4   שָׁאֵרִית for שְׁאֵרִית.

     11   Blank equal to the space of one word between לבו and ויודע.

     20   חוק for חֹק.

p. 2, l. 3   ותושיה may also be read ותושייה.

     9   קציתם may also be read קציהם.

     15   כאשר may perhaps be read באשר.

     20   Supply after בשר the word אשר.

p. 3, l. 1   ומשפחות for ומשפחה, the ת, however, is doubtful.

     21   Omit interrogation mark after והלוים.

p. 4, l. 17   Blank equal to the space of a short word after הזנות.

     17   ההין for ההון, after which we have a blank equal to the space of a short word.

     21   אותם for אותם.

p. 5, l. 3   נפתח twice, but the first is cancelled.

     12   לאמר for לאמר.

     13   זיקי for זיקות.

     16   בעלילותם for בעלילותיהם.

p. 6, l. 1   מאחר for מֵאַחַר.

     2   ויקח for וַיָקֶם.

     5   ויגורו for ויגרו.

     10   הרשיע may be also read הרשוע.

     18   לחול for לחול.

p. 7, l. 5   יסורו may be also read יסודו.

     8   היסורים may be also read היסודים.

     16   Supply blank equal to space of short word after הנפלת.

p. 8, l. 7   להון for להין.

     10   Blank equal to space of one word after העמים.

     17   הועירו may be also read היעירו.

p. 9, l. 2   אמר. It seems that the scribe wrote originally אשר but corrected it into אמר.

     3   רעהו for רעהו.

Heb. p. 9, l. 14   The blank is before הכל, and it is not impossible that this word was cancelled by the scribe and corrected by the following וכן.

22   ההון for החוק.

22   בלו .., for כלו .., but there is no real certainty about it.

23   יקום, but not certain. May perhaps also be read יקומו.

p. 10, l. 15   Before השישי we have the letters מי cancelled by the scribe.

18   ורק may also be read ודין.

20   חפצי may also be read חפצו.

p. 11, l. 2   כלי, but the י is hardly discernible now.

13   תפול may also be read תפיל.

23   ת... is very doubtful.

p. 12, l. 3   במשפט for כמשפט.

p. 13, l. 5   משפט for משפש.

10   דים, the letter ד very doubtful.

14   ברית אל ישאל אל אל ישא ואל יתן for ברית אל ישאל אל יתן. The first אל is probably to be pointed אֵל.

16   At the end of this line are traces of something like a ה and then of an א and a ל.

18   ענוהו very doubtful.

18   חט. The ט very doubtful.

18   יטה, may be read יטור. The ו after the ט is certain.

19   נקשר, the ר very uncertain.

22   ה.., looks something like השפטים. The ש and the פ are fairly certain.

p. 14, l. 8   לחברם, may also be read לדברם.

14   ביד for בה.

16   After עבודת, room for one word before ולא. The last letter is still visible, representing a ך, something like a י preceding it. There is also some sign which may be taken as a פ. This would suggest the remainder or corruption of בפרך.

19   Before אהרן we have the letter ח, undoubtedly the remainder of משוח.

p. 15, l. 1   שבועה may also be read שבועת.

2   Some traces of such letters as זה and על, perhaps also פי, after כי at end of line.

5   The אש at end of line is followed by a ר thus making אשר. Then there are at the end some signs which may perhaps be taken as עו.

TEXT B.

Heb. p. 19, l. 26   Between עדתו and ואשר, blank of two words.

35   ובכתבו, last letter of this word not quite certain.

p. 20, l. 1   At the beginning of the line there are signs of some letters now illegible, but, as it would seem, they were cancelled by the scribe.

12   Before ואמנה, sign of one or two letters cancelled by the scribe.

20   After יעלה, sign of one or two letters cancelled.

25   קדשו for קָדֶש: followed by a blank of two words.

33   אל חקי, doubtful.

ADDITIONS AND CORRECTIONS TO TRANSLATION AND NOTES

P. 2, l. 7   Heb. מקדם עולם. Cf. Ps. **74** 2, and Prov. **8** 22 מקדמי ארץ.

10   Heb. עד מה. It was suggested to me by the Rev. J. A. Montgomery that it is probably equal to the Syriac עדמא, and has to be translated *until that.*

p. 4, l. 8   Interpretation of the Law. Heb. כפירוש התורה cf. p. 6, ll. 14, 18 and 20, and p. 13, l. 6. On p. 20, l. 6 we have מדרש התורה. Cf. also p. 7, l. 18 about the דורש התורה. Cf. also p. 7, ll. 1, 2, and 3 where משפט seems = פירוש, the Sect insisting that the particular laws mentioned there (p. 6, l. 18— p. 7, l. 3) should be observed according to their own פירוש or משפט. This suggests the possibility of our having in p. 20, ll. 31 and 32 ...והתיסרו במשפטים אשר נשפטו וכו' a parallel to our passage in p. 4, l. 8 והתיסרו would then mean "to be instructed." The פירוש or מדרש is contained in the Book of Jubilees and similar Apocrypha which the Sect considered authoritative.

p. 5, l. 19   (note 35). In connection with this subject, the following extracts from the Jerahmeel MS. in Oxford, kindly copied for me by the Rev. M. Segal, will not be uninteresting :

ועוד שני אנשים מכשפים היו בהם ושמותם יוחני וממרא וכשנכנסו
בים וראו שהמים מסבבין אותם מה עשו הרבו (?) בכשפיהם ופרחו באויר
עד לרקיע ואין לך ברייה בעולם ומכשפים יותר ממצרים שכן אמרו חכמים
עשרה קבין מכשפות ירדו לעולם תשעה נטלה מצרים ואחת לכל העולם
כולו. והללו יוחני וממרא היו שרי כשפים ומרוב כשפים שהן יודעים
היו עולין עד לרקיע ולא היו יכולין מיכאל וגבריאל לעשות להם כלום
מיד צעקו מיכא' וגבריא' להב̈ה בתחנ̈נים ואמרו לפניו רבונו של עולם
רשעים הללו שישעבדו בניך בשעבוד קשה עומדים כל כך לא היו חוששים
אלא אף עליך הם עומדים ומנין שירד הקב̈ה במצרים שנ̇ ארד עמך

h 2

מצרימה אלא אם רצונך רבן העולמים עשה דין לבניך מיד אמ' הקֹבֹה
למטטרון הורד אותם והפילם והזהר שלא יפלו אלא בים מיד הפילם
מיטטרון בתוך הים בעל כרחן באותה שעה פתחו ישר' ואמרו שירה וברוב
גאונך תהרום קמיך"

Cf. Dr Gaster, *The Chronicles of Jerahmeel*, LIV. and p. 159. London, 1899.
Cf. also Sec. וארא ציוני.

p. 6, l. 2   Heb. ויקח, read ויקם, "and He raised up."

p. 10, l. 18   (note 4). Cf. also Jub. **49** 8, "or whoever says he will do something on it," but the meaning is not quite clear to me.

p. 11, l. 10   (note 28). Perhaps מושבת is in contradistinction to מחולל, a term occurring sometimes in Karaitic literature. It would then mean even in a locality which has the advantage of being מושבת in which he may move all other things he must not move rock or earth.

p. 12, l. 13   (note 4). Add—Meaning obscure. Perhaps we have in this law a protest against the Rabbinic interpretation of Lev. **11** 36 according to which not only the fountain or pit remained clean but also the water therein. Cf. D. Hoffmann, *Das Buch Leviticus*, p. 349, and other commentaries ancient and modern.

p. 15, l. 8   Heb. יפקדוהו. Perhaps it has here the meaning of "to remind him."

p. 19, l. 12   Heb. נאנחים ונאנקים. An expression which the Karaites applied to their own sect. Cf. Pinsher, *Lekute Kadmoniyoth Nispachim*, p. 101.

TITLES OF SOME OF THE WORKS QUOTED IN THE INTRODUCTION AND NOTES, BUT NOT GIVEN IN FULL

Abul-Fath, *Abufathi Annales Samaritani*, ed. Eduardus Vilmar, Gothae, MDCCCLXV.

Beer, *Das Buch der Jubiläen und sein Verhältniss zu den Midraschim*, B. Beer, Leipzig, 1856.

Hadasi, אשכל הכפר, by Judah Hadasi, Gozolowa, 1836.

Jost, *Geschichte des Judenthums und seiner Secten*, Dr J. M. Jost, Leipzig, 1857.

J. Q. R., *The Jewish Quarterly Review*, ed. by I. Abrahams and C. G. Montefiore (20 vols.) London.

Jub., The Book of Jubilees...translated and ed. by Dr R. H. Charles, London, 1902.

Kirchheim, כרמי שומרון, *Introductio in librum Talmudicum* "de Samaritanis," Raphael Kirchheim, Frankfurt a.M., 1851.

Kirkisani, Kirkisani, published by Dr A. Harkavy in Memoirs of the Oriental Department of the Imperial Russian Archaeological Society, vol. VIII. (1893–1894) St Petersburg, 1894.

Montgomery, *The Samaritans, The Earliest Jewish Sect*, Dr James Alan Montgomery, Philadelphia, 1907.

Revue, Revue des Études Juives, Paris.

Singer (Wilhelm), *Das Buch der Jubiläen oder die Leptogenesis*, 1. Theil, Stuhlweissenburg, 1898.

Test., or Testaments, The Testaments of the Twelve Patriarchs, translated and ed. by Dr R. H. Charles, London, 1908.

INDEX* TO REFERENCES TO BIBLE, APOCRYPHA AND RABBINIC LITERATURE IN NOTES OF DOCUMENTS OF JEWISH SECTARIES
VOL. I.

* The references in this Index are to the page and line of the Hebrew text and the corresponding notes in the English translation.

LXI

(93)

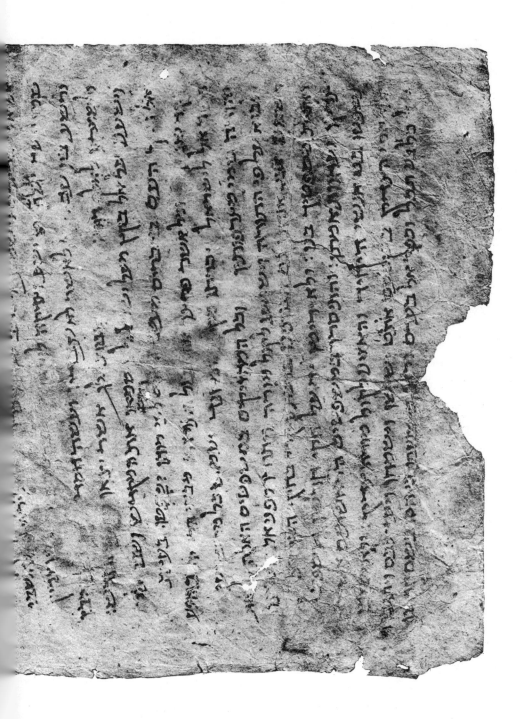

Facsimile of page 20.　Text B

(99)

I　　ועתה שמעו כל יודעי צדק ובינו במעשי

אל כי ריב לו עם כל בשר ומשפט יעשה בכל מנֹאציו

כי במועלם אשר עזבוהו הסתיר פניו מישראל וממקדשו

ויתנם לחרב ובזכרו ברית ראשנים השאיר שארית

5　לישראל ולא נתנם לכלה ובקץ חרון שנים שלוש מאות

ותשעים לתיתו אותם ביד נבוכדנאצר מלך בבל

פקדם ויצמח מישראל ומאהרן שורש מטעת לירוש

את ארצו ולדשן בטוב אדמתו ויבינו בעונם וידעו כי

אנשים אשמים הם ויהיו כעורים וכימגששים דרך

10　שנים עשרים ויבן אל אל מעשיהם כי בלב שלם דרשוהו

ויקם להם מורה צדק להדריכם בדרך לבו ויודע

לדורות אחרונים את אשר עשה בדור אחרון בעדת בוגדים

הם סרי דרך היא העת אשר היה כתוב עליה כפרה סוררה

כן סרר ישראל בעמוד איש הלצון אשר הטיף לישראל

15　מימי כזב ויתעם בתוהו לא דרך להשח גבהות עולם ולסור

מנתיבות צדק ולסיע גבול אשר גבלו ראשנים בנחלתם למען

הדבק בהם את אלות בריתו להסגירם לחרב נקמת נקם

ברית בעבור אשר דרשו בחלקות ויבחרו במהתלות ויצפו

לפרצות ויבחרו בטוב הצואר ויצדיקו רשע וירשיעו צדיק

20　ויעבירו ברית ויפרו חוק ויגודו על נפש צדיק ובכל הולכי

תמים תעבה נפשם וירדפום לחרב ויסיסו לריב עם ויחר אף

אל בעדתם להשם את כל המונם ומעשיהם לנדה לפניו

ועתה שמעו אלי כל באי ברית ואגלה אזנכם בדרכי

רשעים   אל אהב דעת חכמה ותושיה הציב לפניו

ערמה ודעת הם ישרתוהו ארך אפים עמו ורוב סליחות

5 לכפר בעד שבי פשע וכוח וגבורה וחמה גדולה בלהבי אש

בו כל מלאכי חבל על סררי דרך ומתעבי חק לאין שארית

ופליטה למו כי לא בחר אל בהם מקדם עולם ובטרם נוסדו ידע

את מעשיהם ויתעב את דורות מדם ויסתר את פניו מן הארץ

מי עד תומם וידע את שני מעמד ומספר ופרוש קציתם לכל

10 הוי עולמים ונהיית עד מה יבוא עד בקציהם לכל שני עולם

ובכולם הקים לו קריאי שם למען הִתִיר פליטה לארץ ולמלא

פני תבל מזרעם   ויודיעם ביד משיחו רוח קדשו והוא

אמת ובפרוש שמו שמותיהם ואת אשר שנא התעה

ועתה בנים שמעו לי ואגלה עיניכם לראות ולהבין במעשי

15 אל ולבחור את אשר רצה ולמאוס כאשר שנא להתהלך תמים

בכל דרכיו ולא לתוּר במחשבות יצר אשמה ועני זנות כי רבים

תעו בם וגבורי חיל נכשלו בם מלפנים ועד הנה בלכתם בשרירות

לבם נפלו עירי השמים בה נאחזו אשר לא שמרו מצות אל

ובניהם אשר כרום ארזים גָבהָם וכהרים גויותיהם כי נפלו

20 כל בשר היה בחרבה כי גוע ויהיו כלא היו בעשותם את

רצונם ולא שמרו את מצות עשיהם עד אשר חרה אפו בם

בה תעי בני נח ומשפחה . הם בה הם נכרתים

אברהם לא הלך בה ויע . . . הב בשמרו מצות אל ולא בחר

ברצון רוחו וימסור לישחק וליעקב וישמרו ויכתבו אוהבים

לאל ובעלי ברית לעולם   בני יעקב תעו בם ויענשו לפני

5 משגותם ובניהם במצרים הלכו בשרירות לבם להיעץ על

מצות אל ולעשות איש הישר בעיניו ויאכלו את הדם ויכרת

זכורם במדבר להם בקדש עלו ורשו את רוחם ולא שמעו

לקול עֹשֵׂיהם מצות יוריהם וירגנו באהליהם ויחר אף אל

בעדתם ובניהם בֹו אבדו ומלכיהם בו נכרתו וגיבוריהם בו

10 אבדו וארצם בו שממה בו חבו באי הברית הראשנים ויסגרו

לחרב בעזבם את ברית אל ויבחרו ברצונם ויתורו אחרי שרירות

לבם לעשות איש את רצונו   ובמחזיקים במצות אל

אשר נותרו מהם הקים אל את בריתו לישראל עד עולם לגלות

להם נסתרות אשר תעו בם כל ישראל   שבתות קדשו ומועדי

15 כבודו עידות צדקו ודרכי אמתו וחפצי רצונו אשר יעשה

האדם וחיה בהם   פתח לפניהם ויחפרו באר למים רבים

ומואסיהם לא יחיה והם התגוללו בפשע אנוש ובדרכי נדה

ויאמרו כי לנו היא ואל ברוי פלאו כפר בעד עונם וישא לפשעם

ויבן להם בית נאמן בישראל אשר לא עמד כמהו למלפנים ועד

20 הנה המחזיקים בו לחיֵי נצח וכל כבוד אדם להם הוא כאשר

הקים אל להם ביד יחזקאל הנביא לאמר הכהנים והלוים (?) ובני

1—2

צדוק אשר שמרו את משמרת מקדשו בתעות בני ישראל

מעליהם יגישו לי חלב ודם   הכהנים הם שבי ישראל

היוצאים מארץ יהודה והנלוים עמהם   ובני צדוק הם בחירי

ישראל קריאי השם העמדים באחרית הימים הנה פרוש

5 שמותיהם לתולדותם וקץ מעמדם ומספר צרותיהם ושני

התגוררם ופירוש מעשיהם   הקודש שונים אשר כפר

אל בעדם ויצדיקו צדיק וירשיעו רשע וכל הבאים אחריהם

לעשות כפרוש התורה אשר התוסרו בו הראשנים עד שלים

הקץ השנים האלה כברית אשר הקים אל לראשנים לכפר

10 על עונותיהם כן יכפר אל בעדם ובשלום הקץ למספר השנים

האלה אין עוד להשתפח לבית יהודה כי אם לעמוד איש על

מצודו נבנתה הגדר רחק החוק ובכל השנים האלה יהיה

בליעל משולח בישראל כאשר דבר אל ביד ישעיה הנביא בן

אמוץ לאמר פחד ופחת ופח עליך יושב הארץ   פשרו

15 שלושת מצודות בליעל אשר אמר עליהם לוי בן יעקב

אשר הוא תפש בהם בישראל ויתנם פניהם לשלושת מיני

הצדק הראשונה היא הזנות השנית ההון השלישית

טמא המקדש העולה מזה יתפש בזה והניצל מזה יתפש

בזה   בוני החוץ אשר הלכו אחרי צו הצו הוא מטיף

20 אשר אמר הטף יטיפון הם ניתפשים בשתים בזנות לקחת

שתי נשים בחייהם ויסוד הבריאה זכר ונקבה ברא אותם

5

ובאי התבה שנים שנים באו אל התבה   ועל הנשיא כתוב
לא ירבה לו נשים ודויד לא קרא בספר התורה החתום אשר
היה בארון כי לא נפתח בישראל מיום מות אלעזר
ויהושע ויושֵע והזקנים אשר עבדו את העשתרות ויטמן
נגלה עד עמוד צדוק ויעלו מעשי דויד מלבד דם אוריה
ויעזבם לו אל וגם מטמאים הם את המקדש אשר אין הם
מבדיל כתורה ושוכבים עם הרואה את דם זובה ולוקחים
איש את בת אֵחיהם ואת בת אחותו   ומשה אמר אל
אחות אמך לא תקרב שאר אמך היא ומשפט העריות לזכרים
הוא כתוב וכהם הנשים ואם תגלה בת האח את ערות אחי
אביה והיא שאר   וגם את רוח קדשיהם טמאו ובלשון
גרופים פתחו פה על חוקי ברית אל לאמר לא נכונו ותועבה
הם מדברים בם כלם קדחו אש ומבערי זיקי קורי
עכביש קוריהם וביצי צפעונים ביציהם הקרוב אליהם
לֹא ינקה כהר ביתו יאשם כי אם נלחץ כי אם למילפנים פקד
אל את מעשיהם ויחר אפו בעלילותם כי לא עם בינות הוא
הם גוי אבד עצות מאשר אין בהם בינה כי מלפנים עמד
משה ואהרן ביד שר האורים ויקם בליעל את יחנה ואת
אחיהו במזמתו בהושע ישראל את הראשונה
     ובקץ חרבן הארץ עמדו מסיגי הגבול ויתעו את ישראל
ותֵישַם הארץ כי דברו סרה על מצות אל ביד משה וגם

(114)

במשיחו הקודש וינבאו שקר להשיב את ישראל מֵאחר

אל ויזכר אל ברית ראשנים   ויקח מאהרן נבונים ומישראל

חכמים וישמעם ויחפורו את הבאר באר חפרוה שרים כרוה

נדיבי העם במחוקק הבאר היא התורה וחופריה הם

5 שבי ישראל היוצאים מארץ יהודה ויגורו בארץ דמשק

אשר קרא אֵל את כולם שרים כי דרשוהו ולא הושבה

פארתם בפי אחד   והמחוקק הוא דורש התורה אשר

אמר ישעיה מוציא כלי למעשיהו   ונדיבי העם הם

הבאים לכרות את הבאר במחוקקות אשר חקק המחוקק

10 להתהלך במה בכל קץ הרשיע וזולתם לא ישיגו עד עמד

יורה הצדק באחרית הימים   וכל אשר הובאו בברית

לבלתי בוא אל המקדש להאיר מזבחו ויהיו מסגירי

הדלת אשר אמר אֵל מי בכם יסגיר דלתו   ולא תאירו מזבחי

חנם אם לא ישמרו לעשות כפרוש התורה לקץ הרשע ולהבדיל

15 מבני השחת ולהנזר מהון הרשעה הטמא בנדר ובחרם

ובהון המקדש ולגזול את עניי עמו להיות אלמנות שללם

ואת יתומים ירצחו ולהבדיל בין הטמא לטהור ולהודיע בין

הקודש לחול ולשמור את יום השבת כפרושה ואת המועדות

ואת יום התענית במצא .. באי הברית החדשה בארץ דמשק

20 להרים את הקדשים כפירושיהם לאהוב איש את אחיהו

כמהו ולהחזיק ביד עני ואביון וגר   ולדרוש איש את שלום

אחיהו ולא ימעל איש בשאר בשרו להזיר מן הזונות

כמשפט להוכיח איש את אחיהו כמצוה ולא לנטור

מיום ליום ולהבדל מכל הטמאות כמשפטם ולא ישקץ

איש את רוח קדשיו כאשר הבדיל אל להם כל המתהלכים

5 באלה בתמים קדש על פי כל יסורו ברית אל נאמנות להם

לחיותם אלף דור   ואם מחנות ישבו כסרך הארץ ולקחו

נשים והולידו בנים והתהלכו על פי התורה   וכמשפט

היסורים כסרך התורה כאשר אמר בין איש לאשתו ובין אב

לבנו וכל המואסים בפקד אל את הארץ להשיב גמול רשעים

10 עליהם כבוא הדבר אשר כתוב בדברי ישעיה בן אמוץ הנביא

אשר אמר יבוא עליך ועל עמך ועל בית אביך ימים אשר

באו מיום סור אפרים מעל יהודה בהפרד שני בתי ישראל

שר אפרים מעל יהודה וכל הנסוגים הסגרו לחרב והמחזיקים

נמלטו לארץ צפון   כאשר אמר והגליתי את סכות מלככם

15 ואת כיון צלמיכם מאהלי דמשק   ספרי התורה הם סוכת

המלך כאשר אמר והקימותי את סוכת דוד הנפלת המלך

הוא הקהל וכינוי הצלמים וכיון הצלמים הם ספרי הנביאים

אשר בזה ישראל את דבריהם   והכוכב הוא דורש התורה

הבא דמשק כאשר כתוב דרך כוכב מיעקב וקם שבט

20 מישראל השבט הוא נשיא כל העדה ובעמדו וקרקר

את כל בני שת   אלה מלטו בקץ הפקודה הראשון

והנסוגים הסגירו לחרב וכן משפט כל באי בריתו אשר

לא יחזיקו באלה לפוקדם לכלה ביד בליעל הוא היום

אשר יפקד אל היו שרי יהודה אשר תשפוך עליהם העברה

כי יחלו למרפא וידקמום כל מורדים מאשר לא סרו מדרך

5 בוגדים ויתגוללו בדרכי זונות ובהן רשעה ונקום ונטור

איש לאחיו ושנוא איש את רעהו ויתעלמו איש בשאר בשרו

ויגשו לזמה ויתגברו להן ולבצע ויעשו איש הישר בעיניו

ויבחרו איש בשרירות לבו ולא נזרו מעם ויפרעו ביד רמה

ללכת בדרך רשעים אשר אמר אל עליהם חמת תנינים יינם

10 וראש פתנים אכזר   התנינים הם מלכי העמים ויינם הוא

דרכיהם וראש הפתנים הוא ראש מלכי יון הבא לעשות בהם

נקמה ובכל אלה לא הבינו בוני החוץ וטחי התפל כי

מבוהל רוח ומטיף כזב הטיף להם אשר חרה אף אל בכל עדתו

ואשר אמר משה לא בצדקתך ובישר לבבך אתה בא לרשת

15 את הגוים האלה כי מאהבתו את אבותך ומשמרו את השבועה

וכן המשפט לשבי ישראל סרו מדרך העם באהבת אל את

הראשנים אשר הועירו אחריו אהב את הבאים אחריהם כי להם

ברית האבות   ובשונאי את בוני החוץ חרה אפו   וכמשפט

הזה לכל המואס במצות אל ויעזבם ויפנו בשרירות לבם

20 הוא הדבר אשר אמר ירמיה לברוך בן נרייה ואלישע

לגחזי נערו   כל האנשים אשר באו בברית החדשה בארץ דמשק

*   *   *   *   *   *   *   *

כל אדם אשר יחרים אדם מאדם בחוקי הגוים להמית הוא

ואשר אמר לא תקום ולא תטור את בני עמך וכל איש מביאי

הברית אשר יביא על רעהו דבר אשר לא בהוכח לפני עדים

והביאו בחרון אפו או ספר לזקניו להבזותו נוקם הוא ונוטר

5 ואין כתוב כי אם נוקם הוא לצריו ונוטר הוא לאויביו

אם החריש לו מיום ליום ובחרון אפו בו דבר בו בדבר מות

ענה בו יען אשר לא הקים את מצות אל אשר אמר לו הוכח

תוכיח את רעיך ולא תשא עליו חטא   על השבועה אשר

אמר לא תושיעך ידך לך איש אשר ישביע על פני השדה

10 אשר לא לפנים השפטים או מאמרם הושיע ידו לו וכל האובד

ולא נודע מי גנבו ממאד המחנה אשר גנב בו ישביע בעליו

בשבועת האלה והשומע אם יודע הוא ולא יגיד ואשם

כל אשם מושב אשר אין בעלים והתודה המושב לכהן

והיה לו לבד מאיל האשם הכל   וכן כל אבדה נמצאת ואין

15 לה בעלים והיתה לכהנים כי לא ידע מוצאיה את משפטה

אם לא נמצא לה בעלים הם ישמרו   כל דבר אשר ימעל

איש בתורה וראה רעיהו והוא אחד אם דבר מות הוא ויודיעהו

לעיניו   בהוכיח למבקר והמבקר יכתבהו בידו עד עשותו

עוד לפני אחד ושב והודיע למבקר אם ישוב וניתפש לפני

20 אחד שלם משפטו   ואם שנים הם והם מעידים על

דבר אחר והובדל האיש מן הטהרה לבד   אם נאמנים

הם וביום ראות האיש יודיעה למבקר ועל ההון .. כלו שני

עידים נאמנים   ועל אחד להבדיל הטהרה ואל יקום

2

עוד לשופטים להמית על פיהו אשר לא מלאו ימיו לעבור
על הפקודים ירא את אל   אל יאמן איש על רעהו
לעד עובר דבר מן המצוה ביד רמה עד זכו לשוב
וזה סרך לשפטי העדה עד עשרה אנשים ברורים
5 מן העדה לפי העת ארבעה למטה לוי ואהרן ומישראל
ששה מבוננים בספר ההגו וביסודי הברית מבני חמשה
ועשרים שנה עד בני ששים שנה ואל יתיצב עוד מבן
ששים שנה ומעלה לשפוט את העדה כי במעל האדם
מעטו ימו ובחרון אף אל ביושבי הארץ אמר לסור את
10 דעתם עד לא ישלימו את ימיהם על הטהר במים אל
ירחץ איש במים צואים ומעוטים מדי מרעיל איש
אל יטהר במה כלי וכל גבא בסלע אשר אין בו די
מרעיל אשר נגע בו הטמא וטמא מימיו במימי הכלי
על הש..ת לשמרה כמשפטה   אל יעש איש ביום
15 השישי מלאכה מן העת אשר יהיה גלגל השמש
רחוק מן השער מלואו כי הוא אשר אמר שמור את
יום השבת לקדשו וביום השבת אל ידבר איש דבר
נבל ורק אל ישה ברעהו כל אל ישפוט על הון ובצע
אל ידבר בדברי המלאכה והעבודה לעשות למשכים
20   אל יתהלך איש בשדה לעשות את עבודת חפצי
השבת אל יתהלך חוץ לעירו אד על אלף באמה
אל יאכל איש ביום השבת כי אם המוכן ומן האובד
....ה   ואל יאכל ואל ישתה כי אם היה במחנה

בדרך וירד לרחוץ ישתה על עומדו ואל ישאב אל
כל כלי אל ישלח את בן הנכר לעשות את חפצו ביום השבת
אל יקח איש עליו בגדים צואים או מובאים בגו כי אם
כיבסו במים או שופים בלבונה אל יתערב איש מרצונו
5 בשבת אל ילך איש אחר הבהמֿה לרעותה חוץ מעירו כי
אם אלפים באמה אל ירם את ידו להכותה באגרוֿף אם
סוררת היא אל יוציאה מביתו אל יוציא איש מן הבית
לחוץ ומן החוץ אל בית ואם במובה יהיה אל יוצא ממנה
ואל יבא אליה אל פתח כלי טוח בשבת אל ישא איש
10 עליו סמנים לצאת ולבוא בשבת אל יטול בבית מושבת
סלע ועפר אל ישא האומן את היונק לצאת ולבוא בשבת
אל ימרא איש את עבדו ואת אמתו ואת. שוכרו בשבת
‎־אל אל יילד איש בהמה ביום השבת ואם תפול אל בור
ואל פחת אל יקימה בשבת אל ישבית איש במקום קרוב
15 לגוים בשבת אל יחל איש את השבת על הון ובצע בשבת
וכל נפש אדם אשר תפול אל מֿיֿם‎ מקום מים ואל מקום
אל יעלה איש בסולם וחבל וכלי אל יעל איש למזבח בשבת
כי אם עולת השבת כי כן כתוב מלבד שבתותיכם אל ישלח
איש למזבח עולה ומנחה ולבונה ועץ ביד איש טמא באחת
20 מן הטמאות להרשותו לטמא את המזבח כי כתוב זבח
רשעים תועבה ותפלת צדקם כמנחת רצון וכל הבא אל
בית השתחות אל יבא טמא כבום ובהרע חצוצרות הקהל
יתקדם או יתאחר ולא ישביתו את העבודה כולה ...ת

קודש הוא   אל ישכב איש עם אשה בעיר המקדש לטמא
את עיר המקדש בנדתם   כל אֲשֶׁר ימשלו בו רוחות בליעל
ודבר סרה כמשפט האוב והידעוני ישפט וכל אשר יתעה
לחלל את השבת ואת המועדות לא יומת כי על בני האדם
5 משמרו ואם ירפא ממנה ושמרוהו עד שבע שנים ואחר
יבוא אל הקהל   אל ישלח את ידו לשפוך דם לאיש מן הגוים
בעבור הון ובצע   וגם אל ישא מהונם כל בעבור אשר לא
יגדפו כי אם בעצת חבור ישראל   אל ימכר איש בהמה
ועוף טהורים לגוים בעבור אשר לא יזבחום   ומגורנו
10 ומגתו אל ימכר להם בכל מאדו ואת עבדו ואת אמתו אל ימכור
להם אשר באו עמו בברית אברהם   אל ישקץ איש את נפשו
בכל החיה והרמש לאכל מהם מעגלי הדבורים עד כל נפש
החיה אשר תרמוש במים והדגים אל יאכלו כי אם נקרעו
חיים ונשפך [ד]מם וכל החגבים במיניהם יבאו באש או במים
15 עד הם חיים כי הוא משפט בריאתם   וכל העצים והאבנים
והעפר אשר יגואלו בטמאת האדם לגאולי שמו בהם כפי
טמאתם יטמא הנוגע בם   וכל כלי מסמר מסמר או יתד בכותל
אשר יהיו עם המת בבית יטמא בטמאת אחד כלי מעשה
סרך מושב ערי ישראל על המשפטים האלה להבדיל בין
20 הטמא לטהור ולהודיע בין הקודש לחול   ואלה החקים
למשכיל להתהלך בם עם כלהו למשפט .. ועת וכמשפט
הזה יתהלכו זרע ישראל ולא יוארו   וזה סרך מושב
..... תהל ....בקץ הרשעה עד עמוד משוח אהרן

*   *   *   *   *   *   *   *

וישראל עד עשרה אנשים למועט לאלפים ומיאיות וחמשים

ועשרות ובקום עשרה אל ימש איש כהן מבונן בספר ההגו על

פיהו ישקו כולם   ואם אין הוא בחון בכל אלה ואיש מהלוים בחון

באלה ויצא הגורל לצאת ולבוא על פיהו כל באי המחנה   ואם

5 משפט לתורת נגע יהיה באיש ובא הכהן ועמד במחנה והבינו

המבקר בפרוש התורה   ואם פתי הוא הוא יסגירנו כי להם

המשפט   וזה סרך המבקר למחנה ישכיל את הרבים במעשי

אל ויבינם בגבורות פלאי ויספר לפניהם נהיות עולם בפרתיה

וירחם עליהם כאב לבניו ויש . . . לכל מדחובם כרועה עדרו

10 יתר כל חרצובות קשריהם ל . מי . . דים עשוק ורצוץ בעדתו

וכל הנוסף לעדתו יפקדהו למ . שיו ושוכלו וכוחו וגבורתו והונו

וכתבוהו במקומו כפי יהותו בגורל ה . . .   אל ימשול איש

מבני המחנה להביא איש אל העדה . . פי המבקר אשר למחנה

ואיש מכל באי ברית אל ישאל אל יתן . . בני השחר . .

15 אם כף לכף   ואל יעש איש . . לם . . ולם . . מכר . . אם . . .

למבקר אשר במחנה ועשה . . . נה ולא י .   . . . . .

. . . . . . ה וכן למגרש והוא י . .   . . . .

. . . . ענוהו ובאהבת חסד . . אל יטה . . הב . .

. . . . . הם ואת אשר איננו נקשר ב . .   . . . .

20 . . . . וזה מושב המחנות . כל . .   . . . .

. . . . . . לה לא יצליחו לשבת בארץ . . . . .

. . . . לה ה . . למ . . ל . . . . . .

אשר לא באו מיום סור אפרים מעל יהודה וכל המתהלכים באלה
ברית אל נאמנות להם להנצילם מכל מוקשי שחת כי פתאום ונענ..
וסרך מושב כל המחנות יפקדו כלם בשמותיהם הכהנים לראשונה
והלוים שנים ובני ישראל שלישתם והגר רביע ויכתבו בשמותיהם
5 איש אחר אחיהו הכהנים לראשונה והלוים שנים ובני ישראל
שלושתם והגר רביע וכן ישבו וכן ישאלו לכל והכהן יפקד
א̇ש הרבים מבן שלושים שנה ועד בן ששים מבונן בספר
... בכל משפטי התורה לחברם כמשפטם   והמבקר אשר
לכל המחנות מבן שלשים שנה ועד בן חמשים שנה בעול בכל
10 סוד אנשים ולכל לשון רם . פרי .. על פיהו יבאו באי העדה
איש בתרו ולכל דבר אשר יהיה לכל האדם לדבר למבקר ידבר
לכל ריב ומשפט   וזה סרך הרבים להכין כל חפציהם שכר
תרומתן הם לכל חדש . המ ... ט ונתנו על יד המבקר והשופטים
ממנו יתנו בעד .. עם ו . מני יחזיקו בה עני ואביון ולזקן אשר
15 ... לאיש אשר יגע ולא .. ישבה לגוי נכר ולבתולה אשר
ר אין לו דורש כל עבודת .. ולא ..
וזה פרוש מושב
.וזה פרוש המשפטים אשר
אהרן וישראל ויכפר עוננו .
20 ר קר בממון והוא יודע ו .
ענש ימים ששה ואשר ידבר .
א במש

.. ע וגם באלף ולמד וגם באלף ודלת כי אם שבועה הב ..

באלות הברית   ואת תורת משה אל יזכור כי . . . .

ואם ישבע ועבר וחלל את השם   ואם באלות הברית . . .

השפטים   ואם עבר אשם הוא והתודה והשיב ולא ישא . . . .

5 מות .   והבא בברית לכל ישראל לחוק עולם את בניהם אש . . . .

לעבור על הפקודים בשבועת הברית יקומו עליהם   וכן

המשפט בכל קץ הרשע לכל השב מדרכו הנשחתה ביום דברו

עם המבקר אשר לרבים יפקדוהו בשבועת הברית אשר כרת

משה עם ישראל את הברית לש . . ל . . . שה בכל לב . .

10 נפש אל הנמצא לעשות בם . . . ז . . . ואל יידיעהו איש את

המשפטים עד עמדו לפני המבקר . א . יתפתה בו בדרשו אתו

וכאשר יקים אותו עליו לשוב אל תורת משה בכל לב ובכל נפש

. . . ים . . ממנו אם ר . . . ל . .   וכל אשר נגלה מן התורה לריב

. ש . . בו . . . . . המבקר אותו וצוה עליו וי . . .

15 בד . . . מים . . לפ . . ע . . המתו א . . . ה ומשוגע וכל . .

וכא . . ל . . עד . . . אל

בת

20

עמכם ברית ועם כל ישראל על כן יקום האיש על נפשך לשוב אל

תורת משה כי בה הכל מדוקדק　　　ופרוש קציהם לעורון

ישראל מכל אלה הנה הוא מדוקדק על ספר מחלקות העתים

ליובליהם ובשבועותיהם וביום אשר יקום האיש על נפשו לשוב

5 אל תורת משה יסור מלאך המשטמה מאחריו אם יקים את דבריו

על כן נימול אברהם ביום דעתו　　　ואשר אמר מוצא שפתיך

תשמור להקים　　　כל שבועת אסר אשר יקום איש על נפשו

לעשות דבר מן התורה עד מחיר מות אל יפדהו　　　כל אשר

. . . . איש על נפשו ל . . . .　　　עד מחיר מות אל יקימהו

10 . . . שבועת האשה אשר אמ . . . שה להניא את שבועתה אל

יניא איש שבועה אשר לא . דע . . דם להקים הוא　　　ואם להניא

אם לעבור ברית הוא יניאה ואל יקימנה　　　וכן המשפט לאביה

על משפט ה . . . ות אל ידור איש למזבח מאום אנום וגם

. . הנים אל יקחו מאת ישראל . . . . יקדש איש את מאכל

15 . . . ל . י הוא אשר אמר איש את ע . דו . . ו חרם　　ואל

יק . . . . מכל . . . .　. . . . . . . אחזתו

. קדש . . . .　. . . . . . . יענש

הנודר . . . .　. . . . .

לשופט . . . .　. . . . .

. . . . 20

　　＊　　　＊　　　＊　　　＊　　　＊　　　＊　　　＊　　　＊

Fragment—Text B.

נאמנות להם לחיותם לאלפי דורות :   כב שומר הברית והחסד
לאהֲב ולשמרי מצוֹתי לאֶלֶף דור :   ואם מחנות יֵשֽבֽוּ כֵּחֹקי
הארץ אשר היה מקדם ולקחו נשים במנהג התורה והולידו בנים
ויתהלכו על פי התורה :   וכמשפט היסודים כסרך התורה
5 כאשר אמַר בֽ"ו איש לאשתו ובין אב לבנו וכל המאסים במצות
ובחקים להשיב גמול רשעים עליהם בפקד אל את הארֶץ
בבוא הדבר אשר כתוב ביד זכריה הנביא חרב עורי על
רועי ועל גבר עמיתי נאם אֵ הך את הרעה ותפוצינה הצאן
והשיבותי ידי על הצוערים :   והשומרים אותו הם עניי הצאן
10 אלה ימלטו בקץ הפקדה והנשארים ימסרו לחרב בבוא משיח
אהרן וישראל :   כאשר היה בקץ פקדת הראשון אשר אמר יחזקֵּא
ביד יחזקאל וההתוֽ להתות התיו על מצחות נאנחים ונאנקים
והנשארים הֹסֽגרוֹ לחרב נוקמת נקם ברית :   וכן משפט לכל באי
בריתו אשר לא יחזיקו באלה החקים לפקדם לכלה ביד בליעל
15 הוא היום אשר יפקֹד אֵ כַּאֽשֶֽׁר דֺבֺֽר אֵ היו שרי יהודה כמשיגי
גבול עליהם אשפך כמים עברה :   כי באו בברית תשובה
ולא סרו מדרך בוגדים ויתעללו בדרכי זנות ובהון הרשעה
ונקום ונטור איש לאחיהו וֽשֽנֹֽא איש את רעהו ויתעלמו איש
בשאר בשרו ויגשו לזמה ויתגברו להון ולבצע ויעשו את
20 איש הישר בעיניו ויבחרו איש בשרירות לבו ולֹא נזרו מעם
ומחטאתם :   ויפרעו ביד רמה ללכת בדרכי רשעים :   אשר
אמר אֵ עליהם חמת תנינים יינם וראש פתנים אכזר :   התנינים
מלכי העמים וײנם הוא דרכיהם וראש פתנים הוא ראש
מלכי יון הבא עליהם לנקם נקמה ובכל אלה לא הבינו בוני
25 החיץ וטחי תפל כי הולך רוח ושקל מֹוֽפֽﬡ סֹופות ומטיף אדם
לכזב אשר חרה אף אל בכל עדתו :   ואשר אמר משה
לישראל לא בצדקתך וביושר לבבך אתה בא לרשת את הגוים
האלה כי מאהבתו את אבותיך ומשמרו את השבועה :   כן
משפט לשבי ישראל סרו מדרך העם באהבת אל את הראשנים
30 אשר העידו על העם אחרי אֵ ואהב את הבאים אחריהם כי להם
ברית אבות   ושונא ומתעב אֵ את בוני החיץ וחרה אﬡ אפו בם ובכל
ההלכים אחריהם וכמשפט הזה לכל המאס במצות אֵ
ויעזבם ויפנו בשרירות לבם כן כל האנשים אשר באו בברית
החדשה בארץ דמשק וֽשֽבֽוּ וֽיֽבֽגֽדֽו ויסורו מבאר מים החיים :
35 ל . יֵֽחֽשֽבֽוּ בסוד עם ובכתבם לֹא יֵֽכֽתֽבֽוּ מיום הֵֽאֹֽסﬡ יֺוֽﬧ מורה

מורה היחיד עד עמוד משיח מאהרן ומישראל   וכן המשפט
לכל באי עדת אנשי תמים הַקֹדֶש וִיקֹוץ מעשות פקודי ישרים
הוא האיש הנתך בתוך כור :   בהופע מעשיו יִשָׁלַח מעדה
כמו שלא נפל גורלו בתוך למודי אל כפי מעלו יַה יזכירווהו אנשי

5   מעוט עד יום ישוב לעמד במעמד אנשי תמים קדש אֲשֶׁר אֵין
גֹורלֹו בֹתֹוֹך ובהופע מעשיו כפי מדרש התורה אשר יתהלכו
בו אנשי תמים הקדש אל יַת יֵאֹות איש עמו בהון ובעבודה
כי אֹרֹרֹוּהֹו כל קדושי עליון וכמשפט הזה לכל המאס בראשונים
ובאחרונים אשר שמו גלולים על לבם וִיֹשֹׂימוּ וילכו בשרירות

10   לבם אין להם חלק בבית התורה :   כמשפט רעיהם אשר שבו
עם אנשי הלצון יִשָׁפֹטֹו כי דברו תועה על חקי הצדק ומאסו
בברית ואמנה אשר קימו בארץ דמשק והוא ברית החדשה :
ולא יהיה להם ולמשפחותיהם חלק בבית התורה   ומיום
האסף יורֹיֹה היחיד עד תם כל אנשי המלחמה אשר הלכו

15   עם איש הכזב כשנים ארבעים :   ובקץ ההוא יחרה
אף אל בישראל כאשר אמר אין   מלך ואין שר ואין שופט ואין
מוכיח בצדק ושבי פשע י...שמרו ברית אל אז...נד...איש
אל רֹעֹ..ל...ן...אַחֹיֹו את אחיו יתמך צעדם בדרך אל ויקשב
אֵל אל דבריהם וישמע ויכתב ספר זכרן..ליראי אל לחושבי

20   שמו . עד יֵֹעֹלֶהֹ ישע וצדקה ליראי אל ושבתם וראיתם בין צדיק
ורשע בין עבד . ל לאשר לא עבדו :   ועשה חסד ..לאוהביו
ולשמריו לאלֶף דור :   מביתפלנ אשר יצאו מעיר הקדש :
וישענו על אל בקץ מעל ישראל וטמאו את המקדש ושבו עד
אל :   נסיך העם בדברים מעט...לם   לפי רוחו יִשָׁפֹטֹו בעצת

25   קדש :   וכל אשר פרצו את גבול התורה מבאי הברית בהופע
כבוד אל לישראל יכרתו מקרב המחנה ועמהם כל מרשיעי
יהודה בימי מצרפותיו   וכל המחזיקים במשפטים האלה לצאת
ולבוא על פי התורה וישמעו לקול מורה ויתודו לפני אל ..אנו
רשענו יַם..אנחנו גם אבותינו בלכתם קרי בחקי הברית

30   ואמת משפטיך בנו :   ולא ירימו יד על חקי קדשו ומשפט
צדקו ועדוות אמתו :   והתיסרו במשפטים הראשונים אשר
נשפטו בני אנשי היחיד והאזינו לקול מורה צדק :   ולא ישיבו
אל חקי הצדק בשמעם אֹתֹם ישישו וישמחו ויעז לבם ויתגברו
על כל בני תבל וכפר אל בעדם וראו בישועתו כי חסו בשם קדשו

T-S. 10 K 6

1 ..ועתה שמעו כל יודעי צדק ובינו במעשי
אל כי ריב לו עם כל בשר ומשפט יעשה בכל מנאצו
כי במעלם אשר עזבוהו הסתיר פנו מישראל וממקדשו
ויתנם לחרב ובזכרו ברית ראשנים השאיר שאירית
לישראל ולא נתנם לכלה ובקץ חרון שנים שלש מאות
ותשעים לתיתו אותם ביד נבוכדנאצר מלך בבל
פקדם ויצמח מישראל ומאהרן שורש מטעת לירוש
את ארצו ולדשן בטוב אדמתו ויבינו בעונם וידעו כי
אנשים אשמים הם ויהיו כעורים וכמגששים דרך
שנים עשרים ויבן אל אל מעשיהם כי בלב שלם דרשוהו
ויקם להם מורה צדק להדריכם בדרך לבו וידע
לדורות אחרונים את אשר עשה בדור אחרון בעדת בוגדים
הם סרי דרך היא העת אשר היה כתוב עליה כפרה סוררה
כן סרר ישראל בעמוד איש הלצון אשר הטיף לישראל
מימי כזב ויתעם בתוהו לא דרך להשח גבהות עולם ולסור
מנתיבות צדק ולסיע גבול אשר גבלו ראשנים בנחלתם למען
הדבק בהם את אלות בריתו להסגירם לחרב נקמת נקם
ברית בעבור אשר דרשו בחלקות ויבחרו במהתלות ויצפו
לפרצות ויבחרו בטוב הצואר ויצדיקו רשע וירשיעו צדיק
ויעברו ברית ויפרו חוק ויגודו על נפש צדיק וכל הולכי
תמים תעבה נפשם וירדפום לחרב ויסיסו לריב עם ויחר אף

Facsimile of page 1.   Text A

(119)

Fragment—Text A.

DOCUMENTS OF JEWISH SECTARIES

VOLUME II

קונטרסים מספר המצות לענן

FRAGMENTS OF THE BOOK OF THE COMMANDMENTS BY ANAN

EDITED

FROM HEBREW MANUSCRIPTS IN THE CAIRO GENIZAH COLLECTION
NOW IN THE POSSESSION OF THE UNIVERSITY
LIBRARY, CAMBRIDGE

AND PROVIDED WITH

A SHORT INTRODUCTION AND NOTES

BY

S. SCHECHTER, M.A., Litt.D. (Cantab.)

President of the Jewish Theological Seminary of America in New York

CONTENTS

INTRODUCTION

THE matter published in this volume under the title of קונטרסים מספר המצות לענן (The Fragments of the Book of the Commandments by Anan) represents four different manuscripts, marked as *A, B, C,* and *D.* They bear class-marks T-S.16.359—365 MS. A; T-S.16.366 MS. B; T-S.16.367*a* MS. C; T-S.16.367*b* MS. D.

A, extending from page 3 to page 29, consists of 14 leaves or 28 pages, the last page of which is blank. Each leaf measures in full $9\frac{1}{2} \times 7\frac{1}{2}$ inches, but, unfortunately, we have only one or two complete leaves, nearly all the rest being mutilated and torn off at the edges, or at the bottom, as indicated by dots. The writing is inclined towards cursive, and there is a strong resemblance between it and the writing of the manuscripts of the Genizah fragments published by Dr A. Harkavy in his *Studien und Mittheilungen*, part 8 (לקוטי קדמוניות 2nd part, St Petersburg, 1903). I suspect gaps between several leaves, and certainly there are gaps at the end of pages 22, 24, 26 and 28. I had great doubts even as to the sequence of the leaves, as they were found at various times and scattered over a large area of the Genizah; I consulted Dr Poznanski on this point, but, unfortunately, his letter was lost.

B, extending over pages 30 to 32, consists of two leaves or four pages, one page of which is blank. They are only remainders of leaves, but what remain measure $6\frac{3}{4} \times 5\frac{1}{2}$ and $7\frac{1}{4} \times 5$ inches respectively. The writing is in square characters, very ancient, hanging from ruled lines. A special peculiarity in it is the fact that the Tetragrammaton is written in full, which is a rare occurrence.

C, extending over pages 33 and 34, consists of one leaf or two pages. It is likewise the remainder of a leaf, but what remains forms the bottom of the leaf and measures $4\frac{3}{4} \times 4\frac{3}{4}$ inches. The writing is in ancient square characters and has some similarity with MS 3 in Dr Harkavy's publication.

D, extending over pages 35 and 36, consists of one leaf or two pages. It measures $9\frac{3}{8} \times 7\frac{1}{4}$ inches. The writing is in square characters, fairly ancient.

The last few pages of this volume are taken up by references to the Scriptures. (The reference for p. 3, ll. 10—16, to Lev. **29** should read Lev. **27**.) These fragments are certainly in need of a commentary, but this task must be left to specialists such as Dr Poznanski, who, I hope, will soon furnish us with the necessary explanation to the contents of these fragments as well as with an essay bearing on their relation to the works of other early Karaitic writers.

S. SCHECHTER.

New York,
June 1910.

4

. . . . תין .

. . . . מעשר בקר . . . . מי חב .

פניה קדשו לא . . . . חלופיה ואי מה

כל מעשר לבר מן בקר וצאן מן דפריק מיניה יהיב . . . .

5 . . . דכֿ ואם גאל יגאל וגֿ ואם גאל יגאל בתרין לישני לאדעך

. . י למפרק מיניה קאים לאפוקי מעשר דבקר וצאן דלא שרי

. . . א איש אמאי אשה היכא דאית לה ממונא אי זרעא מאי

. . . והלי והבכל מילי מחיבין במעשר כי היכן דפרישנן אילא

. . . נא דארעא קאים בלשון איש לאדעך דאשה לא

10 . . . לק בארעא אבל היכא דאית לה מידי מחיבא למיתן מעשר

. . . ואמא ממעשרו דמן מעשר דיליה הוא דאיפריק מיניה יהיב

. . וה אבל קא באעי למיזבן מלוי מידי ממעשר דאחריני כד

. . . צריך טפויי חומשיה ובהמה טמאה נמי ועבדים מחיבין

כל אשר תתן לי וכֿת ויפרץ האיש מאד מאד וגֿ והם כי דומיא

15 . . . ד דבקר וצאן מפריש מעשר דבהמה טמאה ועבדים דכֿ וממחצית

. . אחוז מן החמשים מן האֿ מן הבֿ מן החֿ ומן הצֿא מכל הבהמה

. . לאפרשותא דקדש מן אדם ומן בהמה טהורה ומן . . . . אה

. . אחוז מן החמשים קא אמא בהון אף אפרשתיהו לכ . . . . הו

. . אי בעי מיפרק מן עבדים או מן בהמה טמאה דמ . . . ו . . ליה

20 . . . ומוסיף חומשיה עליה ופריק ליה דכֿ אף בבור אשר יבכר

. . . טמאה ופֿ בעֿ ויסף חמש עליו מה ההו דגבי שור ושה לא

. . . דגבי טמאה קא אמא דנוסיף חומשיה על פורקניה ומפ . . .

. . . . . בקר דקמא לא צריכת לאקדושיה גבי בהמה טמאה . . .

. . . . פורקניה ופריק ליה׳ ואף עבדי נמי כי גונא דבהמה טמא

. . כל את . . דכֿ ואם כל בהמה טמאה אשר לא יקריבו . .

25 . . . . קא אמא בהמה טמאה לא ידעינן דלא למקרב מינה . . . .

. . . ים דכֿ . . . . די הו בר איקרובי מיניה קורבן הוא . . .

לֵוִי .

מֵעַ

כִּי .. שׁ ‏ ‏ ה

5   התם דע ‏ ‏ ם כתב כל מעשר ביש

דעל מעשר ‏ ‏ כולהן ישראל קאים והיכ

יש אית להון ארעא דב והתנחלתם את הארץ בגורל ..מ

מעשר דלא קביעא נמי קאים דב הביאו את כל המעשר ו ..

כייל ליה לכל מעשר ואפילו מעשר דלא קביעא וקא אמא

10   לכל דפלח בביתי בין לויים ובין יש ‏ ובארץ יש מפרשינן מ

ב ב מעשר חד מעשר ללוים וחד מעשר אכלין ליה מ

דב עשר תעשר וג ואכלת לפני יי אהיך ב א יב לשכן ש

מעשר יש אכלין ליה קא אמא ואכלת לפני יי אהיך והלא מע

דב ולבני לוי אילא על תנין מעשר קאים מישום האכי אקד

15   בתרין לישאני לאפרושי תרין מעשר חד מעשר ללוים וחד מעש

בעלים בבית המקדש כי היכן דאמרן וקא אמא את כל תבא

זרעים ופירות הוא דמפרשינן תרין תרין מעשר ולאו מן בהמה וכ

דומייהו וקא אמא היצא השדה דאי אית ליה לאיניש גינאי א

מיחייב בתרין מעשר וקא אמא שנה שנה ולא אמא שנה בש

20   ראזים בכל שתא ... מחיבינן לעשורי כל דאית לן והכא ..

או מ.. דאשתני מן היכן דהוה כד איעשר אבל מידי דאית ..

איתחלף מן היכן דהוה כד איעשר ואף על גב דינט ...ה ..

לא צריך עישוריה דכל מידי חדא זימנא הו דמחייב עיש

אעשרנו לך דגבי יעקוב לאו כי האי עשר תעשר ..בהא .

25   וכל אשר תתן לי קא אמא מישום דכל מידי..ל .

אמא עשר אעשרנו האכי קא אמא כב .

דמתבעי ‏ לעשוריה כי דפריש במידי מידי אבל ה..ת .

זרעים ‏ ופירות קאים דקא אמא תבואת .

יתור הוא ‏ ולהאכי אייתי לא

30   מעשר כי היכן דפרשן .

אפרשנון לקמיה בין דאדם ובין

קא אמא קדש לי דבעיתו לאפרוש

. . . .

יב . . . .

. . . .

. . . . . . אמא א . . . . . .

באדם . . . ה דאקדים כתב 5

יה דכת . . . . דמודרע ביני יש לא

ה. וכת כל הבכור ..מא לי הוא ואף על גב דלא מקדש

הז ת ליי אהיך קא אמא אשר יולד לאדעך דעל בכור

תלודי ביני יש קאים ולאו דמודרע אזדרועי וקא אמא

אהיך דצריכת לאקדושיה וקא אמא בתריה לפני י' אהיך 10

לך דהאיי בכור דאיתלודי הוא דאיתליד ביני יש ולאו

רע ביני יש מרואתיה נאכלוה בבית המקדש שנה בשנ

א מיבעי משבקיה משתא לשתא וכת אך בכור אשר

מא אשר יבכר ל בבהמ לאדעך דעל בכור דמן כד אזדרע

תא קאים והינו בכור דמודרע אזדרועי ביני יש וקא אמא 15

ש אתן דלא צריך אקדושיה וכת כל פטר רחם לכל בשר

א אמא באדם ובבהמה יהיה לך קא אמא לך דבכד מודרע

יש לכהן יהבינן ליה והאיי דקא אמא באדם בישרא היכא

ו באדם דלאו ביני יש מיזדרע דיכא בכור דגיורת

שהיא מעוברת דגר נמי כישרא . . . . דכ כאזרח מכם 20

וקא אמא אך פדה תפדה ההוא פדיה בא . . . .

ש למפירקיה לבכור ומאן דלא פריק מ ..א . . . .

שב הוא למיפרק נפשיה וקא אמא את בכור הבהמה . . .

שי ..דבהמה לאו דרכה למפרק הי נפשה אמא בה

דמחיבת למיפירקה לבהמה וקא אמא 25

בא . . . ב . . . ופדיו מבן חדש תפדה

ש חדש על . . ק ליה למפירקיה טפי ביה הי

מיקמי דלהוי בר ח יומי

כר באדם וביום הש ימול

ל ..מה בהמה עד יום 30

עד יום שמיני לא אית ביה

ביד האוי בר ח יומי ולא מיחשב

‫בב . . . . התם ה . . . . כה ב‬

‫לא כ . . . . בת יומיה ק.טיל מש‬

‫יומיה . . . . ואי יהיב מומא בגוה יה.‬

‫5 כאשר יתן . . . . אמא באדם ולא טפי ביה הי‬

‫באדם אפילו . . . . יהבינן ביה כואתיה ואפילו מ‬

‫ואפילא לה ואידיעא או זכר או נקבה אפילא לה ים‬

‫ואם אסון יהיה וג' אבל הכא אמא בכור הבהמה טפ‬

‫דהאוי בר ח' יומי לא פריק ליה הטמאה טפי ביה הי מ‬

‫10 חמור תפדה בשה טפי האכא הי לאדעך דעל כל ב‬

‫והאיי דפרט התם בחמור מישום דכל בהמה טמאה‬

‫דכת שורך וחמרך וכל בהמתך אמא מבהמה טהור‬

‫טמאה חמור ואמא בתריה וכל בהמתך בّاﻟّה לבהמ‬

‫שור ולבהמה טמאה בהדי חמור ומישום האכי כת וכל ב‬

‫15 לאדעך דעל כל פטר רחם דבהמה טמאה קאים ואף בכור‬

‫ובכור דשבי ובכור דגירת בעונן למפרקנון דכ הכא‬

‫את בכור האדם וכת התם והכיתי כל בכור מה אדם‬

‫אית ביה בכור האכא . . . בכור שבי דכת עד בכור השפחה‬

‫התם . . . . ע . . . השבי אשר בבית הבור אף‬

‫20 אית . . . בכור דשפחה ובכור דשבי וכת כי לי כל בכ‬

‫בא מّ הّק לי כל בכור ביש קא אמא לך כי היכן דפרי‬

‫האכן דקדיש לקמי בכרי דישרا בכרי דישראל הולכך בעונן למשק‬

‫ולבכור דשבי ובכור דיש פריק ליה בחמשה מיש‬

‫מה יש דשויה לערך דיליה נ' מתקלי דכ מתקלי דכ ביה‬

‫25 עשרים ש' וגו פריון דבכור דיליה שויה ה'‬

‫לערך דיליה ל' מתקלי דכ אם עבד יגח השור‬

‫מתקלי הוא ומתקלא כ' קיראטי האוי דכ ע‬

‫אלמא דבעלמא האכי איתיה למתקלא וב‬

‫כ' קירטי חשבין ליה ומן ידא דבכור ש . . ע‬

‫30 בכור בני יש לקח את הכסף קא אמא א . . הכ‬

‫מّצא‬

דכ . . . . . . ואילא . . . איל .

ך דעל . . . ק וערפתו . . מור

. . . טמאה קאים וקא אמא . . . . . .

ניכסיה : . . . . ואם לא תפדה וערפתו דא . . . . .

5 . פרקים וכד . . . בנחלא דלא אתו ביה מיא . . . . .

. . . ו ביה מיא נפישי דב הכא וערפתו וכת' התם וערפו שם

. . . ההי עריפא דעגלה בנחל ואף הא עריפא דחמור בנחל

. . . עגלה בנחל דאתו ביה מיא נפישי דב ביה אל נחל איתן

. . . עגלא בנחלא דלא וישב הים לפנות בקר לאיתנו אף הי

10 . . . לא דאתו ביה מיא נפישי מה ההי עריפה דעגלה בנחלא

. . . בגויה כי היכין דלא מזדרע זרעא עליה דב אשר לא

. . . רע אף הא עריפא דחמור בנחלא דלא מעכבי מיא

. . . דלא מיזדרע זרעא עליה אבל רחיצת ידים דכתיבה בעגלה

. . . ינן מיניה מידי לעריפא דחמור דב ברחיצה דעריפה

15 . . . שפכה את הדם הזה ובכור דבהמה טמאה דמזדרע

. . . . א אית ליה כהן ופריק ליה מריה בפורסניה וטפי

. . . . א . . פריק ליה מריה מזדבן בפורסניה דב על

. . . מה טמאה וגו האיך א . . . . . הוא איתליד . . בני

. . . . ד חמור ופטר לי שנא . . . . תלודי

20 . . . . . . אמא ביה ואם בבהמה ה . . . . . .

. . . . בבהמה הוא והאיך דאיתלודי א . . . . . .

. . . . . . ופורקניה בעלים אכלין ליה בבית

. . . . . . זדרועי אזדרע בני יש לא צריך אקדושיה

. . . . שלא ליה וכן בכור דשפחה ובכור דשבי ובכור

25 . . . . . א דאיתליד בני יש צריכי אקדושנן

. . . . ליה בבית המקדש וכל דאזדרועי

. . . . בי אקדושנן ופורקנהו כהן שקיל ליה

. . . . ור בבהמה טהורה בתמניה יומי האכי

. . . . ט . . . . בתמניה יומי וכי היכין דמיפריק

. . . . עליה וכֿ

. . . . . מיפריק . . . כור דשבי ובכור דגירת . . . .

. . . עליהון . . . . קנהון מן ידיהון דכֿ באדם ובֿ . . .

. . לבכור דא . . . י הדאדי למיגמר מיהדדי וכליה ל . . .

5 . . . . הדדי למיג . . . מיהדדי ומאי דפריש בהאי לא

. . . גמרינן אדם מאדם ובהמה מבהמת ואי אמרת . . .

. . . חדש בר ירחא דיומי קא אמא אי האכי חו . . .

. . . קא כתיב כי דכֿ התם עד חדש ימים אבל האכֿ . . .

. . . . כתב ימים לאדעך דעל חֹדֶשׁ חֲדָתָא ימים קאים וכו . . .

10 . . . שׂ דמיזדרע ביני יש אף כי אית ביה מומא כהן שי . . .

. . . . . . יהיה לך וגו קא אמא ובשרם וקא אמא כחזה . . .

. . . . קא ראזים לאשוינהו לבוכרי לחזה התנופה וש . . .

. . . כֿ ביה מומא אשויה לחזה התנופה מה חזה התנופה . . .

. . אף אכלין ליה כי הדדי דכֿ והיה החזה לאהרן ולבניו

15 . . אֿ ביה מומא כולהון אכלין ליה כיהדאדי ובכור דלא . . .

. . . . . אשויה לשוק דאמי דתרויהו אית ביה זריק

. . . . דכֿ ליה אכיל . . . ל . . . מֿ דם כהן דזריק . . .

. . . . כהן מומא ביה אית דלא בכור אף

. . . . קא מֿ לכהן יהיה לך אמא ודקא . . .

20 . . ח . . קדש . . איכא דלא והידנא דפרישנן . . . .

. . . דמתלודין אתלודי ביני יֹשׂ ולא אית בהן מום . . . .

. . . . בכור דשפחה ודשבי ודגירת ופודהו כבכ . . .

. . . . . דאית ביה מומא ובין דלא אית ביה מומא ד . . .

. . . . . . יֹשׂ דחזי למיכלנון בעלים בבית המקדש . . .

25 . . . בין דלא אית בהן מומא דמיתיהבין לכהן ובין . . .

. . . . . . עֿ אילין דמזבנין ומתעביד בדמיהון . . .

. . . . ש בקדשים וכי ירבה ממך הדרך כי לא תוכל . . .

אֿ לא . . . כי לקדשים לזבוננון שארי דכא כיון

. . . מ . . . . יכא בית המקדש . . . . .

. . . א נמי . . . . . הון בעבידתא דבית כניש

. . י' קרבן ת . . . . ה קורבן נמי לבית כנישתא . .

. . הכסף דכֹ לי . . . כידהב נמי וכספא אצֹ זהֹ כלי א

עבורא חדתא . . . וכד בעינן למיכל לחמא

אשר האֹרץ אל בבאכם דכֹ אכלינן והדר לכהן . . . .

וגֹ ערסתיכם מראשית וגֹ ערסתיכם ראשית וגֹ כם . .

אל תבאו כי קרבן גבי וכֹת וגֹ הארץ אל בבאכם לה . .

בין מפרשינן דחלה לאדעך אשה ועשיתם גֹ . . .

בארץ אילא מקרבינן לא וקרבן אחריתי ארעא . . . .

קא האכי שמה אתכם מביא אני אשר הארץ ת . . .

ישרֹ בארץ דבין לאשמועך לכון דממטֹנא רעא . . .

משבתיכם ארץ כתיב קרבן וגבי אמא קא . . תי א א . .

דקא יֹשֹ דבארץ לאשמועך לכון יהיבנא דקא לארעא . .

בבאכם דאמא בתר הֹא מֹל באכלכם . . . . אמא קא . .

לכון ממטינא . . לארעא עיליתו כד אמא קא האכא . . .

אפרישו חדתא עבורא ביה למיכל דבעיתו מא . . . .

חלה אפרישו . . עומר דביום

הֹ . . . . כתב לא הזה עֹהֹ עֹ ת' לֹ וכרֹ וקלֹ לחם כֹת אמר . .

האכי חלה מפרשת כד חדתא א . . . ל למיכל דבעיתו . . .

אמא וקא חלה אפרישו מיכלכון כי בה לך אמא . . .

משערי חלה בראשא אפרושי בעונן וכרמל דקלֹ . .

אנֹ מיכל והדר קליא ודלא דקליֹא מחיטֹ . . . .

וקֹ מֹצ מֹה הארץ מעבור ויֹאכלו דכֹת . . עֹם ת . . הנֹ

ממחרת אמא דקא לה אפינן ומצה . . מפרשֹ

דאכלינן הוא ומצות אכלינן ֹדשערי קמא

ראזים קא זמני תרתֹין לתרומה כתבה . . . . . .

דחיטי לחמא למיכל בעונן כד מחיטי כל . . . . . .

דקא אמ . א דחיטי נמי אקר . . . .
יקא אמא . ם . וקא אמא מראשית ערם ב . . . .
ומלישיה להו . . . ש תוב לדילן בתריה מן ההן קמחא א . . .
קמחא דחלה . . . א לה חלה ראשית ומראשית וקא קרו לה . . .
5 לאפרושי חלה תרין עמרי דכֿ האכא חלה וכֿת התם שני . . .
האחת ועשרון עמר הוא דכֿ והעמר עשירת גֿ וקא אמא ת . . .
תרין זמני קא ראזים דכי היכי דמפרשת חלה דשערי בתח . . .
ביום הנפֿת עמר דכֿ ביה והבאתם את עמר וֿג האכי אפריש . . .
בתחלת הצדא דחיטי ביום חג שבעות דכֿת ביה וחג שב . . .
10 וקא אמא כתרומת גרן מה גרן חדא זימנא דמפרשים מיניה . . .
חדא זימנא דמפרשינן לה בשתא ולאו כל אימת דאביתו ל . .
תתנו לייי תרו לדר : דחלה בעלים בעי מיתנה לכהן ולא . . .
דחיטי חמץ אפונן לה ובתרין כוכי אפונן לה דכֿ ממנ . . .
קא אמא בכורים לייי וחלה נמי בכורים הוא וחלה דשערי א . . .
15 כוכי דכֿ ואיש בא מבעל שלשה ויבא לאיש האלהים לחם . . .
וקא אמא לחם וחלה נמי בכורים היא בין חלה דחיטי ובין חלה דשערי
דלחמא דקמחא מפקונן להו דכֿ מכל חלבו את מק מֿמ וש . . .
כי הדרי מפקינן ליהו בין חלה דחיטי ובין חלה דשערי . . .
ושיעורא דחלה בֿ עומרי כי היכי דפרישנן ולהאכי אש . . .
20 חלה אחת לאדעך דעל שיעורא . . . ל . קא מפקיד . . .
והאיי דאפינן לה בֿחֿד בֿוֿבֿא מיש . . דאמח . . לשו . . .
הוה קא אמא הוה כאתיב קמֿ . . אות . . אל . . מעוב . . .
דחלה דקא קרי לה לערבתא דמישחא בה . . קמחא . . .
ההין לרם את הסלת וקא קרי ליה לֿלישא . . . חלה . . .
25 האיי רם דלאו רם הוא רם הוא דמרים במיא . . . . .
במישחא וכי היכין דאסיר לן למיכל מן לחמא . . . לא . .
חלה דשערי האכי אסיר לן מן לחמא . . . . . .
לחמא דחיטי דכֿ תרימו תרומה דתרויהו קא . . . . .
ובעונן מיתן ראשית מכל מידי לכהן בכור . . . . .

2—2

וכל תרומת כל . . . . . יה וראשית . . . . . .

כהן להניח ברכה אל ביתך: קא . . . דבעינן למיתן . . . .

מילי בין מן אכלין ובין מן מילי אה . . . . וקא אמא בכורי . . . .

הוא דבעינן למיתן ליה ראשית דכל הינו . . . ראשית דבכרים . . . .

5 . . . . . קלי ובין מן בהילא דבכורים לאו מידי דא . . תעורי הוא אבל

דממונא ובין

. . . ר בין דאוכלין ובין דבהמה ודכל מידי דמחייב במעשר לא

שות עד דמלא מאה דב לתרומת ולראשית ולמעשרות לכנוס בהם . . .

מנאות התודה לכהנים וללוים קא אמא לראשית לישאנא דחד . . .

דיה ולמעשרות לשאנא דתרין לאדעך דלא בעי למיתן ראשית . . .

10 . . . מלי למישקל מיניה תרין מעשר מעשר דלוים ומעשר

. . . ים והינו מאה דשקלין לוים מיניה מעשר עשרה ויהבין

. . . מעשר חד הולכך יהבינן ראשית מן דהבא ומן כספא

. . . דמאלי מאה מתקלי יהבינן מיניה חד מתקלא ומן חיטי ומן

. . . ן מאי דמאלי מאה אפות יהבינן מיניה חדא איפה ומן חמרא

15 . . . הון מאי דמאלי מאה בתים יהבינן מיניה חדא בת ומן כיתנא

. . . . מאי דמאלי מאה מני יהבינן מיניה חד מניא ומן בהמה

. . . מאה מיינא יהבינן מיניה חד דדהבא וכספא במתקלי

. . . . איפות מיכאלי וכיתאנא ועמרא במני מתקלי ובהמה

. . . ראשית מפקינן לה בראשא ומנונן לה בהדי מינינא

20 . . . מן מאי דחלי עשר ומנונן ה . . כא . . לין מתקלי וכילי

. . . . . מעשר והיכא דנפיש מן מאה בין מתקלי

. . . יא . . א . . אר . . דמפקינן מיניה ראשית אילא חדי דלא

. . . ת נקבל מידי ומידי אילא חד ראשית איפה

. . . א והעמד עש ג גבת כי איפה היא דכ האיפה

25 . . . . ומניא שיתין מתקלי האוי במתקלא בר עשרין

. . . עשרים גרה עשרים שקלים חמשה ועשרים שקלים

. . . המנה יהיה לכם: ודקא אמא וכל תרומת כל מכל

. . . א . עה לוים קאים דבעו אפרושי ראשית ומעשר

. . . דמפרשי יש דקא אמא תרומת כל תרומה

30 . . . כת כן תרימו גם אתם וג עד יש : ומעשר נמי

. . . . . מעשר בני יש עד תרומ ואף כל מתנות דשקלין

מן יש מפרשין מיניה ראשית ומעשר דכׄ מכל מתנו . . . .

מתנות אחרניאתא וקא אמא תרימו את כל תרומת יי׳ דמחיבי ב . . .

ודקא אמא וראשית ערסתיכם תתנו לכהן בתר דאמא ליה תפׄ . . .

לאגמורי דמחיבין לויים למיתן חלה כישראל ואמא בראשית . ל . . .

5 יהיה ובעריסתיכם אמא תתנו לכהן דראשית ובכורים אימ . והב . . א . .

ידי שליח לא נפקא מיניה וחלה בעלים יהבין ליה לכהן כי היכין ד . . שנ . . .

ומדחייבינון ללוים למיתן חלה כל בכורים נמי יהבין דחלה מן בכורים חשיב . .

דכׄת לחם בכורים ולהכי כתב תרימו את כל תרומת יי׳ לאיתויי חלה . . . .

דאי על ראשית ומעשר הוא דקא אמא הא כתב ליה מיקמי הא . . .

10 לכם תרומתכם וגׄ וכל גרן וכל יקב מחיבין בראשית ומעשר א . . א . .

כתב תרימו את כל תרומׄ יי׳ לחיבונן בחלה ובכורים ובכל תרומ . . .

אבל מיפרק בכרי דבניהו ואפרושי בכרי דבעירהו לא מחיבין דאינון ח . .

בכרי דישראל מפרישי ובעיריהו חלופי באכרי דבעירא ד . . . . לקהל

הלוים לי אני יי׳ וגׄ אבל אי מאטי להון אמתא ממעשר וילדה בכור . . .

15 ממעשר וילדי בכרי מחיבונן למיפרקנון ואפרשנון כישר . . . .

בוכרי ממתנות דקא שקלין מיׄש דכׄ מכל מתנתׄ עד י׳ ובוכ

ובכורים ומעשר מחיבין לאפרושי בין בארץ יׄש ובין בא . . .

דכל מתנות דכהנים תדירא מחיבין יׄש לאפרושנון ד . . .

הקדשים וגׄ קא . . . כל תרומות וקא אמא לחק עולם . . .

20 תרומות חק על יׄש דכׄ הכא ברית מלח עולם . . וכת . . .

לאדועך דמחיבין בתרומות כי מילה דכׄ ברית . . .

מלח וכל מעשר ומתנות דלוים בהדי מתנות דכהנים . . .

מישקל כהנים מן לויים מכל מתנותם ראשית . . . .

ולויים אכלין ליה למעשר בכול דוכתא טהורים דילה . . .

25 דכׄ ואכלתם אתו בכל וגׄ אבל כהנים לא אכלין לׄת . . .

במקום טהור וכל איניש טהור דכׄ כל טהור ב . . .

לא אכלין ליה אי לאו זכרים דכהנים ולא אכלין ליה . . .

דכׄ כל קרבנם לכל מנחתם וגׄ ובקדש הקדשים . . .

למיתן דמי חטאת ודמי אשם לכהנים דכׄ כסף . . .

30 הכא נמי יהבין להון מאן דאית עליה חט . . .

. . . . . . כל זכר ובבית כנישתא וכיון דדמי הוא דקא שקלין
ול . . . . כיהדדי אכלין ליה דכ בחטאת הכהן המחטא א יא וכת באשם
הכהן . . יכפר בו לו יהיה הולכך כי לא איכא המחטא אתה וכי לא איכא
. . . . בו כלהו כהני כיהדדי שקלין ליה כיכול כי תרומות והיכא דלא שכיח
5 כהן למיתן ליה תרומות ובכורים ובכורות ולא שכיח לוי למיתן ליה מעשר
. . . . . נן להון לכולהון ומזבנינו להון וממטינן להון לדמיהון ללוים ולכהנים
מה בקדשים וכי ירבה ממך הדרך כי לא תוכל שאתו וכת בהון ונתת בכסף
. . . . התם שרא לזבוני קדשים ואמטויי דמיהון כי לא מידרי ליה
. . . . אף כל היכא דאיכא קדשים מזבנין להון וממטונן דמיהון
10 . . . רו לן קדשים ודמי בכור דאית ביה מומא אכלין ליה כהנים
. . . . וטמאים בכל דוכתא דכ וכי יהיה בו מום וגו בשעריך תא
. . . . בכורות דאכלין ליה בעלים בבית המקדש כד לא אית להון מומא
. . . . ית בהון קא אמא דנכלוה טהורים וטמאים במתיהון אף
. . . . יהיב לכהן דכי לא אית ביה מומא מיקרב לקרבן והיכא
15 . . . . ומא אכיל ליה טמא וטהור דכהנים והשתא דלא מצא
. . . . א דקנינא ודתורי היכא דמתרמי דיהבין להון בכור
. . . . מומא דתורא או דקנינא מזבנין ליה ואכלין ליה לדמיה
. . . . כרים דכהנים בכל דוכתא אכלי דמי בכורים בהמה
. . . . יהבין לכהנים טהורים דכהנים אכלין ליה במקום טהור
20 . . . . רים דכת את בכור האדם ואת וג שויה לקדושיה
. . . . ם ודפריון בהמה טמאה כי הדאדי : ואסיר
. . . . מומא בבוכרא דכ וכי יהיה בו מום קא אמא וכי יהיה
. . . . אויי ביה מומא מנפשיה אלמא דאסיר לך לדילך
. . . . מומא וכל דלאו כהן הוא לא אכיל קדש ותותביה
25 . . . לא אכיל קדש דכ וכל זר לא יאכל קדש וג אבל
. . . . אכלין דכ וכהן כי יקנה נפש וג קא אמא ויליד ביתו
. . . . ל . . . . אינון ובניהון למיכל לחמא מן גביה
. . . . אב . אי סמיכין על מידעם אחרינא דלחמיהון לאו

מיגביה ודוא לא אכלין קדש ולהאכי דק כתב הם . . .

בלחמו דבין עבדא דזבין ליה מן שוקא ובין עבדא דמתי . . .

סמיכין על לחמיה דאכלין קדש וברתיה דכהן דהוא לגברא . . .

לא אכלא קודש דב ובת כהן כי תהיה לאיש וגו ובת כהן דהוא . . .

5 דמגרשא וברא וברתא לא אית לה והדרא לגבי אבות אכלא . . .

כהן כי תהיה אלמנה וג וכל דלאו בר קדש^{מיכל} הוא משתלי ואכיל קד . .

חומשיה עליה ויהיב ליה לכהן דב ואיש כי יאכל קדש בש . . .

דאמרנן דאכיל קדש בטהרה אכלין ובמקום טהור אכל . . .

דיחשבנון ולא יחללו את קדשי וג לאדעך דלא נכלו כולהון . . .

10 בטהרה: פקידינן רחמ למיתן פורקן נפשתן . . .

פלגיה דמתקלא כספא ומיתן תוב כל שתא פלגיה דמתק . .

דב כי תשא וג כוליה פיסקא קא אמא כי תשא וקא אמא . . .

נפשו ל בפ א דכל אימת דמימנו באע^ו למיתן פורקן נפש . . .

ולא יהיה בהם נגף בפ אתם קא ראזים דאילא יהבין פורקן . . .

15 האוי מיתנא בהן וקא אמא זה יתנו כל העבר על הפק מ . . .

דבעא למיתן פלגיה דמתקלא וקא אמא עשרים גרה . . .

מחיבין ק . . . א וקא האני אמא מחצ השקל תרומה לייי . . .

ב . מ . . ל . . . . . . כספא תרומה לייי בלא מו . .

. . ל . לא . . . . . לם ת . . . . . בה חלה דב בה תרומה

20 לאפרוש . . חלה אף מחצית השקל דב ביה תרומה . . .

שב . . לא מימננון פלגיה דמתקלא דא . . . בימים . .

מ . . ש האכי זה יתנו אילא להאכ . . תנא . . . . ומחצית . .

ותנא כתב בחדא . . . . העבר על וג . . . .

מפקיד לבר מן מי אפקיד למיתן כד מ . . . כת . .

25 הראש ויאמר לו מדוע לא דרש על הלוים . . . .

^{וכת ויתנו...}

עבר הא^להים והק ליש לאם להביא לייי את משאת משה . . .

במדבר קא מגמר לן דכל שתא בעינן נש . . . .

העשיר לא ירב וה ל ימע ממ הש כת . .

דתרויהו קאים דבין פלגיה^ד מתקלא הב . .

30 דיהבי כל שתא לא עתירא באעי טפ . . .

לכפר על נפֹש דהאי פלניה דמתקלא האוי כפרה על יֹש וכי ..

.. מימנא מבר עשרין שנין וכמא דסליק דיהיב פלניה דמתקלא ..

אי נמי מבר בֹ שנין וכמא דסליק דיהיב פלניה דמתקלא דכתב ..

.. שנה ומעֹ וֹג ופלניה דמתקלא דיהבין כד מימנא יֹש פסקון ליה

5 .... מתקלא ויהבין פלניה דֹב בקע לגלגלת וֹג קא אמא בקע ובקע

מיפסק הוא דֹב ונטה את ידך על הים ובקעהו וקא אמא לֹש ..

.. ושלשת וֹג לאדעך דיֹש הוא דיהבי ולא יהבין בהדיהון כהנים

אמא מקמיה וכסף פקודי העדה לאדעך דאמנויי אמנו ..

.. ה דמתקלא דיהבין כל שתא לאצריפין מיפיסקיה מיפסק

10 .. בין ליה ישראֹל וכהנים ולוים דֹב משאת משה עבד יֹיֹ

.. לישראֹל וקא אמא משאת ומשאת לישֹנא מליא הוא דֹב הרב

.. לותם משאת העשן מן העיר יֹוקא אמא והקהל ליֹש דיהבי אף

.. דֹב הכא והקהל וכֹת התם ושחטו אתו כל קהל עֹ יֹש

.. ל דפסח ישראֹל וכהנים ולוים מיחייבין בפסח אף האיֹי

15 .. שאת ישראֹל וכהנים ולוים מיחיבין למיתן וכֹת בתחלה איש

.. בסופא לכפר על נפשתיכם דבתחילה על יֹש לחודיהו

.. בפקוד אתם וניתן כפר בפקידה ישראֹל הוא דיהבין כי

.. כֹת בסופא על יֹש וכהנים ולו ... יֹם דֹב לכפר

.. וכפרים כהנים ולוים נמי ... כין בישראֹל דֹב ועל הכֹה

20 .. קא אמא ועל הכהנים טפי ביה הי רבי רחמנא

.. הנים ולוים וקא אמא ועל כל עם הק יכפר אף כד

.. מדכר בהדיהון כהנים ולוים .. לכך כל שתא יהבין

.. כל דהוה ליה בר בֹ שנין פלניה דמתקלא כספא

.. עה בתשרי מיקמי יומא דכיפורי בֹ יומי דֹב האכא

25 .. מאת בני יֹש וֹב התם ומאת עדת בני יֹש יקח

.. פלניה דמתקלֹא כסף כפורים כי היכין

.. ורים לאדעך דגבי יום הכפורים

.. ף מאת כי היכי דֹב בחטאת יום

לאדעך ... ם דמתפרשא חטאת דיום הכפרים

תרין יומי מיקמי יום כפורים דכל קורבן תרין יומי . . . . .

שלישי מיקרב אף האיי פלגיה דמתקלא יהבינן ליה מן . . . .

דכיפורי בׄ יומי וקא אמא ונתת אתו על עבׄ אׄ מועׄ דלא עׄ . .

אילא עבידתא דבית כנישתא וקא אמא והיה לבני ישׄ לׄ . . . .

5 וכתׄ ביום הכפורים יכפר עליכם לטהר וגׄ וכתׄ בתרוייהו כמ . .

בתרוויהו לפני ייׄ וכתׄ בהאיי פלגיה דמתקלא לזכרון לאדעך דל . .

פלגיה דמתקלא דוכרנא ליש קמי רחׄ לכפורי להון עונות . . .

ולדכינון לקמיה כיעבדת יום הכפרים וכל כסף דיהבינן לק . . .

ביני איקׄשׄי יהבינן דבׄ הכא שקל וכתׄ התם שקל כסף עב . . .

10 האיך שקיל כסף זוזי דסאגו הוא דבׄ ביה עבר לסחר אף . . . . .

כסף דהכא זוזי דסאגו הוא הולכך גמרינן דשרי למעב . . . .

ומתן בזוזי דסאגו ואף על גב דציר עליהון צורת בעלי ח . . . . . .

וכן פשיטי דבׄ עבר לסחר : ∘∘∘

פקידינן רחׄ דלא למינסב גברא מקרובות דיליה ולא . . . .

15 התם לק . . בי . . לׄ . . דבׄ איש איש אל כל שאר וגׄ קא אׄ . . .

. . . לאדעך . . לׄ . . שׄ . שלׄ . קא מזהר דלא למינסב ק . . .

. . . לׄ . . . . . . אמא : קא קארי ליה לקטון . . . . .

ז . . ד ולׄ . . . . שא הוא דבׄ ויחפש בגדול וגׄ קא . .

וב . . . . . שישד . . . . . ופות וקא אמא אל כל שאר . . . .

20 מ . . . לך . בעל ונשא .נפיק מן זרעיה קא מפקוד לא . . .

ד . מ.שת . . . בתו ובת בנו . . . בת כל קא מגמר . . .

ז . .את . . שאר בשר אסיר ליה אם . . במי . .הוא . . .

בנות בנת . . שבות . . . . במא כי ושא . . . . אׄ.לׄ.ן . . .

דבׄ ונהמת באחריתך וגׄ וזרע . . . . . .

25 וקא אמא לא תקרבו לגלות . .בׄ.אׄ . . . . . אׄ . .בׄ . לגב . . . .

קא מגמר לן דשרי ליה לאיניש . .מׄ . . . . .

ואף על גב דאסיר ליה למינסב . . . .

בלשון יחיד וכתׄ לא תקרבו בלשון . .

דאסיר ליה לגברא למינסב מׄ . . . .

30 לאיתתא לאנסובי לקרבה דילה . . . .

‫‪. . . .‬‬ ‫ולבני בנה כמא דנחית וקא אמא אני יי׳ דאי משמעי‬

‫‪. . .‬‬ ‫פריצותא בהדי קרבותיו הואיל ודיר גביהו דאיין ליה רחמ‬

‫‪. . .‬‬ ‫א אני יי׳ וכת׳ התם ובכל אלהי מצ אעשה שפֿ אׁ יי׳׳ מה אני‬

‫‪. . .‬‬ ‫ם דינא הוא אף אני יי׳ דהכא דינא. ‫וכתׄ ערות אביך‬

5 ‫‪. . . .‬‬ ‫אמך לא תגׄ וג קא אמא ערות אביך אמאי זכר אוחרנא משרי‬

‫‪. . .‬‬ ‫לא ההו שאר בשרו הוא דאמא דקא מפריש לך והאי ערות‬

‫אביך על בת קאים דאסיר לה לאנסובי לאבוה וקא אמא וערות אמך‬

‫אזהר ליה לבן דלא למינסב אימיה וכתׄ וערות אמך טפי ביה‬

‫אשויה לאיסורא דאב לבת ואסורא דאם לבן כיהדדי‬

‫‪. . . .‬‬

10 ‫‪. . .‬‬ ‫דעך דכי היכי דתתקף איסורא דאיש למינסב קרובותיו האכי‬

‫‪. . .‬‬ ‫קיף אסורא דאשה לאנסובי לקרוביה וקא אמא אמך היא‬

‫‪. . . .‬‬ ‫כתׄ אמך בׄ זמני וכתׄ לא תגלה בׄ זמני קא ראזים לך‬

‫‪. . .‬‬ ‫מך הוא כמא דסליק אסירן לך וכתׄ הוא וקרונן היא‬

‫‪. . .‬‬ ‫זים דאמות דאב נמי כמא דסאׄליק אסירן לך וכן‬

15 ‫‪. . .‬‬ ‫ורה לאנסובי לאבות דילה ולאבה דאימא כמא דסליק‬

‫‪. . .‬‬ ‫דאסיר איש בקרובותיו הכי אסירא אשה בקרבותיה‬

‫‪. . .‬‬ ‫דפרישנן ודאסיר בשאר בשרו בנות לאב ובנים‬

‫‪. . . .‬‬ ‫ר הכא אבות לבת ואמ‪. .‬אׁ ל‪. . .‬ תרויהו אסורן חד‬

‫‪. . .‬‬ ‫לחיבנון דינא לאב‪. . .‬בין כ‪. .‬ דדי‬

20 ‫‪. . .‬‬ ‫מנסבין כיהדדי וכן כל קרובים וכל קרובות‬

‫‪. . .‬‬ ‫הדרי חיובא דאשה וחיובא דאשתו דינא כיהדדי:‬

‫‪. . .‬‬ ‫הכתׄ ערות אשת אׁ ל׳ תגׄ‪. . .‬אביך הי קא אמא ערות‬

‫‪. . .‬‬ ‫יך‪. .‬אסיר ליה איתתיא דא‪. . .‬י ואפילו גרשה אבוי‬

‫‪. . .‬‬ ‫אבוי דאי כד איתה גבי אבוי היא הא הא כל נשי גברי‬

25 ‫אסירן ואפילו בחימוד דכׄ אב לא תחמד אשת **אשׁ**‬

‫‪. . .‬‬ ‫ערות אביך הוא קא ראזים דאסיר ליה למנסב‬

‫‪. . . .‬‬ ‫גבֿ‪. . .‬תת אבוי דמן דקא משוי ליה לאיתת‬

‫‪. . . .‬‬ ‫בעלה נמי ערוה דילה היא הולכך אסירא‬

‫‪. . .‬‬ ‫דבעל אשת אביו וכתׄ הוא וקרנון הוׄא קא‬

30 ‫‪. . .‬‬ ‫לך דכי היכי דאסיר ליה לאיש למינסב אשת‬

בע . . אשת אביו הא . . . ר ליה למנסב אשת בעל . . . .
אסירא לאנסובי לבעל אימה ולבעל אשת בעל אימה ו . . . .
אביה דאשה אסירא לקרובים כאיש לקרובותיו :
ערות אחותך בת אביך או בת אמך וֹג קא אמא ערו . . . .
5 בת אֹ או בֹ אֹ דאסירא ליה אחתיה בין בת אבוי ואימיה . .
אבוי ולא בת אימיה ובין בת אימיה ולאו בת אבוי וקא . . .
בית או מוֹ חוץ בין דאתלידא בכשרות ובין דאתליד . . .
דאיתליד מן עבד ובין דאתליד מן אמה דאתליד בֹ . . .
ליה מולדת בית דכֹת אשתך כגפן פוריה בֹ בית דא . . .
10 קרי לה מולדת חוץ דכֹ פֹעֹם בחוץ פעֹ וגֹו וקא אמ . . .
דכוליהי אסירן ליה כיהדדי וקא אמא ערותן בלשֹ . . .
לך מישום דלא אמא בת אביך ואמך ולא אמא בת . . .
בת אמה אמא ערותן בלשון רבים קא אמא לך . . . .
אינון אסירן לך בין דהשבין לך ובין דלא חשבין לך . . .
15 אסירא לאההא אף . . מן זנות . . או דמן עבד או דמ . . .
. . . וכֹת ערות בת בנך או בת וגֹו קא אמא עֹר . . .
בת בנך דא . . . ליה למינסב בת בנו או בת בתו . . .
מן עבד . . . . מן כשירה . . . הא חֹש . . .
ה . . . . רן . . . . דפרישנן אילא הא . . .
20 האכא . . . . ב . . ה . או . ה . . . .
ליה מיקמיה מילדת בֹ . . . . כא . . . .
בנו ובת בתו נמי דמן זֹנ . . . את . . . .
וקא אמא כי ערותך הנה קֹא א . . . .
זנות ועבד ואמה כי הנך דמֹ . . . .
25 למנסב בנות בניו או בנות בנותיו . . . .
עבד או מן אמה כמא דנחית . . . .
בניו ובנות בנותיו דמתילדין מן מֹ . . . .
לאנסובי לבני בנה ולבני בנתהֹ די . . . . .מֹי
הנה אשויה לאיסוריהו לאים . . . .

3—2

בת ·· אשת אביך מולדת וג קא אמא ערות בת . . . .

אשת אביך מול א דאסירא ליה בת איתתא דאבוי דמן . . .

אוחרינא כד הוי לה לאיתתא דאבוי ולד מן אבוי דקא אמא . . .

אביך ואי על ברתה דילידתה מן אבוי היא הא כתב ליה . . .

אחותך בת אביך אילא על ברתה דילידתה מן גברא . . .   5

א קאים ואי מאית אבוי כד לא הוה לה לאשתו ולד מיניה . . .

ליה ברתיה דמן גברא אוחרנא דכי קא אסר לה לברתה . . .

ילדא ולד מן אבוי הוא דקא אסר לה אבל לא ילדא ולד . . .

שריא ליה ברתיה וקא קרי לה לברתה כד ילדא ולד . . .

אחותך דכיון דילדא לה ולד מן אֵבוי הוה ליה וההו . . .   10

אבוי תרויהו אחיה דההו ולד דילידא ליה מן אבי . . .

לה ההי בת אשת אביו כי אחתיה וקא אמא אחותך . . .

גל ערותן ולא אמא לא תגלה ערותה אחותך היא . . .

ים דכֹ בת אמך היא לא תגֹ ערותה ולאשת בן דכֹ ביה . . .

היא ל תגֹ ערותה קא ראזים דאחות אשת אביו . . .   15

אל.. כד ילדא אשת אביו ולד מן אבוי דכיון . . .

שת אביו ולד מן אבוי הויא . . . ביה ח .. אמו . . .

ב..ל אחיו הוה . . . יר אחות א .. ו . . . . .

תה ילד .. ובת כ . . דא ליה כד . . . . . .

ו בנ..ד ב ..ד ילדא ב .. ו ולד מבנותיה.. . .   20

ולד ו . . . ב.. ניסב בת כלתו הוה ליה . . . .

ס . האכי דמיה לכלתו וכתיב . . . . . .

כי היכין דאסירא ליה בתה . . . . . .

כא אד.. ולד מן אבוי האכי אסירא . . . .

אמ... דילדא אמו ולד מיניה וכי היכי   25

דא ..לתי ולד מבנו מבנו האכי . . . .

תד . . . . לדה בתו ולד מיניה וכן אשה . . .

ב . . . . א את..א דאשת אביה כד ילדה . . .

ביה ולבן כלתה כד ילדה כלתה ולד . . . . . .

.. לב .. או לא .. דבעל אמה כד ילדה

. . . . ה ולב .. . על בתה כד ילדה בתה

. . כלתה וכ . . . ערות אחות אביך ל' תג שאר ...

אביך היא : קא אמא ערות אחות אֹ לֹ תג דאסירא

5 ליה אֹחֹתֹיה דאבוי וקא אמא שאר אביך היא : קא ראזים

דאחות אביו דמן אביו קא אסר דקא אמא שאר אביך

האכי קא אמא דהוא ואבוך מן חד זרעא אינון וכתיב הוא ...

היא קא ראזים דכי היכין דאסירא ליה אחות אביו דמן ד ...

אסירא ליה אחואתיה דאימיה דמן אביה וכן אשה אסיר ...

10 לאחי דֹ אביה דמן אביה ולאחי אביה דמן אביה :

ערות אחות אמך ל' תג כי שאר אמך הוא : קא אמא ער ...

אמך לא תג בתר דרזמה בההיא אחות אב כי היכין ד ...

ולבת בתו בתר דרזמה בשאר בשרו לשויה להדא ...

בת בנו ובת בתו מה התם על בת בנו ובת בתו . . . ...

15 אף הכא על אחות אמו דמן פסולה קאים הול . . . ...

אחות אמו אף . . . . פסולא וקא אמא מ . . . .

. . . . ום .. אף דמן פ . . . תא דאימיה . . ..

אף . . ק . . . אמא . . . . . ביא . . . .

. . . . חד זרעא . . . .

20 מקשיה שאר אב . . ..

דמן פסולה כי ה . . ..

אביך מן זרעא . . . .

דאבוהא הוא וכל . . ..

ליה אחות אמו . . . .

25 דמן פסולה וכן א . . .

אף דמן פסולה : . . . . ..

קא אמא ערות אחי . . . .

לאדעך דהאי דאב . . . . .

ליה אשת אחי אבי . . תליה באחי אביו לאו . .

דכל קרובות דומייא . . רי אסירין נשים דלהון

כי אחי אביו דדמיא דאחות אביו הוא ואסרה

לאשתו וכן אשה כל קרוביה דומיהו כנשים אסירין

5 להון בעלים דלהון דכי היכי דאסיר איש בקרובותיו

. אבי אסירא אשה בקרוביה וקא אמא לא תקרב דשרי

. . יה למידר גבה וקא אמא דדתך הוא דאסירן ליה אחואתיה

. . מן אביה בין מכשירה ובין מפסולה כי דדתו וכת הוא וקרונן

ה'א קא ראזים דכי היכי דאסירא ליה אשת אחי אביו

10 . . . ו אמיה האבי אסירא ליה אשת אחי אמו ואחואתיה דמן

בין מכשירה ובין מפסולה וכן אשה אסירא לאנסובי . . .

. . . אחות אביה ולאחיו דמן אביו בין מכשירה ובין מפסולה

. . . . אמה ולאחיו דמן אביו בין מכשירה ובין

. . . . . וכת ערות כלתך ל תג אשת וג קא אמא

15 . . . . רא ליה כלתיה בין גרשה בנו ובין מת בנו

. . . בני הוא ה . . גברי אסירא

. . . . וכן כלם . . מישום

. . . . . . ובין . . ת

. . . . . . עג כתב . .

20 . . . . איש לר . . .

. . . . . . א ו . . . ונן

. . . . . . דנחית אסירן לך

. . . . . . על בת בנה כמא

. . . . . . אף אשת אב אסירא

25 . . . . . האיי דפרט באסור

. . . . . קרבים וקרובות דטפי

. . . . . אשת אב באשת אב

דכֿ אך בשר ואף על גב דדם לא אית . . . דאית להון וכֿת . . .
תאכל הנפש כֿתב הנפש וטפי ביה הי לאדעך דכל נפש אסיר .
למיכל בהדי בשר בין דאית ליה דם ובין דלא אית ליה דם אי . . .
מיתו להון אי דאית בהו חי ומטוו להון או דצליק להו או דמלח ל . . .

5 ולבתר דנפקא נפשיהו אכֿיל להון ומאן דנגע בנבלת בהמה
טהורה מטמי עד דערבא שימשא וסאחי ודאכֿי ומאן דאכֿיל
מנבלתה מיחייב כֿיבוס ומאן דדארי לה לנבילתה מיחייב
כֿיבוס דכֿ וכֿי ימות מן הבהמה והאכֿל מנבלתה ולא אמא ביה
כל לאפוקי מטומאה דיליה כל דלא האוי בר כֿ שנה לא מטמיא

10 ליה נבלתה ואמא הנגע האוכֿל הנושא טפי בהו הי הי דנגע
לכתחילה לא מיטמו ועד דדארי על כפיה לא מיחיב כֿיבוס
ועד דאכֿיל כֿידע דנבלה היא לא מיחיב כֿיבוס ואמא והנשא
עד דדארי לה לנבילתה כי דאיתה לא מיחיב כֿיבוס ואמא
והאכֿל מנבלתה דאפילו אכֿיל מקצת נבילה איחיב ליה כֿבום

15 וחיביה כֿיבוס לאוכֿל ולנושא לאדעך דנפיש אסורא
דנושא כאוכֿל ואמא וכי ימות מן דאי שאחיט לה לבהמה
בעידנא דקא בעיא מימת כנבלה היא מישום הכֿי אמא מיתא
יומת בלשון זכֿר לאדעך דלאו על בהמה דמֿיֿמֿת קאים
אילא על בהמה דשחטין לה בעידן מיתא קאים דבהמה

20 בלשון נקבה איקריא דקא אמא זאת הבהמה והואיל
ושחיטה זכֿר דשחיט מישום הכֿי אמא יומת בלשון זכֿר
ואמא הבהמה טפי בהֿ הי דעד דהויא בת הֿ יומי לא מטמיא
ולאכֿילה נמי לא שריא ולא שרי לן למיכֿל אילאו בהמה דלא
מריעא דכֿ וזבחת מבקרך ומצאנך הכא קא אמא דלא

25 תזבח אילאו בהמה דשויה בריותה בבקרך ובצאנך
והידנא אסיר לן למיכֿל בקר וצאן דכֿ וזבחת מבקרך דק
קראה וכֿתֿ בשעריך לאדעך דבשעריך הוא דשרי לך
למיכֿל צאן ובקר בלא שעריך לא והידנא לא איכא
בשעריך דשעריך ארץ ייֿ דאיקריא כד איתה בידי

30 דישראל דכֿ שפטים ושטרים אבל עוף . . . . . .

דשריא לן למ . . . . פנינא שני .. אולא וטביא .. ות .. שרי לן
למיכל דלא פרשו קרא בשעריך .. לא בבקר וצאן אבל בעידנא
דקא באעי מימת אסיר לן מישחטנון ומיכלנון דב וכי ימות מן
דק קראה וכתב היא דכל בהמה דשריא לכון למיכלה אסיר

5 לכון מישחט בעידן מיתותה ומיכלה ויונא ושפנינא וטביא וכל
חיה דשרי לן למוכלה לא שחטינן לה אילאו מקדלה בין ראשה
לאפכותה דב ביה בעוף ומלק את ראשו וכי דירכא דמשתחטין
בה לעולה שחטינן להין לאכילה דב בבקר ובצאן מזבח
אדמה וכת וזבחת מבקרך קריה לשחיטת צאן ובקר בין

10 לגבי עולה ובין לגבי אכילה זביחה לאדעך דכי דירכא
דמשתחטין בה לעולה כה הו דירכא משתחטין לאכילה
מה שחיטת בקר וצאן בין לעולה ובין לאכילה כיהדרי
משתחטין ואף שחיטת חיה אשויה קרא לש . ט . . .
עוף דכת דכח אשר יצוד ציד קא אמא בתרויהו ושפך א . .

15 דמו לאדעך דשחיטה תרויהו כיהדרי הוא ואפקות . .
לשחיטה דידהו בלשון ושפך לאדעך דלאו כדרך צאן
ובקר משתחטין ושחיט ליה בין ראשית לאפקותין
עד דשחיט קניא ומאטי לעיקבא דלישנא דב ומלק
קא אמא דבעי למישיחטיה מיקדלית עד דמאטי גבי

20 ליקא דיליה וליקא בלישנא הוא דב ילוק בלשונו ואמא
ולא יבדיל דלא למי בעי למפסקיה לצוריה כוליה אשתכח
דבעי מישחט עד עיקבא דלישנא אבל בקר וצאן שחיט
ליה מצוריה בין עיקבא דלישנא לקניא עד דפסיק ליה
לושטא דב ויקח את המאכלת אמא מאכלת לשחוט

25 לאדעך דבמקום אכילה דבעי מישחט דא לאו חרב הוה
קרי לה אילא קריה מאכלת לאדעך דשחיטה במקום
אכילה בעי מישחט וטעם אכילה בחיכא הוא דאיתיה
דב וחיך יטעם לאכול אשתכח אשחיטה דבקר וצאן
מצוורא הוא להדי חיכא ובעי מפסקיה לושטא כוליה

30 ואמא נמי בעוף ממול ערפו טפי ביה מם לאדעך
. . . מל . . . היכא דקא אמא למישחט עוף מקדליה להדי

מצוות דרחמנ דכׄ וראיתם אותו מן שמירה דציצת מד . . .

פסח ומן פסח מדכרת יציאת מצרים הוא דכׄ תזבח את הפ . .

ומיגו דמדכרת יציאת מצרים מדכרת יׄ דברות דתחלת יׄ . . .

דברות יציאת מצרים כתוב בו דכׄ אנכי יי׳ ומתמניה אטרפׄי

5 דציצת מדכרת מילה דכׄ וביום השמיני ימול ומן גדלא

דציצת מדכרת שרשרת דחשן ומגו דמדכרת חשן מדכרת

כל דיניה דחשן דכל דיניה בגויה מפרשין דכׄ ונתת אל חשן

המשפט ומתלתה חוטי דגדילתא מדכרת תורה דכתבה רחמ . .

בתלתה אפׄי ומיגו דמדכרת תורה מחזקת למידעה וקׄיומה

10 דכׄ הלוא כתבתי להודיעך קושטׄ ומחוורה דציצת מדכרת

יום הדין דכׄ חזה הוית עד די כרסון רמיו נהר דינור נגד ונפיק

ותרין אטרפׄי דציצת מדכרת מטה אהרן ומיגו דמדכרת

מטה אהרן מדכרת לחות העדות הוה דכׄ יתבא השב את

מטה אהרן ועדות לוחות אינן דכׄ שני לוחות העדות ומאורכא

15 . . . ת מדכרת ציץ נזר הקודש דכׄ עליה קדש לייׄי וכתיב

. . . עליך ומיגו דמדכרת קדש לייׄי מדכרת שבת דכׄ

. . . שבת קדש ומדכרת מ . עדים דכׄ אלה מוע . . .

. . . עשרות וקדשים דכׄ וכל מעשר הארץ . . .

כׄ קדש לי כל בכור וכׄ וכל מ . . . . כי

20 . . . . אימדושי ל . . . לי קדשתו

. . . . תכלת . . ומשולחן

. . . . נפשך לקמי . אקרי טהור דכׄ

ע . . . חן הטהור ומלחם הפ . . . דכׄ את קרבני לחמי

ומן ציבעא דתכלת מדכרית . . . יד רחמנ לאנהורי ליש

25 בציון דכׄ נאם יי׳ אשר אור לו . . . ציון וכׄ כי עין בעין יראו ומ

דלא לבשין ינוקי גלימא דת . . ת מדכרת שמירה וטהרה

דשבת דכׄ ושמרו בני יׄש את השבת ומארבעי קרנתא דגלימא

מדכרת גאולה דכׄ ונפצות יהודה יקבץ ומיגו דמדכרת

גאולה מיחזקת למעבד תשובה דגאולה לבעלי תשובה

30 דהויה דכׄ . . . בא לציון גואל ולהכין כׄ וזכרתם את כל מ .

ANAN 4

.. כי מצוות דאוריתא איכא אדכרתיהו בציצת וקא אמא לא
תתורו אחרי לבבכם דאסיר ליה לאיניש לעיוני במילי דאורית'
ואתקונניו על מאי דהני ליה לליביה ורגיג להו לעיניה וקא
אמא אשר אתם זונים אחריהם דלא טעי אינשי אילא כד
5 אזלין בתר מאי דהני ליה לליבהון ורגיג ליה לעיניה וקא אמא
לא תתורו בתר וזכרתם את כל מצות יי' וטפי ב . . . א
בלא דתלייה בתר מצות יי' דאמא מיקמיה ותתורו לשאנא
דעינתא הוא דכ הכא תתורו וכת התם וימירו את ארץ
כנען מה האיך ויתורו עיוני הוא אף האיי תתורו עיוני הוא
10 ודרגיג להון לעיני מאי הוא מיכלא דכת נחמד למראה וטוב
למאכל קא תלי ליה למיכלא בחזוותא ודהני ליה לליביה מאי
היא זנותא דכ כי יצר לב האדם קא תלי ליה ליצר בל . . .
אשתכח דאסיר לאתקונניון למילי דאוריתא על זנ . . .
ועל מיכלא אילא על מילי דדחלות שמיא וכי יו . . .
15 זכי לן רחמנא ומברכנן ועבדינן כל מצוות . . . .
. . . . ק . רחמנא . . . בתר האכי למען . . .
. . . ל . מצו . . . ooo

היום הזה . . . . קא אמא קרא . . . .
נחיתה תורה . . . . אף מ שנה קאים דכ וא . . . עים
20 שנה בעשתי א' . . . . קא אמא בתריה את יי' האמרת
היום קא אמא להו היו . . . ה יי' אלהיך דכל אימת דמקימין
יש אוריתא הכי דמו קמי . . . כמן דאינהו קבלוה מהר
סיני : פקידין רח . . לקדושה לשבתא דלא למעבד
בה שום עיבידתא דכ זכור את יום השבת לך אמא מישום
25 דפקיד ליה לנטורי שבת מיקמי האכי : ואמא התם מילי
בשבת דלא קא מדכר להין הכא ' קא אמא .. דכר לנטורי

ונא הוא דמוקמין חאבוקיי בארע . . . .

גדדו כמשפטם בחרבות וברמחים עד . . . .

דקא אמא דמאהו בבשריהו בחרבות . . . .

כת . . . ביה דמחתא דספסירא ורומחא ודאי . . . . . .

בחרבות וברמחים ע̇ . . . דם עליהם איל̇א אמא 5

רומחא ודספסירא קאים איל̇א על מחתא . . . .

ביקיי קאים מחתא נפשיהו בקליל אית לא . . . . . .

דכד מחו נפשיהון בקשיותא אתי דמא מבשרהון . . . . .

ברמחים סימאנא דקא מסר לך אמא לך הא . . . . . .

ליה בעידנא דמיתו . גויה ספפסירי ורומחי 10

עבדין חאבוקיי אילאו באספידא דמית . . . . . .

גמרין דגדידא חאבוקיי הוא וקא אמא . . . . פס . . .

לא תשימו קרח . . ב . . . . . . ת דאף כל מילי דגרמין לכן לאסתלוקי

מילי דשמיא מבין עיניכון . . . עבדון על מת דמילי דשמיא קבֿל עינן

בעינן שויאנין כי דכת̇ ושמתם את דברי אלה ואקדים כתב גדידא וקרחה 15

ב . . עיניכם מיקמי ז̇ לד . . . מת לאגמור . . . בלא על מת נמי אסיר

. . . למעבד גדידא וקרחה בין עינים דת . . רא מחיבין לשויאנין

. . . מילי דשמיא קמן כ . . דכת שויתי יי̇ לנגדי תמיד ס

. . . דינן רחמֿ דמאן . . . ך ליה חבריה ומוזיף ליה חבריה זוזי אסיר

ליה אוזופיה בריביתא דבֿ אם כסף תלוה וגֿ קא אמא אם כסף בר יש 20

דמוזיף בר יש ו . . . תב את העני עמך . . לעני דישראל̇ מצוה לאוזופיה

טפי ביה הי בעני עני דידיע לך דודאי עני הוא דמחיבת לאוזופיה ו . . .

ליה עמך . . עני קא מחיב דענ . . דב לנבך טפי מיחיבת ביה מעניא

דמרחק מינך וקא אמא . . . . . . כנשה בלשון יחיד דאסיר לך לאוזפיה

בריבית לחד מן איל . . . . . לאו עני ובין דעני דמרחק מנבך 25

ובין דמקרב לנבך ואמא תרין ליש . . . י̇ לא תהיה לו כנשה וגֿ לא תהיה לו

כנשה דאסיר לאיגד . . . עליה הוא י̇ . . מסקת ביה לא תשימון עליו נשך

דאסיר לך לאוזפיה בריבֿת . . לא כתב וא בלא תשימון לאגמורך דאי

מינגדרת עליה ריבית . . . א שקלת מיניה ואמא לא תשימון בלשון

א ‏.. קא מזהר לן דאי איכא איניש ‏...
דמיגדר עליה כד מסיק ביה מחיב ‏...
קא אמא אם חבל תחבל שלמת ר ‏...
ובין דלאו עני כד שקלת מיניה לבושא במ ‏...
5 אמא עד בא השמש ‏.. לן מיקמי מעיל ש ‏...
דעילא שימשא הוא הוה כֿתיב כבוא ‏...
דעם דמטיא שימשא למיעל תייר ליה ‏...
לבדיה וגٔו קא אמא כי היא כסותה לבדה ‏... יא ‏...
כסות ואמא שמלה דבֿין גלימא ובין לב ‏...
10 בעית לתיוריה ליה וקא אמא בכסות ‏.. ל ‏...
ושקלת חד מינהון לא צריכת לת ‏...
דאי שקלת מיניה ההו לבושא דלביש ‏...
אבל לביש תרין לבושי ושקלת ההו ‏... לבושיה לא ‏...
לתיוריה ואמא היא שמלתו לערו ול ‏... מא והיא שמלתו דכד לא אית
15 ליה אילא חד גלימא או חד לבושא תרויהו כחד מביא ‏.. חשיבי
ומתיבת לתיורי ת ‏.. כתֿ הוא וקרונ ‏... א בין לגברא ובין לאיתתא
כד שקלת לבושא מינ ‏... כי הדדי חשיבין בין תיורי להון ובין א ‏...
לתיורי להון וכתֿ כסותה ו ‏.....ן כסותו דכסות דחזיא ‏.. לא בֿעית
לתיוריה לאיש וכסות דחזיא ‏.. אשה בש ‏.. לאשה ואלמנ ‏...
20 שרי למשקל מינה ‏.. מאנא ב ‏..שכו נא ‏... לא תחבל בגד אלמנה ‏...
וקא אמא במה ישכב לאדעך דעל מן דלא אש ‏..ד מאני ‏... ן קיים
‏.. בעית לתיורא ליה וקא אמא והיה כי יצעק וֹגֿ דאי לא מתיר ליה
מקבֿיל לה לרחֿם לצעקת ‏.... בתר ה ‏.... בין לאיש ובין לאשה
אילא מתירת ליה משתמע ‏.... כתֿ וכי ימוך אחיך ומטה וגٔו
25 קא אמא וכי ימוך אחיך וׂמ ידו ‏.. ‏... ‏.ן אחיד וממעט ממוניה
ומצטרך לדילך וקא אמא ‏... חזקת ‏..גר ‏..תושֿ וחֿי עֿ ולא אמא וגר
ותושב וחֿי עֿ לאדעך דהאי והחזקת ו ‏.. ודקא אמא על אדוריה
ואותביה גבך ואחייה בהדרך קאים ‏... ‏.. ה חיזוק דכמא דיכלת
בעית לאחזוקי בהדריה ואמא גר ות ‏.. ‏.. ב בין דבעי למידם גבך

פרש . . . . יתר . . . .

יבי ומן . . . .

מיקא ויגד ומן . . . .

חקיך ומן . . לי עד רישיה . . משיח

בדתי ומן מי אני עד וישמע יתרו 5

שית עד כתב לך ומן כתב . . . עד :

א עד קח את אהרן : ומן . . . . . .

עשה ארץ ומן במעשה עד . . . בד

חומשיה וידבר ו . . ן וידבר ר . . .

קח קרח ומן ויקח עד וישלח משה . . . 10

מטות ומן ראשי . . ריש חומשה

שמע יש ומן שמע ועד עשר תעשר . . .

רא עד אתם נצבים ועד לסופא . . .

חכ . . . בן בפיסחא ○ וכל עْ יומי דצום . . .

. . . שֿן ואמרין פסקי י . . רא מן קומו ברכו עד ותבואתה 15

. . . הושיענו ז זמני וברוך אלהי יש ד זמני וקרבין כהני

. . . ן מאני דקדש וק . . . ן בי . . לם לתכתקא דכהני ואמר

מני . . היי על עמד ואמרין קהלא ל . . ש יי לא לנו וכד קריב

. . . למימר קומו . . רו אמר ברוך יי אהי יש ברוך יי אלהים אהי

יש וברוך שם : ברוך ע. לעולם : הושיענו ברוך יי והדר אמ . . . 20

א יי לב . . . : ובשבעה בירחי וביומא דכיפורי אמרין . . .

. . . סוקי . . שרא ז פסקי מן ספר תלים . . . ימלל ג . . .

מסים ליה . . קא . . ליה ונפלי . . לאנפיהון ואמר . . .

שם יי עד דמסיْ . . ליה . . פלין . . אנפיהון ואמר ב . . .

ל . . נפֿ ואמר אהב. כי יש עד . . ים ונפֿ על אנפֿ וא . . . 25

כל גוים ונפֿ על אנפֿ ואמר הודו ליْיْ . . מרנא יש עד . . סיים ונפֿ על . .

ובכל דאמרינן פסוקי דעזרא בין ביום הכפורים ובין בשבע . . בירח . . .

ובין בתרין יומי דפורים ובין בשבעין יומים דצומא מכסונן פראכי

ושדרונן קיטמא דצ . . מא ○

B מנא לעשורי לקמיה לכל דאית לן דכ . . . .

ארץ מזרע הארץ מפרי העץ ליהוה הוא . . . .

אבל מעשר הארץ טפי בארץ הי ואקדים כת . . . .

ד דכל דהאוי מן הארץ מחייב במע . . ואמא . . .

5 לויה בתר מות יומת ד . . . .

ב מעשר מחיב למיתה ואמריה בהאיי . . . . .

ץ ולא אמא עשר כל שיהיה מן הארץ דמצ . . . .

דכתיב ויתן לו מעשר מכל ולגבי יעקב כתיב . . .

עשר אעשרנו לך ואי אמרת דיעקב מנדר הוא . . .

10 דכתיב וידר יעקב נדר וכתיב בנדר דיעקב והיה . . .

לי לאלהים וכתיב וכל אשר תתן לי עשר אעשרנו לך . .

בהדי הדאדי לאגמורנו דכי היכי דמ . . אינ . . למית

רחמנא מחיב למיתן מעשר מכל דאית ליה ו . . ית בני

מתבעי למיתניה למעשר דכתיב בראשא והאבן הז . .

15 מצבה יהיה בית אלהים והדר כתיב וכל אשר ת . .

שרנו לך קא מגמר לן אל בית אלהים בעינ . .

שר דכתיב ה . . או את כל המעשר אל בית הא . .

חנוני . . את ואמא קראה מזרע

אשר . . שוינן לה

את בת . . . .

יעקב מה ההיא שכיבא . . . . . אף אהדר

שכיבא דכתיב ביה את בעילה היא ..וק . . . שכבי בלשון

רוּבא קׇא אמא אשה דאסיר לזכר . . . משכב בהדי זכר בכל

5 דרך שכיבא דנפיק בה שכבת זרע והאי דאמא משכבי אשה

ולא אמא משכבי שכבת זרע קא ראז . . דאף בהדי אשה אסיר

לך למשכב בכל דרך שכיבא דנפיק בה שכבת זרע לבטלה

וקא אמא תועבה הוא אמא לך הא מילתא סני לה רחמׄ . .

כי כל תועבת יהוה אשר שנא וכתיב . . . א . . . נן ה . .

10 דכי היכון דאסיר ליה לזכר למבע .

למבעל נקבה וכי היכין דאסיר ליה לזכ

דרך שכיבא דנפיק בה זרעא האכי זכ . .

בהדי אשה בכל דרך שכיבא דנפיק בה וב

לה למשכב בכל דרך שכיבא דנפיק ב

15 הוא על תועב . . . .

דהאו .   .   .   .

לאחר מיתת .   .   .   .   .   איסוריהי כד איתנין גבר

בעליהֹן הוא° .   .   .   . ומזרעך לא תתן להעביר למלך ולֹא תחלל

את שם אלהיך אני .. קא אמא ומזרעך לא תתן להעביר למלך

5 דאסור ליה לאפוקי מן זרעיה לרעותא דנפשיה דאמא ומזרעך

לא תתן כי היכין דאמא מקמוה לא תתן שכבתך לזרע לאידעך

דעל זרע קאים ולא על ולד° להעביר למלך דלא לעבירו זרעות

לרעותא דליביה דמֹלך רעותא דליביה היא כידכתיב וימלך לבי

.   . אמא לא תחלל את שם אלהיך קא רזים לך דמאן

10 ללה לאוריתא דרחמנא כֹולֹה דשם ייי .   .   .   .

א דכתיב ארון האלהים אשר נקרא שם .   .   .   .

י אוריתא הוא דאיכא דכתיב ואשם את .   .   .   .

שיתי ויהיו שם אישתכח דקא קארו לה .   .   .   .

א אמא אני יהוה דדיין ליה רחמנא למאן .   .   .   .

15 יה וכתיב התם .   .   .   .   .   .

C

ע . . . .

בלא . . . .

בלא עת נדתה . . . .

א דצריכא ספירת שבעה אבל כי חזיא עד ש . . . . . .

5 וטמ . . . . . יכא ספירת שבעה׳

בה ואפילו קטנים דידען נפשיהו מיטמו עד דערבא . . . .

דכתיב כל הנגע בה יטמא עד הערב וכל מאני דגניא . . . .

בא עליהון מיטמו וכל דקאדיב לכתחילה מחור מאניה . . . .

תיב עד לפניא דכתיב כל המשכב אשר תשכב עליו כל ימי . . .

10 ה יהיה לה וכל הכלי אשר תשב עליו טמא יהיה כטמאת נדתה . .

ע בם יטמא וכבס בגדיו ורחץ במים וטמא עד הערב כתב קרא וכל . . .

קטנים דידעי נפשיהו הנגע טפי ביה הי דׄאן דלאו לכתחילה נגע . . .

מטמי וטפי ביה הי בערב לאודועך דההיא דמיטמי בהנך . . .

ב וכבס בגדיו . . . שמשא ואף על גב דכל היכ . . .

15 ב וטמא עד . . . מים מחייב למירחץ וכל ה . . .

ביה נמי ורחץ במים מחיב למירחץ . . . פרט ביה רחמנא . .

נן דכל · · · · · · · · · ·

רחיצא כו · · · · · · · · ·

דגניא עליהו · · · · · · · ·

בהון מיסתיב עד דערבא שמשא וסאח · · · · · · ·

5 ...רי דכתיב אם על המשכב הוא או על ה · · · · ·

בנגעו בו יטמא עד הערב׳ מאי אם על המשכ · · · ·

דכתיב ליה מיקמיה כל המשכב אשר תשכב ע · · · ·

הכלי אשר תשב עליו יטמא קא אמא האכא אם · · · ·

קא אמא האכא משכב דאמרית לך על משכב אחו · · · ·

10 ההוא כלי דאמרית לך על כלי אחרנא הוא מאן דקא · · ·

משכב דתותי ההוא משכב או בההוא כלי דתותי ההוא כלי מ ...

עד דערבא שמשא ולא צריך כיבום בגדיו

דפחרא דקרבא בהו תברינן להו וכל מאני דגיזא שבמים ל · ·

דכתיב וכלי ח ... שר יגע בו הזב ישבר וכל כל · ·

15 ריבה נמי · · ת · · · ובהוא דכתיב והזב את · · ·

זובו לזכר · · · · · לאשויה לטמאה ולטהר ..דזב · ·

D . . . . ל . . . אסיר ליה לזכר למינסב אשת אביו . . . . . .

. . . . אביו ואשת בעל אמו ׃ ואסי^{לה}ר לנקבה לאינסוב . . . . . .

ולבעל אשת בעל אמה ולבעל אשת אביה ׃ ואסיר ליה לזכר . . .

אשת בעל אשת בעל אמו דדומיא דאשת בעל אשת אביו בגבב . .

5 בעל אשת בעל אמו הוא והילכך אסירא אשתו ׃ ואסיר לה

לנקבה לאינסובי לבעל אשת בעל אשת אביה דדומיא דבעל

אשת בעל אמה בנשים אשת בעל אשת אביה הוא והילכך

אסיר בעלה והאיי דתניה לאשת אביו לטפויי בהדה איסור

דהלין קרבות וקרבים דפרישנן בהדה ׃ ואסיר ליה לזכר

10 למינסב אחואתיה בין בת אביו ואמו ובין בת אמו ולאו בת אביו

ובין בת אביו ולאו בת אמו בין דמתילדא בכשרות ובין דמתילדא

בזנות בין דמתילדא מן עבד ובין דמתילדא מן אמה ׃ ואסיר

לנקבה לאינסובי לאחהא בין דאיתליד בכשרות ובין דאיתליד

בזנות בין דאיתליד מן עבד ובין דאיתליד מן אמה ׃ ואסיר

15 ליה לזכר למינסב אשת אחיו דדומיא דאחתו בגברי אחיו הוא

והילכך אסירא אשתו ׃ ואסיר לה לנקבה לאינסובי לבעל אחותה

דדומיא דאחיה בנשים אחואתיה היא והילכך אסיר בעלה ׃

ואסיר להון לכל אבות בין דזכרים ובין דנקבות למינסב מן כל

בנותם בין דמן זכרים ובין דמן נקבות או דמתילדא מן זנות אף

20 מן עבד אף מן אמה ׃ ואסיר להון לכל אמות בין דזכרים ובין

דנקבות לאינסובי למן כל בניהן בין דמן זכרים ובין דמן נקבות

אף דמתילדא מן זנות או מן עבד או מן אמה ולהאכי תנאנין ׃

ואסיר ליה לזכר למינסב בתה או אחותה דאשת אביו כד ילדא

אשת אביו ולד מן אביו ׃ ובת כלתו כד ילדא כלתו ולד מן בנו ׃

25 ובתו או אחותו דבעל אמו כד ילדא אמו ולד מיניה ובת בעל

5—2

. . . . . . כד ילדא בתו ולד מיניה ׃ ואסיר ל . . ל . . .

. . . . . לבנה או לאחהא דאשת אביה כד ילדא אשת

. . ביה ולד מן אביה ולבן כלתה כד ילדא כלתה ולד מן בנה

ולבנו או לאחיו דבעל אמה כד ילדא אמה ולד מֵניה ולבן בעל

בתה כד ילדא בתה ולד מיניה ׃ ואסיר ליה לזכר למנסב אשת

בנה או אשת אחיה דאשת אביו כד ילדא אשת אביו ולד מן

אביו ואשת בן כלתו כד ילדא כלתו ולד מן בנו ואשת בנו או

אשת אחיו דבעל אמו כד ילדא אמיה ולד מיניה ואשת בנו

דבעל בתו כד ילדא בתו ולד מיניה דדומיא דבתה דאשת אביו

ואחואתיה בגברי בנה ואחיה אינון ודומיא דבת כלתו בגברי בן

כלתו הוא ודומיא דבתו דבעל אמו בגברי בנו ואחיו אינן

ודומיא דבת בעל בתו בגברי בן בעל בתו הוא והילכך אסירן

נשותיהן ׃ ואסיר לנקבה לאינסובי לבעל בתה או לבעל אחותה

דאשת אביה כד ילדא אשת אביה ולד מן אביה ולבעל בת

כלתה כד ילדא כלתה ולד מן בנה ולבעל בתו או לבעל אחֹתו

דבעל אמה כד ילדא אמה ולד מיניה ולבעל בת בעל בתו כד

ילדא בתה ולד מיניה דדומיא דבנה ואחיה דאשת אביה בנשים

בתה ואחותה אינון ודומיא דבן כלתה בנשים בת כלתה היא

ודומיא דבנו ואחיו בעל אמה בנשים בתו ואחתו אינן ודומיא

דבן בעל בתה בנשים בת בעל בתה היא והילכך אסירין

בעליהֹן ׃ ואסיר ליה לזכר למנסב אחות אביו דמן אביו בין

מכשירה ובין מפסולה ואחות אמו דמן אביהָ בין מכשירה

ובין מפסולה ולאחי אמה דמן אביה בין מכשירה ובין מפסולה ׃

ואסיר ליה לזכר למינסב אשת אחי אביו דמן אביו בין מכשירה

ובין מפסולה ואשת אחי אמו דמן אביה בין מכשירה ובין מפסולה

NOTES

PAGE 3

Line				
3	ויתן לו וג׳	Gen.	**14** 20	
4	וידר	,,	**28** 21	
5	והיה ה׳ וג׳	,,	**28** 20	
5	וכל אשר וג׳	,,	**28** 22	
8	הזאת וג׳	,,	**28** 20.	For the contents of this line and the preceding one, cf. below, p. 30, ll. 1—3.
9	המעשר וג׳	Mal.	**3** 10	
10	מפרי העץ	Lev.	**29** 30	
11	מעשר הארץ	,,	,,	
16	קדש לה׳	,,	,,	For these last 6 lines cf. below, p. 30. See also Harkavy, pp. 131 and 135.
17	מז			Probably מזרע and two or three words more from Lev. **27** 30.
18	טפי . . מם . . דייקי			Reading very doubtful, and so is מיתברא ibid. where the ת can also be taken as a ד
19	בכ . . ב .			Reading doubtful. Perhaps it read בכור של בהמה
20	וכל מעשר וג׳	Lev.	**27** 32	
23	כל אשר	,,	,,	
25	בשבט	,,	,,	(השבט)
26	העבר יהיה קדש	,,	,,	

PAGE 4

5	ואם גאל וג׳	Lev.	**27** 31	
11	ממעשרו	,,	,,	
14	כל אשר וג׳	Gen.	**28** 22	
14	ויפרץ וג׳	,,	**30** 43	
15, 16	וממחצית . . אחז וג׳	Num.	**31** 30	
20	אף בכור וג׳	Lev.	**27** 26	
21	ופ׳ בע׳ וג׳	,,	**27** 27	

(140)

Line 25   כל את   Very doubtful. Some letters are discernible over these words between the lines but they are illegible.

25   ואם כל וג׳   Lev. **27** 11

Page 5

Line	Hebrew	Reference
5	כל מעשר וג׳	Num. **18** 21
7	והתנחלתם וג׳	,, **33** 54
8	הביאו את וג׳	Mal. **3** 10
12	עשר תעשר וג׳ ואכלת וג׳	Deut. **14** 22, 23 Cf. also verse 26.
14	ולבני לוי	Num. **18** 21
16	את כל וג׳	Deut. **14** 22
18	היצא השדה	,, ,,
19	שנה שנה	,, ,,
24	אעשרנו	Gen. **28** 22
24	עשר תעשר	Deut. **14** 22
25	וכל אשר וג׳	Gen. **28** 22
32	קדש לי	Exod. **13** 2

Page 6

Line	Hebrew	Reference
7	לי הוא	Exod. **13** 2
7, 8	כל הבכור וג׳	Deut. **15** 19
10	לפני ה׳ וג׳	,, **15** 20
12	שנה בשנה	,, ,,
13, 14	אך בכור וג׳	Lev. **27** 26
15, seq.		See Harkavy, p. 128. The quotation given there in the name of Kirkisani refers probably to this case.
16	ש . . אתו	Lev. **27** 26
16	כל פטר וג׳	Num. **18** 15
17	באדם וג׳	,, ,, Cf. Num. **8** 17
20	כאזרח מכם	Lev. **19** 34
21	פדה תפדה	Num. **18** 15 ההוא doubtful.
23	את בכור וג׳	,, ,,

Line 26	ופדויו וג׳	Num. **18** 16	The ב . . בא are very doubtful.
29	וביום הש וג׳	Lev. **12** 3	

PAGE 7

5	כאשר יתן	Lev. **24** 20
8	ואם אסון וג׳	Exod. **21** 23
8	בכור הבהמה	Num. **18** 15
9	הטמאה	,, ,,
10	חמור וג׳	Exod. **13** 13
12	שורך וג׳	Deut. **5** 14
13	וכל בהמתך	,, ,,
17	את בכור האדם	Num. **18** 15
17	והכיתי וג׳	Exod. **12** 12
18	עד בכור השפחה	,, **11** 5
19	השבי אשר וג׳	,, **12** 29
20, 21	כי לי וג׳	Num. **3** 13
Marg. line	בערכך	See Lev. **27** 6 and verse 27
25	עשרים ש׳	Lev. **26** 5
26	אם עבד וג׳	Exod. **21** 32
30	בכור בני וג׳	Num. **3** 50

PAGE 8

2	וערפתו	Exod. **13** 13, **34** 20	
4	ואם	,, ,, ,,	
6	וערפו וג׳	Deut. **21** 4	
8	אל נחל וג׳	,, ,,	
9	וישב וג׳	Exod. **15** 27	The line above עגלא בנח׳ דלא indicates that these words have to be cancelled.
11	אשר לא	Deut. **21** 3	
15	שפכה וג׳	,, **21** 7	
17, 18	על . . . הטמאה	Lev. **27** 11	Reading doubtful; probably we should read כל instead of על.
20	ואם בבהמה	Lev. **27** 27	

PAGE 9

Line 3	באדם ובב ‥	See Exod. **13** 2, Num. **8** 17, **18** 15
6	מבהמת	See Num. **3** 41, 45
8	עד חדש וג׳	Num. **11** 20
11	יהיה לך	„ **18** 17
11	כחזה	„ „
14	והיה החזה וג׳	Lev. **7** 31
19	לך יהיה	Num. **18** 18
22	כבכ ‥	Reading doubtful.
27	וכי ירבה וג׳	Deut. **14** 24
28	כי לא ‥	„ „ אשר ‥ א Reading doubtful.

PAGE 10

3, 4	ת׳ קרבן ‥ זה׳ אצ׳	Num. **31** 50
4	לי הכסף	Hag. **2** 8
6, 7	בבאכם וג׳	Num. **15** 18, 20, 21
8, 9		„ **15** 2, 3
11	הארץ אשר וג׳	Lev. **20** 22
13	ארץ משבתיכם	„ „
15	באכלכם וג׳	„ **15** 19
19	לחם וקלי וג׳	Lev. **23** 14
24	ויאכלו וג׳	Jos. **5** 11
25	ממחרת וג׳	„ **5** 12

PAGE 11

2	מראשית וג׳	Num. **15** 21
5, 6	שני ‥ האחת	„ **24** 5
6	והעמר וג׳	Exod. **16** 36
8	והבאתם וג׳	Lev. **23** 10
9	וחג שב ‥	Exod. **34** 22
10	כתרומת גורן	Num. **15** 20
12	תתנו לה׳ וג׳	„ **15** 21
14	בכורים לה׳	Lev. **23** 17

Line 15	ואיש בא וג׳	2 Kin. **4** 42
17	מכל חלבו וג׳	Num. **18** 29
24	ההין לרם	Ezek. **40** 14
28	תרימו תרומה	Num. **15** 19

PAGE 12

1, 2	..וכל תרומת כל...ביתך	Ezek. **44** 30
7, 8	לתרומת...וללוים	Neh. **12** 41
24	והעמר עש׳...האיפה	See Exod. **16** 36, Ezek. **45** 11. ובת גבת read
26, 27	עשרים גרה וג׳	Ezek. **45** 12
30	כן תרימו וג׳	Num. **18** 28
31	מעשר בני וג׳	„ **18** 24

PAGE 13

1	מכל מתנ׳	Num. **18** 29
2	תרימו את וג׳	„ „
3	וראשית עריסתיכם וג׳	Ezek. **44** 30
4, 5	בראשית...יהיה	See Num. **18** 12, 13
6	ד..שן	Very doubtful, perhaps דפרשינן
8	לחם בכורים	2 Kin. **4** 42
10	לכם תרומתכם	Num. **18** 27
13	לקהל	Very doubtful
14	הלוים לי וג׳	Num. **3** 45
16	מכל מתנת׳	„ **18** 29
19	הקדשים..כל תרומת ..} לחק עולם }	„ **18** 19
20	ברית מלח וג׳	„ „
25	ואכלתם אתו וג׳	„ **18** 31
26	כל טהור	„ **18** 11, 13
28	כל קרבנם וג׳	„ **18** 9
28	בקדש וג׳	„ „
29	כסף...	See 2 Kings **12** 17

ANAN 6

PAGE 14

Line 2	הכהן המחטא וג׳	Lev.	**6** 19
3	הכהן...יכפר וג׳	„	**7** 7
7	וכי ירבה וג׳ ונתת בכסף	Deut.	**14** 24, 25
11	וכי יהיה וג׳ בשעריך	„	**15** 21, 22
20	את בכור וג׳	Num.	**18** 15
22	וכי יהיה וג׳	Deut.	**15** 21
25	וכל זר וג׳	Lev.	**22** 10
26	וכהן כי וג׳	„	**22** 11

PAGE 15

1, 2	הם...בלחמו	Lev.	**22** 11	
4	ובת כהן וג׳	„	„ 12	
6	כהן כי וג׳	„	„ 13	
7	ואיש כי וג׳	„	„ 14	
9	ולא יחללו וג׳	„	„ 15	
12	כי תשא	Exod.	**30** 12	
13	נפשו ל׳ וג׳	„	„	
14	ולא יהיה וג׳	„	„	
15	זה יתנו וג׳	„	**30** 13	
16	עשרים גרה	„	„	
17	מחצית השקל וג׳	„	**30** 15	ק...א...האני Very doubtful.
19	תרומה	Num.	**15** 20	
20	תרומה	Exod.	**30** 13	
25, 26	עבד...לאלם	2 Chron.	**24** 6	Read לאהל for לאלם, the reading of which is very doubtful.
26, 27	להביא...במדבר	„	**24** 9	
28	העשיר וג׳	Exod.	**30** 15	

PAGE 16

1	לכפר וג׳	Exod.	**30** 15
4	שנה ומע׳	„	**30** 14
5	בקע וג׳	„	**38** 26

Line 6	ונטה את וג'	Exod.	**14** 16
6, 7	לשש...ושלשת	„	**38** 26
8	וכסף פקודי וג'	„	**38** 25
10	משאת משה וג'	2 Chron.	**24** 6
11, 12	הרב...העיר	Jud.	**20** 38
12	והקהל	2 Chron.	**24** 6
13	ושחטו אתו וג'	Exod.	**12** 6
15	איש	„	**30** 14
16	לכפר על וג'	„	**30** 12
17	בפקד אתם	„	„
18	לכפר	„	**30** 15
19	ועל הכה'	Lev.	**16** 33
21	ועל כל וג'	„	„
25	ת בני יש'	Exod.	**30** 16
25	ומאת עדת וג'	Lev.	**16** 33
26	כסף כפורים	Exod.	**30** 16

PAGE 17

3	ונתת אתו וג'	Exod.	**30** 16
4	והיה וג'	„	„
5	יכפר עליכם וג'	Lev.	**16** 30
6	לפני ה'	See Exod. **30** 16 and Lev. **16** 30
6	לזכרון	Exod. **30**
9	שקל...שקל כסף	See Exod **30** 13 etc. and Gen. **23** 16
10	עבר לסחר	Gen. **23** 16
15	התם לק..בי..ל	Very doubtful
15	איש איש וג'	Lev. **18** 6
18	ויחפש וג'	Gen. **44** 12 All the letters as far as רכ' very doubtful.
19	אל כל שאר	Lev. **18** 6 All the letters and words as far as וקא very doubtful.
24	ונהמת וג'	Prov. **5** 11
25	לא תקרבו וג'	Lev. **18** 6

6—2

PAGE 18

| Line | 1 | אני ה׳ | See Lev. **18** 5, 6 |

3   ובכל אלהי וג׳   Exod. **12** 12

4, 5   ערות אביך...אמך וג׳   Lev. **18** 7   Cf. Harkavy, p. 97 for the next 16 lines.

11   אמך היא   ,,   ,,

12   לא תגלה   ,,   ,,

13   הוא..היא   ,,   ,,

21   דאשתו   Very doubtful. Probably it reads דאיש. Cf. Harkavy, p. 98 for the next 8 lines.

22   ערות אשת וג   Lev. **18** 22

25   לא תחמד   Exod. **20** 17   The dots on אב probably indicate that those letters have to be cancelled.

26   ערות אביך   Lev. **18** 7

29   הוא...הוא   ,,   ,,

PAGE 19

4   ערות אחותך וג׳   Lev. **18** 19   Cf. Harkavy, pp. 98, 99 for the next 11 lines.

7   בית או וג׳   ,,   ,,

9   מולדת בית   ,,   ,,

9   אשתך כגפן וג׳   Ps. **128** 3

11   ערותן   Lev. **18** 9

12   The dot on לך indicates that the word has to be cancelled. Cf. Harkavy, p. 99.

16   ערות בת וג׳   Lev. **18** 10   Cf. Harkavy, pp. 99, 100 for the next 15 lines.

23   כי ערותך הנה   ,,   ,,

PAGE 20

1   בת..אשת וג׳   Lev. **18** 11   Cf. Harkavy, pp. 100, 101 for the next 9 lines.

5   אחותך בת וג׳   ,,   **18** 9

12, 13   אחותך..גל ערותן   ,,   ,,   ים דכ׳ very doubtful.

15   לא תג׳ ערותה   ,,   **18** 15

PAGE 21

Line 3, 4	ערות אחות...היא	Lev.	**18** 12
5	שאר אביך היא	,, ,,	Cf. Harkavy, p. 101 for the next 5 lines.
7	הוא	,, ,,	
10	ד אביה		Probably to be cancelled. See Harkavy, p. 101 for the next 16 lines.
11	ערות..ל' תג' כי וג'	Lev.	**18** 13
12	אמך לא תג'	,, ,,	
14	בת בנו וכו'	See Lev. **18** 10	
27	ערות אחי	See Lev. **18** 14 Cf. Harkavy, p. 102 for the next 16 lines.	

PAGE 22

6	לא תקרב	Lev.	**18** 14
7	דדתך הוא	,, ,,	
8	הוא	,, ,,	
14	ערות כלתך וג'	,,	**18** 15
18	ת	Very doubtful.	
19	עֹב	Very doubtful.	
21		The ו in ונ is doubtful. Perhaps it read פקידינ.	

PAGE 23

1	אך בשר	Gen.	**9** 4
2	תאכל הנפש	Deut.	**12** 23
5		Cf. Harkavy, p. 59 for the next 8 lines.	
8	וכי ימות וג' והאכל מנבלתה	Lev.	**11** 39, 40
10	הנגע האוכל הנשא	See Lev. **11** 24, 25, 40	
11	כפיה	Harkavy p. 59 כתיפיה	
16	וכי ימות	Lev.	**11** 39
18	יומת	,, ,,	Read ימות. See Harkavy, p. 57.
20	זאת הבהמה	Deut.	**14** 4
24	וזבחת מבקרך ומצאנך	,,	**12** 21

Line	26		For the next 5 lines cf. Harkavy, pp. 4, 159, 165.
	27	בשעריך	Deut. **12** 21
	30	שפטים ושטרים	„ **17** 18

PAGE 24

	3	וכי ימות מן	Lev. **11** 39	
	4	היא	„ „	
	7	ומלק וג׳	„ **1** 15, **5** 8. Cf. Harkavy, pp. 136, 144, 153, 155.	
	8, 9	מזבח אדמה	Exod. **20** 24	
	9	וזבחת מבקרך	Deut. **12** 20. See also Exod. **20** 24	
	14	אשר יצוד ציד	Lev. **17** 13	
	14	ושפך	„ „	
	20	ילוק בלשונו	Jud. **7** 5	
	21	ולא יבדיל	Lev. **1** 17, **5** 8	
	24	ויקח את וג׳	Gen. **22** 10	
	28	וחיך יטעם וג׳	Job **34** 3	
	30	ממול ערפו	Lev. **5** 8	

PAGE 25

1	וראיתם אותו	Num. **15** 39
2	תזבח את	Deut. **16** 6
4	אנכי ה׳	Exod. **20** 1, Deut. **5** 6
5	וביום השמיני וג׳	Lev. **12** 3
7, 8	ונתת...המשפט	Exod. **28** 30
10	הלוא כתבתי..להודיעך קושט	Prov. **22** 20, 21
11, 12	חזה הוית...מתמן	Dan. **7** 8, 9
13, 14	השב...אהרן	Num. **7** 25
14	שני לוחות העדות	Exod. **31** 18
15	קדש לה׳	„ **28** 36
17	שבת קדש	„ **16** 23
17	אלה מוע..	Lev. **23** 4
18	וכל מעשר וג׳	„ **27** 30

Line 19	קדש לי וג׳	Exod. **13** 2
19	וכל מ	After the מ there seems to be a trace of a צ reading thus מצות.
23	ע...הן הטהור	Lev. **24** 6
23	את קרבני	Num. **28** 2
25	נאם ה׳ וג׳	Isa. **31** 9
25	עין בעין וג׳	„ **52** 8
27	ושמרו בני וג׳	Exod. **31** 16
28	ונפצות יהודה וג׳	Isa. **11** 12
30	בא לציון גואל	„ **59** 6
30	וזכרתם את וג׳	Num. **15** 39

PAGE 26

1, 2	לא...לבבכם	Num. **15** 39
4	אשר אתם וג׳	„ „
6	ולא תתורו וזכרתם וג׳	„ „
7	מצות ה׳	„ „
8, 9	וימירו את..כנען	„ **13** 2 Read וימירו for ויתורו.
10, 11	נחמד...למאכל	Gen. **2** 9
12	כי יצר וג׳	„ **8** 21
19, 20	וא׳..עים..בעשתי	See Deut. **1** 3
20, 21	את ה׳..היום	Deut. **26** 17
24	זכור את יום וג׳	Exod. **20** 8

PAGE 27

2	..גדדו כמשפטם וג׳	1 Kin. **18** 28
5	בחרבות וג׳	„ „
13	לא תשימו וג׳	Deut. **14** 1
15	ושמתם את וג׳	„ **11** 18
18	שויתי ה׳ וג׳	Ps. **16** 8
20	אם כסף וג׳	Exod. **22** 24
21	את העני וג׳	„ „

Line 24	כנשה	Exod. **22** 24
26	לא תהיה וג׳	,, ,,
27	לא תשימון וג׳	,, ,,

PAGE 28

3	אם חבל תחבל שלמת וג׳	Exod. **22** 25
5	עד בא השמש	,, ,,
8	כי היא כסותה וג׳	,, **22** 26
14	היא שמלתו	,, ,,
15	מביא	Very doubtful.
16	הוא	Exod. **22** 26
20	לא תחבל וג׳	Deut. **24** 17. The letters ב ..שכו נא are very doubtful.
21	במה ישכב	Exod. **22** 26
22	והיה כי יצעק	,, ,,
24	וכי ימוך ..ומטה ידו	Lev. **25** 35
26	וההזקת..גר ותושב וחי וג׳	,, ,,

PAGE 29

5	ומן מי אני עד וישמע יתרו	See Exod. **18** 1
6	כתב לך	Exod. **34** 27
7	קח את אהרן	Lev. **8** 2
8	עשה ארץ	,, **18** 3
10	ויקח קרח	Num. **16** 1
10	וישלח משה	,, **20** 14
11	מטות	,, **30** 2
11	ראשי	,, ,,
12	שמע יש׳	See Deut. **5** 1 & **6** 4
12	עשר תעשר	Deut. **14** 22
13	אתם נצבים	,, **29** 9
15	קומו ברכו...ותבואתה	See Nehem. **9** 5—37. רא.. very doubtful.
16	הושיענו..וברוך אל׳ יש׳	See 1 Chron. **16** 35, 36 ; Ps. **106** 47, 48

Line 18	לא לנו	Ps. **115** 1
19	ברוך ה' וג'	See Ps. **72** 18, 19
20		The letter ע very doubtful.
21	א יי' לב..	Very doubtful.
22	ימלל	Ps. **106** 2
22		The שׁ in שרא is very doubtful.
25	ל. נפ..אהב כי יש'	See Ps. **116** 1
26	כל גוים...הודו	See Ps. **117** 1; **118** 1? The letters סי in סיים are very doubtful.
28		Cf. Harkavy, pp. 40, 130, 149.

PAGE 30

2	מזרע הארץ וג'	Lev. **27** 30
5	בתר	Reading very doubtful. It may also read כתב.
8	ויתן לו וג'	Gen. **14** 20
9	עשר אעשרנו וג'	„ **28** 22
10	וידר יעקב וג'	„ **28** 20
13	ית בני..	Very doubtful.
14, 15	והאבן...אלוהים	Gen. **28** 22
15, 16	וכל אשר...לך	„ „
17	הביאו את וג'	Mal. **3** 10

PAGE 31

1, 2	את בת יעקב	Gen. **34** 7. The word אהדר in l. 2 is very doubtful. It may also be read ההוא.
5	משכבי אשה	See Lev. **18** 22
8	תועבה היא	Lev. **18** 22
9	כי כל וג'	Deut. **12** 31

PAGE 32

3, 4	ומזרעך לא תתן...אני	Lev. **18** 21. Cf. Harkavy, p. 207
6	שכבתך לזרע	„ **18** 20
7	להעביר למלך	„ „

ANAN 7

Line 8	וימלך לבי	Neh.	**5** 7	Cf. Harkavy, p. 207.
9	לא תחלל וג'	Lev.	**18** 21	
11	ארון האלהים	2 Sam.	**6** 2	
12, 13	ואשם...ויהיו שם	Deut.	**10** 5	
14	אני ה'	Lev.	**18** 11	

PAGE 33

1—For the contents of this and the following page, cf. Harkavy, pp. 42, 43 and 44.

3	בלא עת וג'	Lev.	**15** 25	
7	כל הנגע וג'	„	**15** 19	
9, 10, 11	{ כל המשכב...וטמא עד הערב	„	**15** 26, 27	
14	וכבס בגדיו	„	**15** 27	

PAGE 34

5, 6	אם על...עד הערב	Lev.	**15** 23	
7, 8	כל המשכב...יטמא	„	**15** 26	
13	שבמים	Very doubtful, but the ב and the מ are quite visible so that it cannot be taken for שטפין. Cf. Harkavy, p. 44.
14	וכלי ח...שר וג'	Lev.	**15** 12	
15	והזב את וג'	„	**15** 33	

PAGES 35, 36

1 seq.   For the contents of this and the following page, cf. Harkavy, pp. 90, 91, 92, 93 and 95. See also J. Markon, *Texte und Untersuchungen aus dem Gebiete des karäischen Ehegesetzes* (St Petersburg, 1908) p. 100 seq.

A

מיק . . . . . מע . . . . . .

וכל מע . . . . עשר כל . . . . . .

מאברהם אית . . דכׄ ויתן לו מעשר מכל : ולגבי . . .

ואי אמרת דיעקב מינדר הו דינדר מישום דכׄ וידר . . . .

5 דיעקב והיה יי׳ לי לאלהים וכׄ וכל אשר תתן לי עשר . . .

לאגמורנן כי היכי דמחייב איניש למיפלח קמי רחם . . . .

מכל דאית ליה ולבית כנישתא מתבעי למיתניה למע . . . .

הזאת וגׄ קא מגמר לן דלבית אהים בעינן למיתן מעשר . .

המעשר אל בית האוצר ויהי טרף בׄ ובחנוני נא בזאת ואמא . . .

10 ולא כתב ביהוא במפרי העץ דאשינון להארץ ולמזרעה א . . .

כיהדדי למיתן מינהון מעשר הארץ טפי ביה הי דכל דהא . . . .

וכספא ונחשא ופרזלא וכל דמתעביד מארץ מיחייב במעש . . .

דכל דמיזדריע בארץ מיחייב במעשר וטפי ביה הי דאפי׳לו . . .

ואף על גב דלא מזדרעא דכל עׄד רׄי מחיבין במעשר מפ . . ה . . .

15 מחיב במעשר וטפי ביה הי בהעץ דאפי׳לו מאי דנפק . . . . . .

פיר . . א כגון עפצי מיחיב במעשר ליי׳ הוא קדש ליי׳ אמא . . .

כולהו . . ליי׳ היא ועלך רמיא מילתא לאקדושנן ליי׳ ואמא מז . . .

טפי ביה מם מם דייקי כל דמתכיל מיתברא מזרעים ופירות . . . .

בכ . . של . . ב . . . . . כל דמימני אמנויי ההוא דעבר במיניאני . . .

20 . . . . דהא צריכת אנת אקדושיה ליי׳ דכׄ וכל מעשר בקר וצאן . . .

. . . . . דמעשר דהלין נמי ליי׳ הוא כי הלך דאמא מיקמיה ו . . .

. . . אמא עשר כל בקר וצאן דמצוה . . מעשר מיקמי הש . . . .

. . . דפרישנן כל אשר יעבר דקא אמא ולא אמא אשר י׳ . . . .

. . . לקניאנא עד דגאדיל כי היכן דפאריש מאימיה ולא א . . . ב . . .

25 דעבר . . תחת שבט וטפי ביה בשבט הי דמיתבעי למעבריה . . . .

. . ושי ביה מעשר דבקר וצאן העב . . . יהיה קדש ליי׳ . . . . .

קונטרסים מספר המצות לענן

Fragments of the Book of the Commandments

by Anan.

Reviews

RB 78 (1971) 298-99.

CBQ 33 (1971) 608-10.

RevQ 7 (1969-71) 607-608.

JAOS 94 (1974) 515-16.